OXFORD WORLD'S CLASSICS

TO THE LIGHTHOUSE

DAVID BRADSHAW is Reader in English Literature at Oxford University and Hawthornden Fellow and Tutor in English Literature at Worcester College, Oxford. Among other volumes, he has edited *The Hidden Huxley*, Waugh's *Decline and Fall*, Ford's *The Good Soldier*, Huxley's *Brave New World*, and the *Cambridge Companion to E. M. Forster*, as well as Oxford World's Classics editions of Lawrence's *The White Peacock* and *Women in Love*, and Woolf's *Mrs Dalloway* and *The Mark on the Wall and Other Short Fiction*. In addition, he has edited *A Concise Companion to Modernism* (Blackwell, 2003) and, with Kevin J. H. Dettmar, *A Companion to Modernist Literature and Culture* (Blackwell, 2006). He is a Fellow of the English Association and Victorian and Modern Literature Editor of the *Review of English Studies*.

OXFORD WORLD'S CLASSICS

VIRGINIA WOOLF

To the Lighthouse

Edited with an Introduction and Notes by
DAVID BRADSHAW

[Handwritten annotations:]

Lily attempts to transcend time w her painting but she constantly think she is failing.

Mrs Ramsay attempts to make things for the lighthouse.

✱ Mrs Ramsay describes herself as a sponge full of emotions. Note that sponges do not acquire water themselves she is soaking up everyone else's emotions.

OXFORD
UNIVERSITY PRESS

OXFORD

UNIVERSITY PRESS

Great Clarendon Street, Oxford OX2 6DP

Oxford University Press is a department of the University of Oxford.
It furthers the University's objective of excellence in research, scholarship,
and education by publishing worldwide in

Oxford New York

Auckland Cape Town Dar es Salaam Hong Kong Karachi
Kuala Lumpur Madrid Melbourne Mexico City Nairobi
New Delhi Shanghai Taipei Toronto

With offices in

Argentina Austria Brazil Chile Czech Republic France Greece
Guatemala Hungary Italy Japan Poland Portugal Singapore
South Korea Switzerland Thailand Turkey Ukraine Vietnam

Oxford is a registered trade mark of Oxford University Press
in the UK and in certain other countries

Published in the United States
by Oxford University Press Inc., New York

Biographical Preface © Frank Kermode 1992
Editorial material © David Bradshaw 2006
Text © the Trustees of the Virginia Woolf Estate

First published as a World's Classics paperback 1992
Reissued as an Oxford World's Classics paperback 1998
New edition 2006

British Library Cataloguing in Publication Data

Data available

Library of Congress Cataloging in Publication Data

Data available

Typeset in Ehrhardt
by RefineCatch Limited, Bungay, Suffolk
Printed in Great Britain by
Clays Ltd, St Ives plc

ISBN 978–0–19–280560–7

2

CONTENTS

BIOGRAPHICAL PREFACE

VIRGINIA WOOLF was born Adeline Virginia Stephen on 25 January 1882 at 22 Hyde Park Gate, Kensington. Her father, Leslie Stephen, himself a widower, had married in 1878 Julia Jackson, widow of Herbert Duckworth. Between them they already had four children; a fifth, Vanessa, was born in 1879, a sixth, Thoby, in 1880. There followed Virginia and, in 1883, Adrian.

Both of the parents had strong family associations with literature. Leslie Stephen was the son of Sir James Stephen, a noted historian, and brother of Sir James Fitzjames Stephen, a distinguished lawyer and writer on law. His first wife was a daughter of Thackeray, his second had been an admired associate of the Pre-Raphaelites, and also, like her first husband, had aristocratic connections. Stephen himself is best remembered as the founding editor of the *Dictionary of National Biography*, and as an alpinist, but he was also a remarkable journalist, biographer, and historian of ideas; his *History of English Thought in the Eighteenth Century* (1876) is still of great value. No doubt our strongest idea of him derives from the character of Mr Ramsay in *To the Lighthouse*; for a less impressionistic portrait, which conveys a strong sense of his centrality in the intellectual life of the time, one can consult Noël Annan's *Leslie Stephen* (revised edition, 1984).

Virginia had the free run of her father's library, a better substitute for the public school and university education she was denied than most women of the time could aspire to; her brothers, of course, were sent to Clifton and Westminster. Her mother died in 1895, and in that year she had her first breakdown, possibly related in some way to the sexual molestation of which her half-brother George Duckworth is accused. By 1897 she was able to read again, and did so voraciously: 'Gracious, child, how you gobble', remarked her father, who, with a liberality and good sense at odds with the age in which they lived, allowed her to choose her reading freely. In other respects her relationship with her father was difficult; his deafness and melancholy, his excessive emotionalism, not helped by successive bereavements, all increased her nervousness.

Stephen fell ill in 1902 and died in 1904. Virginia suffered another breakdown, during which she heard the birds singing in Greek, a language in which she had acquired some competence. On her recovery she moved, with her brothers and sister, to a house in Gordon Square, Bloomsbury; there, and subsequently at several other nearby addresses, what eventually became famous as the Bloomsbury Group took shape.

Virginia had long considered herself a writer. It was in 1905 that she began to write for publication in the *Times Literary Supplement*. In her circle (more loosely drawn than is sometimes supposed) were many whose names are now half-forgotten, but some were or became famous: J. M. Keynes and E. M. Forster and Roger Fry; also Clive Bell, who married Vanessa, Lytton Strachey, who once proposed marriage to her, and Leonard Woolf. Despite much ill health in these years, she travelled a good deal, and had an interesting social life in London. She did a little adult-education teaching, worked for female suffrage, and shared the excitement of Roger Fry's Post-Impressionist Exhibition in 1910. In 1912, after another bout of nervous illness, she married Leonard Woolf.

She was thirty, and had not yet published a book, though *The Voyage Out* was in preparation. It was accepted for publication by her half-brother Gerald Duckworth in 1913 (it appeared in 1915). She was often ill with depression and anorexia, and in 1913 attempted suicide. But after a bout of violent madness her health seemed to settle down, and in 1917 a printing press was installed at Hogarth House, Richmond, where she and her husband were living. The Hogarth Press, later an illustrious institution, but at first meant in part as therapy for Virginia, was now inaugurated. She began *Night and Day*, and finished it in 1918. It was published by Duckworth in 1919, the year in which the Woolfs bought Monk's House, Rodmell, for £700. There, in 1920, she began *Jacob's Room*, finished, and published by the Woolfs' own Hogarth Press, in 1922. In the following year she began *Mrs Dalloway* (finished in 1924, published 1925), when she was already working on *To the Lighthouse* (finished and published, after intervals of illness, in 1927). *Orlando*, a fantastic 'biography' of a man–woman, and a tribute to Virginia's close friendship with Vita Sackville-West, was written quite rapidly over the winter of 1927–8, and published, with considerable success, in October. *The Waves* was written and rewritten in 1930 and 1931 (published in October of that year). She had already started on *Flush*, the story of Elizabeth Barrett Browning's pet dog—another success with the public—and in 1932 began work on what became *The Years*.

This brief account of her work during the first twenty years of her marriage is of course incomplete; she had also written and published many shorter works, as well as both series of *The Common Reader*, and *A Room of One's Own*. There have been accounts of the marriage very hostile to Leonard Woolf, but he can hardly be accused of cramping her talent or hindering the development of her career.

The Years proved an agonizingly difficult book to finish, and was completely rewritten at least twice. Her friend Roger Fry having died in 1934, she planned to write a biography, but illnesses in 1936 delayed the project; towards the end of that year she began instead the polemical *Three Guineas*, published in 1938. *The Years* had meanwhile appeared in 1937, by which time she was again at work on the Fry biography, and already sketching in her head the book that was to be *Between the Acts*. *Roger Fry* was published in the terrifying summer of 1940. By the autumn of that year many of the familiar Bloomsbury houses had been destroyed or badly damaged by bombs. Back at Monk's House, she worked on *Between the Acts*, and finished it in February 1941. Thereafter her mental condition deteriorated alarmingly, and on 28 March, unable to face another bout of insanity, she drowned herself in the River Ouse.

Her career as a writer of fiction covers the years 1912–41, thirty years distracted by intermittent serious illness as well as by the demands, which she regarded as very important, of family and friends, and by the need or desire to write literary criticism and social comment. Her industry was extraordinary—nine highly-wrought novels, two or three of them among the great masterpieces of the form in this century, along with all the other writings, including the copious journals and letters that have been edited and published in recent years. Firmly set though her life was in the 'Bloomsbury' context—the agnostic ethic transformed from that of her forebears, the influence of G. E. Moore and the Cambridge Apostles, the individual brilliance of J. M. Keynes, Strachey, Forster, and the others— we have come more and more to value the distinctiveness of her talent, so that she seems more and more to stand free of any context that might be thought to limit her. None of that company—except, perhaps, T. S. Eliot, who was on the fringe of it—did more to establish the possibilities of literary innovation, or to demonstrate that such innovation must be brought about by minds familiar with the innovations of the past. This is true originality. It was Eliot who said of *Jacob's Room* that in that book she had freed herself from any compromise between the traditional novel and her original gift; it was the freedom he himself sought in *The Waste Land*, published in the same year, a freedom that was dependent upon one's knowing with intimacy that with which compromise must be avoided, so that the knowledge became part of the originality. In fact she had 'gobbled' her father's books to a higher purpose than he could have understood.

Frank Kermode

INTRODUCTION

A Necessary Act

'I am making up "To the Lighthouse"', Virginia Woolf wrote in her diary on 27 June 1925, '—the sea is to be heard all through it'.[1] More specifically, it was the break of the Atlantic against the rock and sand of Cornwall that Woolf brought to mind as she envisioned her fifth novel and that would resound through its every page. Each summer and early autumn between 1882 and 1894, Woolf's parents, the philosopher and literary critic Leslie Stephen and his wife Julia, had taken their four children from their previous marriages and their own four children to Talland House, their holiday home in the small Cornish fishing town of St Ives, for an eagerly awaited breather from the bustle and bad air of London. The sensuous abundance of those thirteen long vacations, the first thirteen summers of her life, stayed with Woolf for the rest of her days. When they came to a sudden end with the death of her mother in May 1895 the young Virginia Stephen suffered a traumatic double blow.[2] But these were not the only losses Woolf had to contend with during her formative years. In 1897 her beloved half-sister Stella died, probably, like Prue Ramsay, from a pregnancy complication. Then, in 1904, her father passed away, followed in 1906 by her elder brother Thoby, not killed in battle, like Andrew Ramsay, but hardly less shockingly by typhoid. By the age of 24, Woolf still had much to learn about writing but she was already well versed in grieving.

She revisited Cornwall a number of times during her life, and though it was easy to keep in touch with the topography of her childhood summers and savour afresh their sights and sounds, she was all too sorely aware that she could not return to the past. As early as 1905, for example, Woolf, her elder sister Vanessa, and their two

---

[1] *The Diary of Virginia Woolf*, ed. Anne Olivier Bell assisted by Andrew McNeillie (5 vols.; London: Hogarth Press, 1977–84), iii. 34.

[2] 'With mother's death the merry, various family life which she had held in being shut for ever. In its place a dark cloud settled over us; we seemed to sit all together cooped up, sad, solemn, unreal, under a haze of heavy emotion.' Virginia Woolf, *Moments of Being*, ed. Jeanne Schulkind, rev. Hermione Lee (London: Pimlico, 2002), 104.

brothers crept up to Talland House in the fading light of an August evening:

We could fancy that we were but coming home along the high road after some long day's outing, & that when we reached the gate . . . we should thrust it open, & find ourselves among the familiar sights again. In the dark, indeed, we made bold to humour this fancy of ours further than we had a right to; we passed through the gate, groped stealthily but with sure feet up the carriage drive, mounted the little flight of rough steps, & peered through a chink in the escalonia hedge. There was the house, with its two lighted windows; there on the terrace were the stone urns, against the bank of tall flowers; all, so far as we could see was as though we had but left it in the morning. But yet, as we knew well, we could go no further; if we advanced the spell was broken. The lights were not our lights; the voices were the voices of strangers . . . We hung there like ghosts in the shade of the hedge, & at the sound of footsteps we turned away.[3]

This bitter-sweet cameo of a fanciful homecoming, of hungering eyes and a lighted house, of belonging and severance commingled, is not, strictly speaking, a source for *To the Lighthouse*, but the novel's setting in a summer home by the sea and its poignant fusion of mournfulness and rapture, nostalgia and deliverance, is drawn from the same deep well. For St Ives and Cornwall possessed Woolf in the same kind of way (if not quite to the same extent) that Dorset possessed Thomas Hardy. The 'most important of all my memories', she wrote less than two years before her suicide in 1941, was of listening to the sea at Talland House:

If life has a base that it stands upon, if it is a bowl that one fills and fills and fills—then my bowl without a doubt stands upon this memory. It is of lying half asleep, half awake, in bed in the nursery at St Ives. It is of hearing the waves breaking, one, two, one, two, and sending a splash of water over the beach; and then breaking, one, two, one, two, behind a yellow blind. It is of hearing the blind draw its little acorn across the floor as the wind blew the blind out. It is of lying and hearing this splash and seeing this light, and feeling, it is almost impossible that I should be here; of feeling the purest ecstasy I can conceive.[4]

---

[3] Virginia Woolf, *A Passionate Apprentice: The Early Journals and 'Carlyle's House and Other Sketches'*, ed. Mitchell A. Leaska (London: Pimlico, 2004), 282.

[4] *Moments of Being*, 78–9.

'Why am I so incredibly & incurably romantic about Cornwall?', Woolf asked herself on the eve of a later visit to the county. 'One's past, I suppose: I see children running in the garden. A spring day. Life so new. People so enchanting. The sound of the sea at night.'[5] An equally great Modernist, W. B. Yeats, reflecting on his unrequited passion for Maud Gonne in a poem called 'Words', recognized that he would have been only half the poet he was had he not had to come to terms with the pain of her rejection: had she been more responsive, Yeats asks rhetorically, 'What would have shaken from the sieve?' Cornwall and all it stood for played no less a role in the forging of Woolf's art. What shook from the 'sieve' of those thirteen Talland House summers was not only *To the Lighthouse* (1927), *Jacob's Room* (1922), and *The Waves* (1931), but the whole wistful, lyrical, backward-looking, sea-salted, ghost-haunted cast of her genius.

If the lighthouse Woolf had in mind when she conceived her novel is the Godrevy Lighthouse—'my Lighthouse'[6] as she called it in 1930—which shone every night through the windows of Talland House from the other side of St Ives Bay (and is still operational today), and if the cricket playing, guest-glutted summer life of the Stephen family has its direct counterpart in the cricket playing 'hubbub' (p. 91) of the Ramsays' jam-packed residence (where, as at Talland House, there are no fewer than eight children at large[7]), *To the Lighthouse* draws even more profoundly on Woolf's fixation with her dead parents than it does on her enduring heartache for 'the best beginning to life conceivable'.[8] More than anything else, this accounts for the eerie (but unspooky) impression many readers pick up that the novel is peopled by more than its roll of characters. Not only does the Ramsays' summer home creak and groan with unsettled spirits, and clothes keep their 'human shape' (p. 106) in its wardrobes, but it is furnished with the 'crazy ghosts of chairs and tables whose London life of service was done' (p. 25), while 'fumbling airs' move 'ghostlily' (p. 104) about the soon to be abandoned rooms at the beginning of 'Time Passes' and Lily Briscoe is alternately

[5] *Diary*, ii. 103.

[6] *The Letters of Virginia Woolf*, ed. Nigel Nicolson and Joanne Trautmann (6 vols.; London: Hogarth Press, 1975–80), iv. 165.

[7] Andrew, Jasper, Roger, James, Prue, Nancy, Rose and Cam.

[8] *Moments of Being*, 133.

comforted and distressed by the presence of Mrs Ramsay's spirit in 'The Lighthouse'. Furthermore, the Ramsays' property, like its Cornish original, is located near a beach, and the thud of the sea on the shore is sometimes heard by Mrs Ramsay as a 'ghostly roll of drums' (p. 17), just as when Cam looks back at the island in 'The Lighthouse' it seems to be 'wrapped in its mantle of peace; as if the people there had fallen asleep . . . were free like smoke, were free to come and go like ghosts' (p. 140). Before her death, Mrs Ramsay glides through her memories 'like a ghost' (p. 72), while Woolf's description of Mr Ramsay, 'stumbling along a passage . . . one dark morning' with his arms stretched out (p. 105), and his later dream of his dead wife walking on the terrace with her 'arms . . . stretched out to him' (p. 138) are further examples of the novel's mellow haunted-ness.[9] Mr Ramsay's anguish is perfectly expressed in these unconsummated embraces but they also have a mildly Gothic aspect, while the ship which is sighted in 'Time Passes' is described as a 'silent *apparition*' (p. 109), the lights which play on the sea are seen by Mrs Ramsay as a '*phantom* net floating there to mark something which had sunk' (p. 57) and the '*phantom* kitchen table' (p. 22; all emphases added) which Lily always brings to mind when she thinks of Mr Ramsay's work is both a philosophical commonplace and a fitting companion for the 'crazy ghosts' of London furniture that have found their final resting place on the island, such as 'the sofa on the landing', which Mrs Ramsay has inherited from her mother, or 'the rocking-chair (her father's)' (p. 92). *To the Lighthouse* reaches far beyond autobiography, but it would have been a very different novel indeed without Woolf's famished remembrance of things past and her ongoing sense of her parents being both absent and about her, while the 'one-armed man' (p. 13) whom Mrs Ramsay encounters on her way into town, and the mackerel with a 'square [cut] out of its side' which is tossed alive from Macalister's boat (p. 148), give voice at one level to Woolf's feelings of mutilation following the loss of her mother, half-sister, father, brother, and childhood within the short space of eleven years.

---

[9] On the morning of their mother's death, Woolf and her siblings were taken to 'say goodbye. My father staggered from the bedroom as we came. I stretched out my arms to stop him, but he brushed past me, crying out something I could not catch; distraught. And George [her half-brother] led me in to kiss my mother, who had just died.' Ibid. 102.

Though this is by no means a gloomy novel—indeed the majority of its characters are observed smiling, joke-telling, or laughing at one point or another (for example, four of the children (p. 89); Augustus Carmichael, Minta Doyle, and Mr Ramsay (p. 89); and Lily Briscoe (p. 156)) and at its conclusion it is emphatically optimistic—death and dying figure as prominently as ghosts in the book. As well as the deaths of Mrs Ramsay, Prue, and Andrew, for example, the servant Marie's father is dying of cancer in Switzerland (p. 26), whereas the woman in the nearby town whom Mrs Ramsay visits (it is not clear whether she or her daughter is called Elsie) is probably dying of tuberculosis (see below, pp. xxiii–xxiv). Similarly, the wild boar's skull nailed to the wall of the nursery (p. 92) acts as a gruesome memento mori which is complemented by 'the skulls of small birds' (p. 11) in the attics, whereas William Bankes, macabrely, thinks of his long-standing but tricky friendship with Mr Ramsay as being 'like the body of a young man laid up in peat for a century, with the red fresh on his lips' (p. 21). Above all, while the two structures which dominate the novel—the towering Lighthouse and the imposing holiday house—may be viewed from any number of angles, the unoccupied and dilapidated dwelling-place of 'Time Passes' undoubtedly stands in one sense for Woolf's raw feelings of displacement and bereavement following the deaths of her four close relations, just as the Lighthouse beam, gathering up rooms in its 'loving caress' (p. 109) one moment and leaving them dark again the next is a potent emblem both for the brevity of life and the inexorable pulse of grief. Smoothing James's hair, and with 'the monotonous fall of the waves on the beach' in the background, Mrs Ramsay accepts that a sound 'which for the most part beat a measured and soothing tattoo to her thoughts' at other times 'had no such kindly meaning, but . . . remorselessly beat the measure of life . . . and warned her . . . that it was all ephemeral as a rainbow' (pp. 16–17). By 1906, Woolf needed no reminding of this and the publication of both the British and American first editions of *To the Lighthouse* on 5 May 1927, the thirty-second anniversary of Julia Stephen's death, was no coincidence.

Woolf had written about her parents on a number of occasions before she published *To the Lighthouse*. Her first (affectionate and respectful) recollection of her father appeared in a short essay which F. W. Maitland incorporated into his *Life and Letters of Leslie*

Stephen (1906)[10] and the following year Woolf wrote a piece predominantly about her mother called 'Reminiscences', which was not for public consumption.[11] She would go on to incorporate aspects of her parents into her first two novels, *The Voyage Out* (1915) and *Night and Day* (1919)—in her depictions of Helen and Ridley Ambrose and Katherine Hilbery's parents respectively—and would also draw on facets of her own story in her portrayal of Colonel Abel Pargiter and his family in *The Years* (1937). Five years previously she penned a centenary tribute for *The Times* (28 November 1932) entitled 'Leslie Stephen: The Philosopher at Home: A Daughter's Memories'.[12] An act of filial homage, this essay is both warm and moving, but in 1939–40 Woolf produced her most compelling account of her parents and childhood in the candid, lengthy, and unfinished 'Sketch of the Past', in which she recalled that with regard to the influence of her mother in particular, writing *To the Lighthouse* had been cathartic:

It is perfectly true that she obsessed me, in spite of the fact that she died when I was thirteen, until I was forty-four. Then one day walking round Tavistock Square [where Woolf then lived in London] I made up, as I sometimes make up my books, *To the Lighthouse*; in a great, apparently involuntary, rush. One thing burst into another. Blowing bubbles out of a pipe gives the feeling of the rapid crowd of ideas and scenes which blew out of my mind, so that my lips seemed syllabling of their own accord as I walked. What blew the bubbles? Why then? I have no notion. But I wrote the book very quickly; and when it was written, I ceased to be obsessed by my mother. I no longer hear her voice; I do not see her.

I suppose that I did for myself what psycho-analysts do for their patients. I expressed some very long felt and deeply felt emotion. And in expressing it I explained it and then laid it to rest.[13]

In view of this obsession, it is not surprising that *To the Lighthouse* is almost as preoccupied with inheritance as it is with transience and mortality, especially the way in which physical, psychological, and

---

[10] Frederic William Maitland, *The Life and Letters of Leslie Stephen* (London: Duckworth, 1906), 474–6; repr. as 'Impressions of Sir Leslie Stephen' in *The Essays of Virginia Woolf*, ed. Andrew McNeillie (6 vols.; London: Hogarth Press, 1986–), i. 127–30.

[11] See *Moments of Being*, 1–30.

[12] Repr. as 'Leslie Stephen' in Virginia Woolf, *Collected Essays*, vol. iv (London: Hogarth Press, 1967), 76–80.

[13] *Moments of Being*, 92–3.

emotional attributes are passed on from one generation to the next. Our first impression of James, for example, is of a pint-sized version of his father (and, behind Mr Ramsay, Leslie Stephen), a boy 'of stark and uncompromising severity, with his high forehead and his fierce blue eyes ... frowning slightly at the sight of human frailty' (p. 7). Towards the end of the novel, James begins to say things 'to himself, half aloud exactly as his father said it' (p. 166), just as Cam, like her father, plucks a leaf from the hedge as she passes it in 'The Window' (pp. 38, 46) and, in 'The Lighthouse', murmurs 'dreamily, half asleep, how we perished, each alone' (p. 156; see also p. 137), while Prue is a Mrs Ramsay-like 'perfect angel with the others ... [who] took one's breath away with her beauty' (p. 49).

All the qualities Woolf most admired in her mother are embodied in Mrs Ramsay: her beauty, her lovingness, her tender solicitude for those in her care, her concern for the poor and the disadvantaged in her community, her 'delicious fecundity' (p. 33). But Woolf also explores Julia Stephen's limitations in this novel, especially her conventionality, her anti-feminism, her dubious concept of charity, her imperiousness, and her imperialism. Mrs Ramsay is disparaging about Lily's aspirations as a painter (p. 17), for instance, but is quite prepared to entertain the possibility that James might 'turn out a great artist' purely on the strength of his 'splendid forehead' (p. 28). In the same vein, she finds it easy to imagine James, 'all red and ermine on the Bench or directing a stern and momentous enterprise in some crisis of public affairs' (p. 7), but her 'mania ... for marriage' (p. 144) renders her incapable of envisaging her daughters doing anything other than netting husbands and bearing children.

Even her knitting the brown stockings for the son of Sorley the Lighthouse keeper and her visiting the sick in 'The Window' are possibly more problematic activities than they might appear. Julia Stephen was celebrated for her philanthropic good works both in Victorian London and St Ives, but by the Edwardian period ('The Window' is set in September 1909[14]) the whole question of how best to combat the vast and apparently intractable problem of the poor was a matter of impassioned public debate, with a Royal

[14] Lily tells us there is a ten-year break between 'The Window' and 'The Lighthouse' (p. 122), and since 'The Lighthouse' is set in the 'September' (p. 116) after the War has finished, i.e. September 1919, that means 'The Window' is set in September 1909.

Commission on the Poor Laws and the Relief of Distress making a concerted examination of the issue between 1905 and 1909. While there is absolutely no reason to suppose that Mrs Ramsay does not genuinely agonize over 'the eternal problems: suffering; death; the poor' (p. 51) as she visits the infirm and the destitute 'weekly, daily, [on the island] . . . or in London' (p. 11), as I have argued elsewhere, *To the Lighthouse* exposes the insufficiency of her kind of individualistic, Victorian-style philanthropy and sees it as part of the 'vast and benevolent *lethargy* of well-wishing' (p. 12; emphasis added) in which not only Carmichael but the whole leisured class are sunk. As well as the woollen stockings, Mrs Ramsay considers sending to the Lighthouse 'a pile of old magazines, and some tobacco, indeed whatever she could find lying about, not really wanted, but only littering the room' (p. 8) and her haphazard (and slightly disgraceful) thoughts underline the comparative futility of such 'good works'.[15]

Woolf's admiration for and ambivalence about her mother is also reflected, perhaps, in the ambiguous dedications in the books Mrs Ramsay has been presented with over the years (but which she has never read): ' "For her whose wishes must be obeyed" . . . "The happier Helen of our days" ' (p. 25). The first inscription is an allusion to Ayesha, the beautiful and imperious queen of an African tribe whose head-turning allure proves almost fatal to the Englishmen who come across her in Rider Haggard's *She* (1887), just as Mrs Ramsay has been accused of '[w]ishing to dominate, wishing to interfere, making people do what she wished' (p. 49), of being 'tyrannical, domineering, masterful' (p. 50) in the past. It could be that Woolf wants us to see her philanthropy as another indication of her need to control others, and once we are able to picture Mrs Ramsay as a woman who likes to 'dominate' and who gets a kick out of being 'masterful', it becomes easier to sympathize not only with Carmichael's guardedness towards her but also with Mr Ramsay, and to see her husband's unsettling behaviour as a response to his wife's withheld affections. Mr Ramsay undoubtedly acts like a child at times, but it may be that his conduct is neither entirely inexplicable nor utterly unprovoked.

---

[15] The ideas discussed here draw on material from my essay 'The Socio-Political Vision of the Novels', in Sue Roe and Susan Sellers (eds.), *The Cambridge Companion to Virginia Woolf* (Cambridge: Cambridge University Press, 2000), 191–208.

The second dedication, of course, refers to Helen of Troy, a legendary beauty, but a woman to whom many Greek, Roman, and later writers (for example, Virgil, Ovid, Seneca, and Dante) were hostile in that they represented her as being of dubious morality and largely responsible for the decade-long Trojan War (see note to p. 25). Of course, there is no suggestion whatever that Mrs Ramsay's life has been anything other than wholly virtuous (as was Julia Stephen's), but the dedicator could have had something of Helen of Troy's reputation as a misleader of men in mind when writing the inscription. It is just possible, in other words, that whoever wrote it believed, like Charles Tansley, that Mr Ramsay had 'dished himself by marrying a beautiful woman and having eight children' (p. 74). Again, this is not how Woolf saw her parents' relationship, but it does square with her view that her mother and father were in some ways incompatible.

Although Mr Ramsay is probably not 'grinning sarcastically . . . with the pleasure of disillusioning his son and casting ridicule upon his wife' (p. 7) at the beginning of the novel, but only giving that impression to the antagonistic James (we are reminded that James thinks his father 'a sarcastic brute' later on in the novel (p. 155) but we see no evidence of any sarcasm throughout the text), Mr Ramsay is at once a plate-throwing, door-slamming (p. 162) tyrant and 'a figure of infinite pathos' (p. 128), 'venerable and laughable at one and the same time' (p. 39), appealing (bending 'to tickle James's bare calf with a sprig of something' as he walks past him) and rebarbative in equal measure, a 'compound of severity and humour' (pp. 28, 29). With a 'compass on his watch-chain' (p. 99), Mr Ramsay sees himself as the selfless leader of a doomed polar expedition (p. 31) or the commander of a 'forlorn hope' (p. 32) or a valiant but fated horseman: he enlists himself into the 'Charge of the Light Brigade' (by changing 'they' to 'we' (p. 18); see note to this page) not just as an ordinary cavalryman, but 'fell as a thunderbolt, fierce as a hawk at the head of his men' (p. 28). Rather less intrepidly, his career as a philosopher, despite his books and his fame, seems to have ground to a halt, stymied by his feeling of being intellectually marooned near the middle of a figurative alphabet (pp. 30–2). And if the crude linearity of his angst is not absurd enough, when he is not fretting about his own predicament he is 'chuckling' about the Scottish philosopher David Hume (1711–76) getting stuck in a bog (pp. 54, 57, 61).

'Never was anybody at once so ridiculous and so alarming' (p. 18), as Mrs Ramsay says. Yet in line with the mood of reconciliation which dominates 'The Lighthouse' it is noteworthy that when James and Cam do eventually make ready for their excursion with their father he has 'all the appearance', in Lily's eyes, 'of a leader making ready for an expedition'. At long last, Mr Ramsay can stride ahead of his children with a 'firm military tread' (p. 128) that will actually take him somewhere other than up and down the terrace or round and round the garden.

On the day her previous novel, *Mrs Dalloway*, was published (14 May 1925), Woolf wrote in her diary:

I'm now all on the strain with desire to stop journalism & get on to *To the Lighthouse*. This is going to be fairly short: to have father's character done complete in it; & mothers; & St Ives; & childhood; & all the usual things I try to put in—life, death &c. But the centre is father's character, sitting in a boat, reciting We perished, each alone, while he crushes a dying mackerel . . . [16]

By 20 July 1925 she had settled on 'father & mother & child in the garden: the death; the sail to the lighthouse'.[17] Like Leslie Stephen, the calf-tickling Mr Ramsay can be loving and approachable—Cam clambering over her father's shoulder (p. 22) recalls Stephen's moments of uninhibited ease with his own children—but Mr Ramsay, especially in 'The Lighthouse', when he plays 'the part of a desolate man, widowed, bereft' (p. 137) to the full, is modelled chiefly on Sir Leslie Stephen (he was knighted in 1902) the widower, a largely remorseful, self-pitying, and histrionic old man, prone to 'explosions'[18] and in despair that his reputation as a philosopher was already on the wane and would not survive his death. Though Mr Ramsay's antics may be viewed as comical—booming verse at those he bumps into, shouting it so loudly at Mrs Giddings that she 'almost jumped out of her skin' (p. 59), 'screwing his face up' in fury simply because Carmichael asks for another bowl of soup (p. 78), 'talk[ing] by the hour about his boots' (p. 85, see also p. 127), 'whiz[z-ing] his plate through the window' (p. 162) on finding an earwig in his milk—both Lily and his children have learned to be apprehensive

[16] *Diary*, iii. 18–19.
[17] Ibid. 36.
[18] See *Moments of Being*, 115–18, 104; quote from p. 115.

of him, just as Woolf grew to dread her father's bouts of self-lacerating despair. On 28 November 1928, the day on which Sir Leslie would have been 96, she wrote in her diary:

His life would have entirely ended mine. What would have happened? No writing, no books;—inconceivable. I used to think of him & mother daily; but writing The Lighthouse, laid them in my mind. And now he comes back sometimes, but differently. (I believe this to be true—that I was obsessed by them both, unhealthily; & writing of them was a necessary act.)[19]

Wasting Away

Woolf completed the first draft of *To the Lighthouse* 'in dread of "sentimentality" '[20] and when she revised the holograph she toned down many of its more obviously autobiographical elements. Not only did she wish to create some distance between herself and her story, she also wanted to place greater emphasis on the broader cultural and historical issues which her story entailed. In short, she was anxious to exorcize not only the ghosts of her parents in *To the Lighthouse* but also many of the Victorian values they so magnificently embodied.

In the fifth chapter of Woolf's next novel, Orlando is soon alienated by the chilly mores of the nineteenth century, but finds the pestilential dampness of the epoch almost harder to bear:

damp now began to make its way into every house—damp, which is the most insidious of all enemies, for while the sun can be shut out by blinds, and the frost roasted by a hot fire, damp steals in while we sleep; damp is silent, imperceptible, ubiquitous. Damp swells the wood, furs the kettle, rusts the iron, rots the stone. So gradual is the process, that it is not until we pick up some chest of drawers, or coal scuttle, and the whole thing drops to pieces in our hands, that we suspect even that the disease is at work.[21]

To the Lighthouse anticipates this part of *Orlando* in that Woolf critiques the 'disease' of Victorianism through a similar emphasis

[19] *Diary*, iii. 208.
[20] Ibid. 110; see also pp. 36, 106, 134.
[21] Virginia Woolf, *Orlando: A Biography*, ed. Rachel Bowlby (Oxford: Oxford University Press, 1992), 217–18.

on the unhealthy dampness of the Ramsays' summer home and repeatedly draws attention to the escalating soddenness of the island as a whole. We read, for example, that the house 'positively drip[s] with wet' (p. 25) even before it lies empty for ten years, just as Mrs Ramsay knows full well that if she were to leave her green cashmere shawl lying about in the house 'it would be the colour of pea soup' (p. 26) within a fortnight. Outside her home a more fundamental inundation is in progress. Standing on the edge of the lawn, for instance, Mr Ramsay feels himself to be on 'a spit of land which the sea is slowly eating away' (p. 38), thinking again of 'the sea eat[ing] the ground we stand on' shortly afterwards (p. 38). He hopes his children will be able to 'stem the flood a bit . . . the land dwindling away, the little island . . . half swallowed up in the sea' (p. 58), yet when the candles are lit and the uncurtained windows are shut during the dinner scene, the 'panes of glass . . . far from giving any accurate view of the outside world, rippled it so strangely that here, inside the room, seemed to be order and dry land; there, outside, a reflection in which things wavered and vanished, *waterily*' (pp. 79– 80; emphasis added). The diners share a sense of 'making a party together in a hollow, on an island' with 'common cause against the fluidity' beyond the walls of the house (p. 80), and to Mrs Ramsay, when her husband begins chanting 'Luriana, Lurilee', the words '(she was looking at the window) sounded as if they were floating like flowers on water out there' (p. 90).

'One can hardly tell which is the sea and which is the land' (p. 103), Prue says in the third paragraph of 'Time Passes', and although her remark is most obviously a comment on the darkness which has enveloped her, Paul, Minta, and Lily during their after-dinner wave-watching walk on the beach, her words anticipate the symbolic immersion and degradation of the house during the Ramsays' ten-year absence from the island. No sooner have the lamps been extinguished for the night in the middle section of the novel than torrential rain and a 'profusion of darkness' (p. 103) assail the property. Its 'rusty hinges and swollen sea-moistened woodwork' (p. 103) offer no defence against the elements and the 'rain-pipe' above the study window becomes blocked with leaves and lets 'the water in' (p. 111). When Mrs McNab enters the nursery at one point during the years when the house is unvisited it is very 'damp' and even the wild boar's skull has 'gone mouldy' (p. 112): in every room, plaster falls off walls 'in shovelfuls' (p. 113). In the final, post-War part of the novel, however, damp is a problem of the past and its only vestige is associated with the generation (as Mr Ramsay puts it in a comment to Macalister) that 'would soon be out of it' (p. 167): when Mr Ramsay approaches Lily at one point before setting off for the Lighthouse his 'immense self-pity, his demand for sympathy poured and spread itself in pools at her feet, and all she did, miserable sinner that she was, was to draw her skirts a little closer round her ankles, lest she should get wet' (pp. 126–7). The threat of the 'destruction of the island and its engulfment in the sea' (p. 17) is foregrounded near the beginning of the novel and the prospect of its being submerged grows more acute throughout the first two parts: significantly, the only local man who is observed in the neighbouring town in 'The Window' is 'digging in a drain' (p. 15). However, the 'engulfment' of 'Time Passes' is akin to the biblical flood (Genesis 6–8); in 'The Lighthouse' the old world of Victorian and Edwardian certainties has been literally washed away and a new dispensation, where marriage isn't the only option for women and where projects get completed rather than put off or abandoned, has finally come to pass.

The scourge of damp is linked with the threat of tuberculosis in the novel. Between 1901 and 1911 another Royal Commission looked into the causes and prevalence of TB in the United Kingdom and it is important to appreciate that Sorley's son, with his 'tuberculous hip' (p. 8), is symptomatic of a grave national problem. One of the recommended ways of keeping the disease at bay (or of fighting it once it had gained a foothold) was effective ventilation, and so the fact that Tansley overhears Mrs Ramsay tell the occupant (or one of the occupants) of the 'poky little house' she visits that she (or they) 'must keep the windows open and the doors shut' (p. 15), suggests that the invalid in the house could well be another victim of the disease. Fearful of the contagion spreading from the town to her house, Mrs Ramsay tries to enforce the same regimen at home as she recommends for the locals and she grows exasperated with the failure of both her servants and her children to follow her straightforward instruction: 'That windows should be open, and doors shut—simple as it was, could none of them remember it?' (p. 26; see also p. 42).

The spectre of TB stalks the novel in other guises. The boar's skull in the nursery, for example, is redolent of scrofula (the name of this form of tuberculosis comes from the Latin word *scrofa*, meaning a breeding sow, and refers to the distinctive swelling of glands in the victim's neck giving the face a porcine appearance). Significantly, wherever Mrs Ramsay holds her light in the nursery 'there was always a shadow [of the boar's skull] somewhere' (p. 93). As she leaves the room, Mrs Ramsay does her best to ensure that both damp and TB will be excluded: she 'pulled the window down another inch or two, and heard the wind, and got a breath of the perfectly indifferent chill night air . . . and let the tongue of the door slowly lengthen in the lock . . .' (pp. 93–4). Her actions are in line with the advice she dispenses but they also betray her profound anxiety, and the 'profusion of darkness' which seeps into the house during the night, 'creeping in at keyholes and crevices . . . came into bedrooms . . . swallowed up . . . the sharp edges and firm bulk of a chest of drawers' (p. 103), suggests that her precautions may have been to no avail. And the vulnerability of all those asleep in the house, adults as well as children, is only reinforced when we read that at times during the night 'a hand was raised as if to clutch something or ward off something, or somebody groaned' (p. 103). Finally, Mrs Ramsay is keen to see a 'model dairy' built on the island (p. 49) in order to combat the threat of bovine tuberculosis—the earwig in her husband's milk perhaps highlighting the scale of the problem she has on her hands—while the eating away of the island by the sea and the gradual saturation of the house by damp may be read as a synecdoche for the sickness, both figurative and epidemiological, of the whole country,[22] in that 'consumption' was the most common name for pulmonary tuberculosis.

If *To the Lighthouse* is the first of a pair of novels in which the more malign aspects of Victorianism are figured through the trope of damp, it completes a trilogy (*Jacob's Room* and *Mrs Dalloway* are the earlier books) in which Woolf engages obliquely with the First World War. While it may seem strange to suggest that a novel in which the majority of the action takes place on a peaceful Scottish island during the Edwardian period is fundamentally (if indirectly) concerned with the devastation of 1914–18, it is not too far-fetched if we bear in mind the kind of responses which 'Time Passes', the part of the novel in which the Ramsays' 'ramshackle' (p. 103) house testifies to

---

[22] See n. 15, above.

the debacle of European civilization (in the manuscript, Mrs McNab is described at one point as 'nothing but a mat for kings & kaisers to tread on'[23]), may have elicited from the book's first readers. For instance, it is unlikely that Woolf's audience in 1927 would have read the beginning of the final sentence of section 1 of 'Time Passes'— 'One by one the lamps were all extinguished'—without thinking of the famous words of Sir Edward Grey, Foreign Secretary at the outbreak of the War, who remarked on 3 August 1914 (in a phrase which was widely disseminated following Grey's publication of his memoirs in 1925), 'The lamps are going out all over Europe; we shall not see them lit again in our life-time.'[24] In a similar way, the 'downpouring of immense darkness' (p. 103) which is visited upon the house evokes not only the terrible rain of shells beneath which soldiers at the front perished but also the water-logged horrors of trench life, while the 'certain airs' which patrol the sleeping house make sentry-like enquiries of the forlorn objects they encounter, 'Were they allies? Were they enemies?' (p. 104). Nor would it have been possible to read that '[p]oppies sowed themselves among the dahlias' (p. 113) in the late 1920s without remembering the War and its terrible aftermath. The spectacular tendency of poppies to 'sow themselves' on the battlefields of the Western Front had been immortalized in John Macrae's well-known poem 'In Flanders Fields' and the British Legion had launched its annual poppy appeal in 1922 in order to raise funds for those who had survived the conflict but who could not live unsupported in the ensuing peace. Even in 'The Window' there is a curious portent of the 1914–18 war when Lily Briscoe is described as watching Mrs Ramsay at the dinner party 'drifting into that strange no-man's land where to follow people is impossible and yet their going inflicts such a chill on those who watch them that they always try at least to follow them with their eyes as one follows a fading ship until the sails have sunk beneath the horizon' (p. 69). The phrase 'no-man's land' was coined centuries before the First World War, but this striking usage of it in a novel of 1927 was surely intended to evoke the unprecedented slaughter which led to the term becoming ubiquitous.

[23] Virginia Woolf, *To the Lighthouse: The Original Holograph Draft*, transcribed and ed. Susan Dick (London: Hogarth Press, 1983), 214.

[24] Viscount Grey of Fallodon, *Twenty-Five Years, 1892–1916* (London: Hodder and Stoughton, 1925), ii. 20.

Elsewhere in 'Time Passes' the dampness and decay which invade the house are described as the 'advance guards of great armies' (p. 105) and the 'ominous sounds like the measured blows of hammers dulled on felt, which, with their repeated shocks still further loosened the shawl and cracked the tea-cups', coupled with 'the thud of something falling' (p. 109), represent the domestic reverberations of the devastating front-line bombardments which killed many more men than Andrew Ramsay (p. 109), just as the repeated storms which beset the island in section 7 of 'Time Passes' sound 'as if the universe were battling and tumbling, in brute confusion and wanton lust aimlessly by itself' (p. 110).

In many ways *To the Lighthouse* is a recapitulation of *Jacob's Room*. Both novels, for example, begin in September and are set or partly set in either Cornwall or a Hebridean mock-up of it; in both novels an animal's skull acts as a memento mori; the Durrants' summer home with its rooks and pampas grass and dinner party in *Jacob's Room* looks forward to the Ramsays' summer retreat with its rooks, pampas grass (pp. 19–20), and dinner party, and the shambling Mr Wortley, a guest of the Durrants, is the prototype of Augustus Carmichael.[25] Another obvious connection between the two novels is that in *Jacob's Room* the 1914 German naval bombardment of Scarborough is dealt with obliquely and in very similar language to the 'measured blows of hammers' passage in *To the Lighthouse* quoted above.[26] Likewise, fallen leaves, an ancient topos for the fallen, which Woolf employs to powerful effect in *Mrs Dalloway*,[27] make a significant reappearance in 'Time Passes', where 'autumn trees, ravaged as they are, take on the flash of tattered flags kindling in the gloom of cool cathedral caves where gold letters on marble pages describe death in battle and how bones bleach and burn far away in Indian sands'. 'The nights now are full of wind and destruction', we read a few lines further on; 'the trees plunge and bend and their leaves fly helter skelter until the lawn is plastered with them and they lie packed in gutters and choke rain pipes and scatter damp

[25] Virginia Woolf, *Jacob's Room*, ed. Kate Flint (Oxford: Oxford University Press, 1992), 73–84.

[26] David Bradshaw, *Winking, Buzzing, Carpet-Beating: Reading* Jacob's Room (Southport: Virginia Woolf Society of Great Britain, 2003), 13–17.

[27] David Bradshaw, ' "Vanished, Like Leaves": The Military, Elegy and Italy in *Mrs Dalloway*', *Woolf Studies Annual*, 8 (2002), 107–25; see esp. pp. 112–16.

paths' (pp. 104–5). Soon afterwards the spring arrives 'without a leaf to toss' (p. 108), and it is almost certainly Woolf's emphasis in *To the Lighthouse* on both a personal and cultural sense of loss which prompted her to write in her diary on 27 June 1925 when making it up: 'I have an idea that I will invent a new name for my books to supplant "novel". A new——by Virginia Woolf. But what? Elegy? . . .'.[28]

Skye's Romantic Shore

While every page of *To the Lighthouse* is infused with Woolf's memories of her idyllic summers in Cornwall, it is set, of course, not in the south-west corner of England, but on Skye, the largest island of the Inner Hebrides, off the north-west coast of Scotland. Unlike Cornwall, Woolf had neither visited Skye (she first set foot on the island in 1938[29]), nor the Hebrides, nor even Scotland when she began to write this novel in 1925, and her lack of familiarity with the island, the islands, and the country got her into hot water with more than one reader. Soon after the book's publication, for instance, Woolf told Vita Sackville-West that 'An old creature writes to say that all my fauna and flora of the Hebrides is totally inaccurate. Dear me! whats to be done about it?', while she informed her sister Vanessa on 22 May 1927 that another correspondent had written to complain that her 'horticulture and natural history is in every instance wrong: there are no rooks, elms, or dahlias in the Hebrides; my sparrows are wrong; so are my carnations . . .'.[30] 'People in The Hebrides are very angry', she remarked to an old friend the following month. 'Is it Cornwall? I'm not as sure as you are'.[31] 'Remoteness from the world was, of course, essential to Mrs Woolf's theme', the *Glasgow Herald*'s reviewer sniped testily on 26 May 1927. 'But this does not justify her action in describing a place which is very obviously Cornwall and calling it Skye . . . she has depicted a

---

[28] *Diary*, iii. 34.
[29] See ibid. v. 154. On 22 August 1933, Woolf had written to Ethel Smyth, 'I wish I knew the geography of the British Isles. I don't at once visualize Hebrides, Skye, and the rest', *Letters*, v. 218.
[30] *Letters*, iii. 374, 379.
[31] Ibid. 389.

country which has an absurd lack of resemblance to the west coast of Scotland.'[32]

Woolf's curious imposition of Cornwall on Skye and the many improbabilities to which it leads—no sane circus impresario, for example, would have been likely to transport a troupe comprising 'a hundred horsemen, twenty performing seals, lions, tigers' (p. 13) to a large (1,735 square kilometres) and in Edwardian times largely inaccessible island with a relatively small and scattered population—has been explained in terms of her anxiety to avoid a possible charge of 'sentimentality' (see above, p. xxi): setting the novel on Skye, the argument goes, rendered it as remote from the contours of her own life as the Hebrides are from London. However, alongside her allegedly errant 'horticulture and natural history' there are aspects of Woolf's Skye that suggest that she may have taken some trouble to read up about the island. For instance, emigration (p. 77) had long been a problem on Skye and elsewhere in the High-lands and Islands and, more intriguingly, during the First World War 'the steamer service was much reduced and uncertain' in the seas around Skye. 'German submarines were constant visitors round the coast and sank several vessels.'[33] Woolf may have had such submarine warfare against (camouflaged?) Allied shipping in mind when she describes 'the silent apparition of an ashen-coloured ship . . . come, gone' leaving only 'a purplish stain upon the bland surface of the sea as if something had boiled and bled, invisibly, beneath' (p. 109).

But the most interesting question of all is not why Woolf chose to airlift her story from Cornwall to the Hebrides, nor whether she did or did not mug up on the recent history of the islands, but why, despite her lack of direct knowledge of it, she decided to set *To the Lighthouse* on Skye *in particular*. Was the island simply chosen at random, as some critics have argued, or did it hold associations for Woolf and her projected reader in 1927 which might not be shared by the general reader today? The answer, almost certainly, is that Skye did hold such connotations for Woolf and her first readers, and

---

[32] Quoted in Virginia Woolf, *To the Lighthouse*, ed. Susan Dick (Oxford: Blackwell for the Shakespeare Head Press, 1992), p. xx.

[33] J. A. MacCulloch, *The Misty Isle of Skye: Its Scenery, Its People, Its Story* (Stirling: Eneas Mackay, 1927), p. vii.

that she located her novel there because she wanted to evoke not its recent past but its literary heritage and its place in the history of Scotland as part of her critique of imperialism.

When Prince Charles Edward Stuart ('Bonnie Prince Charlie') was defeated by the forces of the Hanoverian crown at the Battle of Culloden in 1746, the last battle fought on British soil, he and his Jacobite followers were crushed by the fire-power of an emergent empire. Having landed in the Hebrides in August 1745, the Young Pretender fled back to the islands after Culloden and was famously rowed to Skye under cover of darkness before fleeing, once more, into Continental exile.[34] Woolf would certainly have known 'The Skye Boat Song', the traditional Scottish ballad which commemorates this event, with its final verse beginning 'Burned are our homes, exile and death | Scatter the loyal men', an allusion to the British Government's brutal suppression of the Highlands and Islands in the aftermath of the Jacobite rising (as well as summary executions, devastations of property and rapes, ancient customs and the plaid were proscribed and the bearing of arms forbidden[35]) and she would also have been aware that when Samuel Johnson and James Boswell made their celebrated journey to the Hebrides in 1773, their most prolonged sojourn was on Skye (2 September to 3 October). While on the island, the two men spent a night at the home of Flora Macdonald, the Young Pretender's companion on his legendary voyage 'over the sea to Skye', and they heard from her the story of the Prince's dramatic escape.

Boswell's Jacobite sympathies led him to incorporate a reconstruction of the Prince's flight in his *Journal of a Tour to the Hebrides with Samuel Johnson, LL.D.* (1785), and Johnson himself, despite his notoriously scornful comments about Scotland and the Scots on other occasions, is highly critical of the effects of Government policy and 'is plainly deeply sympathetic to many of the people and social mores'[36] he encountered on Skye and elsewhere in the Hebrides in his *Journey to the Western Islands of Scotland* (1775).

---

[34] See Frank McLynn, *Bonnie Prince Charlie: Charles Edward Stuart* (London: Pimlico, 2003); Jeremy Black, *Culloden and the '45* (Stroud: Sutton, 2000); Murray G. H. Pittock, *Jacobitism* (Basingstoke: Macmillan, 1998).

[35] Black, *Culloden and the '45*, 182–220.

[36] Pat Rogers, *Johnson and Boswell: The Transit of Caledonia* (Oxford: Clarendon Press, 1995), 192.

Johnson devotes a long central section of the *Journey* to a detailed account of the culture, society, and natural history of Skye and writes movingly about the widespread misery and discontent he and Boswell came across in 1773:

There was perhaps never any change of national manners so quick, so great, and so general, as that which has operated in the Highlands, by the last conquest, and the subsequent laws ... The clans retain little now of their original character, their ferocity of temper is softened, their military ardour is extinguished, their dignity of independence is depressed, their contempt of government subdued, and their reverence for their chiefs abated. Of what they had before the late conquest of their country, there remain only their language and their poverty ... That their poverty is gradually abated, cannot be mentioned among the unpleasing consequences of subjection.[37]

Johnson was particularly horrified by the 'epidemick' of emigration which then gripped not just Skye but the whole region and he deplores it at length in the *Journey* (even Flora Macdonald had been forced to emigrate in 1774, but she returned to Scotland in 1779).[38] However, despite Johnson's criticism of the Government, his very presence on the island testified to England's pacification of Skye, the Hebrides, and Scotland as a whole.

Johnson's and Boswell's accounts of their travels led to Skye and the other Hebridean islands being visited by increasing numbers of Englishmen from then on. And not just Englishmen, for the Hebrides' next famous literary visitor was Sir Walter Scott, who came to the island during his tour of Scottish lighthouses in 1814. This journey inspired Scott to complete 'The Lord of the Isles' (1815), in which his deepest nationalist emotions were aroused in describing King Robert the Bruce's struggle against England and the events leading up to the Battle of Bannockburn (1314), the most decisive military victory in Scottish history. The third canto describes the fugitive Robert, driven out of mainland Scotland by Edward I (so-called 'Hammer of the Scots'), escaping to 'Skye's romantic shore'. While on the island, Robert has a dream:

---

[37] Samuel Johnson, *A Journey to the Western Islands of Scotland* ed. Mary Lascelles, *The Yale Edition of the Works of Samuel Johnson*, vol. ix (New Haven and London: Yale University Press, 1971), 57–8.

[38] Ibid. 95–9; quote from p. 96.

His was the patriot's burning thought,
Of Freedom's battle bravely fought,
Of castles stormed, of cities freed,
Of deep design and daring deed,
Of England's roses reft and torn,
And Scotland's cross in triumph worn,
Of rout and rally, war and truce,—
As heroes think, so thought the Bruce.[39]

Robert's later victory at Bannockburn reaffirmed the independence of Scotland and his successors would reign for the next four centuries, but in the novel Scott had published the year before 'The Lord of the Isles', *Waverley* (1814), he had focused on the 1745 rising, the event which conclusively brought that independence to an end. In his novel, Scott's pronounced sympathies for the Jacobite cause flood out in his portrayal of the noble Highland struggle against the alien forces of the Hanoverians and the devastating consequences for the Highlands in particular and Scotland in general when that resistance failed. As he puts it in the last chapter of his novel:

There is no European nation which, within the course of half a century, or little more, has undergone so complete a change as this kingdom of Scotland. The effects of the insurrection of 1745,—the destruction of the patriarchal power of the Highland chiefs,—the abolition of heritable jurisdictions of the Lowland nobility and barons,—the total eradication of the Jacobite party ... The gradual influx of wealth, and extension of commerce, have since united to render the present people of Scotland a class of beings as different from their grandfathers, as the existing English are from those of Queen Elizabeth's time.[40]

Although *The Antiquary*, the Scott novel which Mr Ramsay reads in *To the Lighthouse*, is not concerned with either Jacobitism or Skye, it does complete a trilogy through which Scott illustrates Scottish history from the 1740s to the 1800s (*Guy Mannering* (1815) is the other novel in question). Like Woolf herself, readers of *To the Lighthouse* in the 1920s, a period when Scott's writings were far more popular than they are today, may have found it easier than us to draw together 'The Skye Boat Song', Boswell's and Johnson's writings about the

---

[39] Canto III, from stanza xxvii.
[40] Sir Walter Scott, *Waverley or 'Tis Sixty Years Since*, ed. Claire Lamont (Oxford: Clarendon Press, 1981), 340.

island, Scott's 'The Lord of the Isles', *Waverley*, and the other novels in which his nationalist leanings are evident, as well as the history of Scotland in the 1745–1800 period, into a provocative configuration. In setting the novel on Skye, and including within it a character reading a work of Scott's, Woolf was able not only to honour her parents, both of whom were great admirers of Scott (see note to p. 86), but also to encourage the reader to recall that what happened on Skye and in Scotland at large after 1745 would be repeated elsewhere in the world; to reflect on how Britain would go on to 'depress' the 'dignity of independence' of other, vaster lands, such as the Indian subcontinent; to ponder how 'conquest' (to recall another of Johnson's words) not only subdued Skye and Scotland, but much of the globe.

Mrs Ramsay's attitude to the Empire, it is worth noting, may be just as questionable as her views on marriage and charity. Once again, textual details that might seem random or incidental to a reader today may well have been regarded differently by Woolf and earlier readers of her novel. James Ramsay's cutting out 'pictures from the illustrated catalogue of the Army and Navy Stores' (p. 7) at the beginning of the novel—and the references to other images from the catalogue further on in 'The Window' (e.g. p. 28)—is a case in point. The Army and Navy Stores was set up by military officers in 1871, had an exclusively Establishment clientele, and was an indispensable resource to those engaged in manning and running the Empire at its zenith. To patronize it, therefore, was to play a minor but unequivocal role in the imperial apparatus, and so what might seem to be a merely disarming and introductory scene is in fact loaded with less innocuous ideological ballast. Moreover, the privileged and powerful customer base of the Army and Navy Stores (see note to p. 7) helps us to appreciate why it is entirely natural for Mrs Ramsay to watch James 'guide his scissors neatly round the refrigerator' and then immediately to picture him 'all red and ermine on the Bench or directing a stern and momentous enterprise in some crisis of public affairs' (p. 7). That an Edwardian refrigerator was a luxury appliance many worlds removed from the drudgery of Mrs McNab's existence is also worth pointing out, of course, but what is most noteworthy is the name and nature of the company through whose catalogue the refrigerator is for sale. The Army and Navy catalogue brought home to the far corners of the Empire and just by having it in the Skye house we are told a great deal about the Ramsays' attitudes and social status and are reminded, perhaps, of the way the Hanoverian forces on Skye and throughout Scotland also needed to be provisioned in the eighteenth century.

During her visit to Elsie's 'poky little house', Mrs Ramsay's head is at one point superimposed on a 'picture of Queen Victoria wearing the blue ribbon of the Garter' (p. 15), suggesting, albeit momentarily, that the entire island, and not just her summer home, are Mrs Ramsay's domain. From 1876 Queen Victoria was formally known as Empress of India and the presence on Skye of an imperialistic Englishwoman who fits the profile of Queen Victoria so snugly needs to be registered, while 'Finlay' (p. 49), the Ramsays' substantial summer residence, serviced by at least six staff and comprising a spacious hall, drawing-room, study, smoking-room, dining-room capable of seating '[t]wenty' people (p. 115), kitchen, nursery, bedrooms, servants' quarters and attics, and boasting within its grounds a drive, terrace, tennis court, orchard, lawn, horticultural nurseries, flower beds and capacious greenhouse, is simply palatial compared with the locals' houses. Moreover, as a site where, among other things, bananas and coffee are consumed and in which an exotic conch shell is laid out for admiration above 'the rich purples of . . . grapes' (p. 88), Finlay is literally a place where the fruits of empire are enjoyed and where Britain's ingestion of other people's lands is formally arranged to please the eye.

This anti-imperialist thrust provides us with another way of thinking about those horticultural aspects of the novel which provoked so much umbrage among its first readers. It is almost certainly Mrs Ramsay (see p. 112), for instance, who has transplanted jacmanna, pampas grass, and red-hot pokers to the island (pp. 18, 20, 56), in the same way that she has planted 'dahlias in the big [flower] bed' (p. 55). These exotic plants would have originally arrived in England as 'bulbs' (p. 56) or 'seeds' (p. 115) from the far corners of the Empire (South Africa, New Zealand) and beyond, and their appearance on Skye is probably yet another way in which Woolf marks the territorial reach of the Empire and its homogenization of cultural and geographical difference. Contrary to what the *Glasgow Herald*'s reviewer had to say, one of Woolf's principal aims in this novel was not to achieve 'remoteness from the world' but to critique the Empire's coercive domestication of the remote.

One of the apparently elusive reasons why Mrs Ramsay has 'the whole of the other sex under her protection' is that they 'ruled India' (p. 9), and this throws an interesting light on her indulgent attitude to the elderly Carmichael. Like Peter Walsh in *Mrs Dalloway* and Bartholomew Oliver in *Between the Acts* (1941), Carmichael was a civil servant in India as a young man[41] and, more recently, he has expressed a 'willing[ness] to teach the [Ramsay] boys Persian or Hindustanee' (p. 12). The British promoted the use of Hindustani as a lingua franca throughout the subcontinent as part of their attempt to bring (their notion of) order to the Indian Empire, and so it is more than likely that earlier readers of *To the Lighthouse*, as well as Tansley, would have been able to respond to Mrs Ramsay's response to Carmichael's offer—'but what really was the use of that?' (p. 12)—by answering that if her boys decided that 'rul[ing] India' was the career they wished to follow, knowing Hindustani before arriving there would undoubtedly give them a head start. Other Indian connections should also be considered at this point. Mrs Bast assumes the boar whose skull has ended up on the nursery wall must have been '[s]hot in foreign parts no doubt', Mrs McNab recalling that the Ramsays 'had friends in eastern countries' (p. 115), while the green shawl Mrs Ramsay wraps round the skull is made from *cashmere* wool. Like the words 'bungalow', 'shampoo', 'verandah', and 'pyjamas', 'cashmere' was imported from the Indian Empire. Indeed, it is more than likely that the shawl was a present from there, like 'the opal necklace, which Uncle James had brought [Mrs Ramsay] from India' (p. 67).

The Lot of the Average Human Being

Despite its reputation as an 'endless summer', the Edwardian era was wintry with social, political, and industrial unrest. Between 1906 and 1915 the relatively radical Liberal Party was in power, but the socialist Tansley abuses it roundly at the dinner table (p. 77), continuing to urge on Bankes 'the policy of the Labour Party' (p. 91) when the two men carry on with their political discussion after

[41] More details of Carmichael's experiences in India, including his meeting with 'a bear, on a pass in the Himalayas', are given in the holograph. See *To the Lighthouse: The Original Holograph Draft*, ed. Dick, 155.

dinner. The first words of 'The Lighthouse', ' "Well, we must wait for the future to show," said Mr Bankes, coming in from the terrace' (p. 103) mark the conclusion of their conversation, but as this Introduction has been at pains to argue, social and political questions were also on Woolf's mind as she wrote *To the Lighthouse* and not least because she knew that her brother-in-law, the well-known art critic Clive Bell, was simultaneously bringing a book entitled *Civilization* to a much-delayed conclusion. Reviewing it for his 'World of Books' page in the *Nation and Athenaeum*, Woolf's husband Leonard took exception to Bell's volume and in particular his claim that civilization 'is to be found . . . only in a small society of leisured persons, of non-producers . . . while the vast mass of the population has remained barbarous'. 'Both [Bell's] method and his assumptions are wrong,' Leonard Woolf declares, 'and are bound to lead to wrong conclusions.'[42] Perhaps Bell's most alarming conclusion is his claim that without slavery there can be no civilization:

How are the civilizing few to be supplied with the necessary security and leisure save at the expense of the many?

The answer is that nohow else can they be supplied: their fellows must support them as they have always done. Civilization requires the existence of a leisured class, and a leisured class requires the existence of slaves . . .'[43]

Both Woolfs were familiar with the argument of *Civilization* long before it was published, and inscribed within *To the Lighthouse* is a pre-emptive strike against such blinkered and divisive nonsense. Tansley thinks 'Women made civilization impossible with all their "charm", all their silliness' (p. 70), whereas Bankes believes 'We can't all be Titians and we can't all be Darwins . . . at the same time he doubted whether you could have your Darwin and your Titian if it weren't for humble people like ourselves' (p. 60), while both sides of Bell's argument are weighed in Mr Ramsay's philosophical mind:

If Shakespeare had never existed, he asked, would the world have differed much from what it is today? Does the progress of civilization depend upon great men? Is the lot of the average human being better now than in the time of the Pharaohs? Is the lot of the average human being, however . . . the criterion by which we judge the measure of civilization? Possibly

---

[42] 'Civilization', *Nation and Athenaeum*, 43/10 (9 June 1928), 331.
[43] Clive Bell, *Civilization: An Essay* (London: Chatto and Windus, 1928), 204–5.

not. Possibly the greatest good requires the existence of a slave class. The liftman in the Tube is an eternal necessity. The thought was distasteful to him. He tossed his head. To avoid it, he would find some way of snubbing the predominance of the arts. He would argue that the world exists for the average human being; that the arts are merely a decoration imposed on the top of human life; they do not express it. Nor is Shakespeare necessary to it. (pp. 37–8).

In her characteristically indirect fashion, Woolf in *To the Lighthouse* argues from a similar standpoint to that which Mr Ramsay will adopt in his forthcoming lecture: she valorizes the 'lot of the average human being' and has Lily make it the finishing touch of her picture when she expresses 'the weakness and suffering of mankind' (p. 169) through her final brush stroke. So although Finlay is a kind of offshore academy, with the distinguished Ramsay and his acolyte Charles Tansley locked in discussion of 'some branch of mathematics or philosophy' (p. 10); with the linguist and philosopher-poet Augustus Carmichael basking meditatively in the garden; with the gentleman botanist William Bankes, 'the first scientist of his age' (p. 144), in daily attendance; with Lily Briscoe trying to reconcile post-Impressionist theory and practice in her pictures, and with numerous references to works of art, art galleries, and great works of architecture punctuating the novel—all this leisured activity and the text's mosaic of cultural allusion is juxtaposed with and underpinned by the labour of average human beings, of 'humble people' like Mrs McNab and Mrs Bast. Unlike Clive Bell, however, Woolf positions these two women at the centre of her novel and makes them integral to her notion of civilization, not just two of its nameless and faceless facilitators. Likewise, we learn that the attics of the house hold both the Swiss servant Marie, distressed at the thought of her father dying of cancer, and the impedimenta of the leisured class, 'bats, flannels, straw hats, ink-pots, [and] paint-pots' (p. 11), side by side. Woolf does not make a big issue of this contiguity but she encourages the reader to do so, in the same way that she very deliberately, it seems, has Mrs Ramsay imagine the rock on which the Lighthouse stands as being 'the size of a tennis lawn' (p. 8). Similarly, Bankes, who has brought his 'valet' (p. 23) with him from London, recalls speaking to Mrs Ramsay on the telephone (about his forthcoming vacation?) at one point and then looking out of the window 'to see what progress the workmen were making with an hotel which they were building at the back of his house' (p. 27). Again, this placing of labour and leisure side by side is hardly acerbic, but it is not without bite.

Above all, if the dubious and discredited values of the Victorian and Edwardian eras are exposed in Finlay's dampness and disintegration, its root and branch refurbishment by Mrs McNab, Mrs Bast, and other 'average human being[s]' in 'Time Passes' powerfully undermines Bell's lofty master-and-slave rhetoric. With her swollen hands, lurching gait, 'grinding . . . boots' and general air of 'witlessness' (pp. 106–7), Mrs McNab embodies 'the eternal problems' of the poor and the disadvantaged: 'It was not easy or snug this world she had known for close on seventy years. Bowed down she was with weariness. How long, she asked, creaking and groaning on her knees under the bed, dusting the boards, how long shall it endure?' (p. 107). Woolf told Vita Sackville-West that she was 'doubtful about "Time Passes" ', adding that it 'was written in the gloom of the [General] Strike'[44] of May 1926 when the country seemed to be on the point of degenerating into violence and class strife, and we can sense not only Woolf's rentier unease in this part of the novel but more profoundly her desire for social reconciliation.

In the central part of the novel it is surely significant that the green shawl with which Mrs Ramsay once veiled the boar's skull gradually loosens and swings free. Her shawl was but one of 'the thin veils of civilization' (p. 29) which Mrs Ramsay held so dear but her veiled world was also a world out of kilter. Tellingly, as 'Time Passes' concludes, the rising sun breaks 'the veil' on the eyes of Lily, Carmichael, and Mrs Beckwith, just as Mrs McNab has torn Finlay's 'veil of silence' near the beginning of 'Time Passes'. The somnolence, metaphorical and actual, of 'The Window' has been left behind by Lily at the end of 'Time Passes' and we see her with her 'eyes opened wide . . . sitting bolt upright in bed. Awake' (p. 117). In the final part of the novel no servants are mentioned, yet the word 'effort' dominates the first paragraph of the last section of 'The Lighthouse', as if Mrs McNab and Mrs Bast are still symbolically at work in the house, and a similar 'effort' enables Lily to imagine Carmichael standing next to her and looking out to sea, 'spreading his hands over all the weakness and suffering of mankind; she

[44] *Letters*, iii. 374.

thought he was surveying, tolerantly, compassionately, their final destiny' (p. 169). These last three words most obviously refer to Mr Ramsay and his children reaching the Lighthouse, of course, but 'their' may be just as readily (if less grammatically) applied to 'mankind'. The key point is that it is a political epiphany which prompts Lily to make her final brush stroke and complete her painting. It is triggered by an almost utopian glimpse of a world based on outreach, sympathy, and the elimination of misery.[45] Indeed, so pronounced is the ideological thrust of Lily's moment of revelation, it brings to mind a passage towards the end of Shelley's visionary *Queen Mab* (1813), where the Fairy Queen reveals to the human Spirit the happier shape of things to come:

> Futurity
> Exposes now its treasure; let the sight
> Renew and strengthen all thy failing hope.
> O human Spirit! spur thee to the goal
> Where virtue fixes universal peace,
> And midst the ebb and flow of human things,
> Show somewhat stable, somewhat certain still,
> A lighthouse o'er the wild of dreary waves.[46]

Woolf's friend the art critic Roger Fry wrote that '[t]he drawn line is the record of a gesture, and that gesture is modified by the artist's feelings which is thus communicated to us directly',[47] and what we have at the end of the novel is Lily's 'record' of her moment of vision. By means of her final, uninhibited stroke, she shows how emphatically she has cast off the manacles that held her back a decade previously and she has finally expressed her 'artist's feelings'.

But to identify Lily's last brush stroke too restrictively with 'the weakness and suffering of mankind' would be to read against the grain of this superb and spacious novel. The line might also be thought to represent the 'razor edge of balance' between 'Mr Ramsay and the picture' (p. 158), his 'exactingness' (pp. 33, 124), his being 'lean as a knife, narrow as the blade of one' (p. 7), his being, in Mrs McNab's eyes, 'lean as a rake' (p. 114). Furthermore, as Lily executes her line immediately after she imagines Mr Ramsay springing

---

[45] See n. 15, above.
[46] Shelley, *Queen Mab*, bk. viii, ll. 50–7.
[47] Roger Fry, *Vision and Design* (London: Chatto and Windus, 1920), 22.

onto the Lighthouse rock, it might signify that the essential connect-
ivity between Mr and Mrs Ramsay, to which the reader has been
privy since the end of 'The Window', but which Lily, hitherto, has
been unable to comprehend, has finally been brought home to her.
Lily is suddenly able to make sense of the Ramsays' 'house full of
unrelated passions' (p. 123) and grasp the symbiotic nature of the
parents' relationship. In a perfectly Victorian way, Mr Ramsay was in
awe of his wife's beauty and she revered his mind; he needed her
pity, she needed his adoration. But it is perfectly clear that in addition to the 'weakness and suffering of mankind', the 'arid scimitar of
the male' (pp. 34, 152), and the mutuality of the Ramsays' relationship, the line also stands for, among other things, 'the line of
the branch' (p. 46) Lily considers moving in her earlier, unfinished
picture; quite possibly the tree, which, recalling 'a moment of
revelation' (p. 122) at the dinner table ten years ago, she remembers
she intended to move 'further in the middle' (p. 70; see also pp. 122,
144) of her canvas; 'the problem of the hedge' (p. 148), and the
Lighthouse itself, 'stark and straight' (pp. 152, 165).

Whichever way(s) we read it, with the death of the angel in the
house an incubus has been removed and things are able not only to
work again but to function properly. The lighthouse is reached,
Carmichael is once again appreciated as a poet, Lily is able to complete her picture, and Mrs Ramsay's preoccupation with marriage—
more or less forcing Paul Rayley into asking Minta Doyle to marry
him (p. 65), deciding on the spur of the moment that Lily and
William Bankes 'must marry' (p. 59)—has been brought up to date
through the possibility of more open relationships, like that of Paul
and Minta (p. 143), and easy, loving friendships, such as the one
between Lily and Bankes (p. 145): Lily has remained single and
'happy like [that]' (p. 143). She speaks Mrs Ramsay's name out loud
(p. 133) at one point in 'The Lighthouse', calls out silently to her
ghost at another (p. 146), feels she is 'sitting beside' (p. 141) her, and
mourns her absence a little further on with a searing intensity which
mirrors Woolf's own grief for her dead mother—' "Mrs Ramsay!"
she said aloud, "Mrs Ramsay!" The tears ran down her face' (p. 148;
see also p. 165)—but Lily increasingly feels an even stronger sense of
release from her 'masterfulness' (p. 159), from 'the astonishing
power that Mrs Ramsay had over one' (p. 144). In the end she is able
to appreciate that Mrs Ramsay was both a paragon of beauty and

motherliness *and* a wilful manipulator of those around her. But even
more powerfully, and in a way that is typical of the novel's accom-
modating roominess, Lily acknowledges that with regard to Mrs
Ramsay, 'Fifty pairs of eyes were not enough to get round that one
woman with' (p. 161).

The liberations, transformations, and resolution of 'The Lighthouse' are not completely unanticipated. They have been presaged,
for instance, in the way Cam, in 'The Window', is 'wild and fierce'.
She would 'not "give a flower to the gentleman" as the nursemaid
told her' (p. 21), and the fact that Prue, Nancy, and Rose, as children,
'sport with infidel ideas which they had brewed for themselves of a
life different from' their mother's; '. . . for there was in all their
minds a mute questioning of deference and chivalry, of the Bank of
England and the Indian Empire, of ringed fingers and lace' (p. 9). At
the beginning of 'The Lighthouse', Nancy forgets to order sandwiches for the expedition and confesses that she has no idea what to
send to the Lighthouse keepers (though in the event she makes the
sandwiches herself and gets together 'parcels for the Lighthouse
men', p. 169), an oversight and an admission that are no less integral
to the novel's visionary, speculative, Mr Ramsay-like leap in the
direction of a less patriarchal and a more just world.

All the tensions which the novel explores between the real and the
phantom, husband and wife, separation and connection are
embodied in the Lighthouse itself. As seen by Mrs Ramsay in 'The
Window', it is 'the hoary Lighthouse, distant, austere' (p. 14) and it
is remembered by James as 'a silvery, misty-looking tower with a
yellow eye that opened suddenly and softly in the evening' (p. 152).
Either way, it is a deeply romanticized and illusory structure befit-
ting Woolf's critique of the pre-War era in general, but when James
approaches it in the final part of the novel he realizes it is no more
than a 'tower, stark and straight . . . barred with black and white . . .
[and with] washing spread on the rocks to dry. So that was the
Lighthouse, was it?' (p. 152; see also p. 165). By reaching the Lighthouse with Mr Ramsay, James, and Cam, the reader is able to see that
it is just another place of work; a thing of utility, not romantic at all.
But this is a moment of triumph rather than disappointment. The
old dichotomies of island and Lighthouse, reality and illusion, even
rich and poor, have been harmonized in blue: seen from the boat, the
island has become merely a 'frail blue shape' (p. 169); seen from the

lawn, the Lighthouse has 'melted away into a blue haze' (p. 169); and between them lies the all-absorbing blue of the sea. In the same spirit, as Lily dips her brush 'into the blue paint, she dipped too into the past there' (p. 141): what has been, what is, and what will be have been reconciled as one.

Just as the Lighthouse, 'with its pale footfall upon stair and mat' (p. 104), keeps watch over the house in 'Time Passes', so Mrs Ramsay, as she reads to James in 'The Window', is described as a kind of human tower of light. She emits 'a rain of energy, a column of spray, looking at the same time animated and alive as if all her energies were being fused into force, burning and illuminating' (p. 33). A little further on her beauty is said to be like a 'torch . . . she carried it erect into any room that she entered' (p. 36) and her three-beat 'old familiar pulse' (p. 69) recalls the three-stroke signal of the Lighthouse (p. 52; see also p. 53). In writing her way 'to the Lighthouse', Woolf was able to arrive at a clearer and more enlightened understanding of not just her parents' relationship but more specifically her mother's role in it. However, just as the meaning of the line cannot be pegged down, so the symbol of the Lighthouse itself cannot be tethered to any single interpretation. As Woolf told Fry shortly after the novel was published:

I meant *nothing* by The Lighthouse. One has to have a central line down the middle of the book to hold the design together. I saw that all sorts of feelings would accrue to this, but I refused to think them out, and trusted that people would make it the deposit for their own emotions—which they have done, one thinking it means one thing another another. I can't manage Symbolism except in this vague, generalised way. Whether its right or wrong I don't know, but directly I'm told what a thing means, it becomes hateful to me.[48]

Significant Form

In 1911 Fry praised Cézanne for having revealed 'a new world of significant and expressive form . . . It is that discovery of Cézanne's that has recovered for modern art a whole lost language of form and

[48] *Letters*, iii. 385.

colour',[49] and three years later Clive Bell went on to promote formalism with all the fervour he could muster in his influential *Art* (1914) and to insist that 'significant form' was the cornerstone of all aesthetic value.[50] As Lily makes clear in her description of her picture in 'The Window' (pp. 45–6), she too is a formalist; her abstract canvas is profoundly post-Impressionist in inspiration in that it is built on 'purely aesthetic criteria in place of the criterion of conformity to appearance' and she has set the greatest store on 'the principles of structural design and harmony',[51] in the same way that Cézanne, Gauguin, and Van Gogh had done in their art. Even though she asks Mrs Ramsay to keep 'her head as much in the same position as possible' (p. 17) during her first attempt at her picture, Lily is not concerned with verisimilitude, but rather with finding a way of expressing her 'vision' (p. 46), making a formal success of it by means of 'a shadow here and a light there' (p. 45). Nevertheless, in reducing Mrs Ramsay to a 'triangular purple shape' (p. 45), Lily reveals, paradoxically, how psychologically acute her formalist approach to painting is. Although she has made no 'attempt at likeness' (p. 45) in either of her pictures, she has caught the essence of Mrs Ramsay, a woman who thinks of herself as 'a wedge-shaped core of darkness' (p. 52) and who makes a final, ghostly appearance in the novel as the unnamed figure in the drawing-room who casts 'an odd-shaped triangular shadow over the step' (p. 164).

There are many similarities between Lily's picture and Woolf's novel, and not least the way the structure of the book mirrors the arrangement of the completed canvas, with the two masses of the 'The Window' and 'The Lighthouse' connected by the 'line' of 'Time Passes'. Woolf even made a diagram of this, representing her work as 'Two blocks joined by a corridor':[52]

And with 'The Window' occupying a September evening and 'The

[49] Roger Fry, 'Post Impressionism', *Fortnightly Review* (1 May 1911), 856–67; repr. in Christopher Reed (ed), *A Roger Fry Reader* (Chicago and London: University of Chicago Press, 1996), 99–110; quote from pp. 109–10.

[50] Clive Bell, *Art* (London: Chatto and Windus, 1914), 8 and *passim*.

[51] Fry, *Vision and Design*, 8.

[52] *To the Lighthouse: The Original Holograph Draft*, ed. Dick, app. A, p. 11.

Lighthouse' a September morning, and with a symbolic, ten-year night in between, it is as if 'The Lighthouse' takes place the day after 'The Window'. This consecutive impression underscores the mood of reconciliation in 'The Lighthouse' and is reinforced in various ways. For example, the first sentence of 'The Window' begins with 'Yes' and the last sentence of the 'The Lighthouse' begins with 'Yes' (a word which in turn evokes that most famous double affirmation of all, the 'Yes' with which Molly Bloom begins and ends the final 'Penelope' chapter of that other great Modernist novel, *Ulysses* (1922)). In a similar fashion, the sound of 'carts grinding past on the cobbles' (p. 14), which greets Mrs Ramsay and Charles Tansley on their arrival in the nearby town in 'The Window', is recalled at the end of 'Time Passes' as Mrs Beckwith, Carmichael, and Lily Briscoe wake to, among other noises, 'a cart grinding' (p. 117).

After Mr Ramsay, Cam, and James have departed for the Lighthouse, Lily turns her eyes to her 'canvas as if it had floated up and placed itself white and uncompromising directly before her' (pp. 129–30), like a blank page. She must bring form to her vision just as Woolf had to bring form to her novel. Both artists desired to 'make of the moment something permanent' (p. 133), and when Lily steps back to look at her nearly finished picture she feels as if she is walking 'a narrow plank, perfectly alone, over the sea' (p. 141); 'No one had seen her step off her strip of board into the waters of annihilation' (p. 148). Woolf invariably experienced similar feelings of anxiety (and occasionally desolation) as her novels neared completion and wrote in her diary on 25 October 1920: 'Why is life so tragic; so like a little strip of pavement over an abyss. I look down; I feel giddy; I wonder how I am ever to walk to the end.'[53] And, in the same way that Lily proceeds by 'tunnelling her way into her picture, into the past' (p. 142), it is likely that Woolf's satisfaction at bringing this novel to a conclusion was largely underpinned by her sense that she had finally tunnelled to the heart of her parents' relationship and represented it in all its complexity. In another diary entry, this time from 1923, Woolf had written of the 'tunnelling process' in *Mrs Dalloway* which enabled her to keep the past and the present in place simultaneously, and she employs a comparable method in *To the Lighthouse*.[54]

[53] *Diary*, ii. 72.   [54] Ibid. 272.

Even though she is unable to reify her vision in 'The Window', Lily envisages 'the colour burning on a framework of steel' in her picture, 'the light of a butterfly's wing lying upon the arches of a cathedral' (p. 42). 'Beautiful and bright it should be on the surface,' she says ten years later, 'feathery and evanescent, one colour melting into another like the colours on a butterfly's wing; but beneath the fabric must be clamped together with bolts of iron. It was to be a thing you could ruffle with your breath; and a thing you could not dislodge with a team of horses' (p. 141). Woolf admired a similar combination of strength and delicacy in Proust, and when she 'embedded' herself in his work in 1925 she noted how his writing blends 'the utmost sensibility with the utmost tenacity . . . He is as tough as catgut & as evanescent as a butterfly's bloom', feeling sure that his 'influence' would be evident in *To the Lighthouse*.[55] It is.

Woolf's technique is often misdescribed as 'stream of consciousness' or 'interior monologue', but a comparison of any page of this novel with Molly Bloom's soliloquy at the end of *Ulysses* reveals that Woolf produced something quite different from Molly's uninhibited ruminations, the most obvious difference being that *To the Lighthouse* is entirely narrated in the third person. Woolf depicts (rather than enacts) subjective consciousness, how the human mind meanders through experience, with a magisterial control of her materials. Her technique is paralleled in the way Mrs Ramsay both reads 'The Fisherman and his Wife' and drifts away from it into her own musings, and also in the way the narrative picks up and lets go 'Luriana Lurilee', 'The Castaway', and *The Antiquary*.

Foreshadowed in shorter works, such as 'The Mark on the Wall' and developed through *Jacob's Room* and *Mrs Dalloway*, Woolf summed up her technique in *To the Lighthouse* as 'oratio oblique [indirect speech]'.[56] The point of view is ultimately always that of the omniscient narrator, but lexis and tone are continuously shifting depending on the character in focus creating the effect of an ever changing narrative standpoint. On page 7, for example, Woolf employs straightforward omniscient narration ('Had there been an axe handy . . . seized it') to begin the paragraph describing James's anger at his father's authoritative prediction of rain the following morning before increasingly allowing the style to take on what we

---

[55] *Diary*, iii. 7.   [56] Ibid. 106.

instinctively know to be Mr Ramsay's verbal idiosyncrasies. There are countless examples of this kind of stylistic diffusion in the novel, and the freedoms it granted Woolf are perhaps best in evidence in section 17 of 'The Window' (pp. 68–90), where the narrative point of view is passed round the dining-table like a bottle of wine. 'The dinner party the best thing I ever wrote', Woolf told Vita Sackville-West, 'the one thing that I think justifies my faults as a writer: This damned "method". Because I don't think one could have reached those particular emotions in any other way.'[57]

Every page of *To the Lighthouse* is illuminated by more than a decade's thinking about the art of fiction on Woolf's part. She had repeatedly condemned the Edwardian novelists John Galsworthy, Arnold Bennett, and H. G. Wells for what she saw as their excessive 'materialism', the great efforts to which they went to achieve 'like-ness to life'. 'Is it not possible that the accent falls a little differently . . .,' she asks in 'Modern Novels' (1919),

> that, if one were free and could set down what one chose, there would be no plot, little probability, and a vague general confusion in which the clear-cut features of the tragic, the comic, the passionate, and the lyrical were dissolved beyond the possibility of separate recognition? . . . We are not pleading merely for courage and sincerity; but suggesting that the proper stuff for fiction is a little other than custom would have us believe it.'[58]

Just as Lily's art has nothing in common with the prettifying twee-ness of the Paunceforte-esque painter in the nearby town, whose work, like his master's, is 'green and grey, with lemon coloured sailing-boats, and pink women on the beach' (p. 14), 'pale, elegant, semi-transparent' (p. 19), so Woolf attempted to represent the actual dissolution of experience through her narrative technique, its disorderliness and simultaneity, 'its vague general confusion', its enthralling meld of 'the tragic, the comic, the passionate and the lyrical', and this also explains, among other things, Woolf's striking use of parentheses in 'Time Passes'. Indeed, when she was writing 'The Lighthouse', which switches repeatedly between Mr Ramsay, Cam, and James in the boat and Lily in the garden, Woolf wondered whether the whole book could culminate in a bracket: 'Could I do it

[57] *Letters*, iii. 373–4.
[58] Repr. *Essays* iii. 30–7; quote from p. 33.

in a parenthesis?', she asked herself of Lily finishing her picture and the Lighthouse being reached, 'so that one had the sense of reading the two things at the same time?'.[59] Woolf rejected this idea, but on completing *To the Lighthouse* she thought it quite possible that she had 'made [her] method perfect'.[60]

Deciding whether Woolf was correct or not and 'tunnelling' into her novel with the aid of all manner of biographical, conceptual, ideological, contextual, philosophical, psychological, and theoretical equipment has kept academic and general readers busy ever since the day it was published. *To the Lighthouse* was favourably received by the reviewers and sold extremely well—so well, in fact, that the Woolfs bought their first car on the strength of it—while the consensus that it was her best novel to date was confirmed when it was awarded the Prix Femina-Vie Heureuse in 1928, the only time Woolf received such an honour in her lifetime.

Since the 1920s the reputation of Woolf's work in general and *To the Lighthouse* in particular have grown exponentially. So much so, that the novel is now recognized not only as one of the greatest achievements of the Modernist movement, but one of the greatest works in the entire canon of English literature.[61] This Introduction has been an attempt to look the novel in the eye and get its measure, to hold it for a moment and feel its pulse, but no single reading is ever going to confine it, let alone keep it captive. For as Woolf once said, mischievously, triumphantly, accurately: 'I'm the hare, a long way ahead of the hounds my critics.'[62]

---

[59] *Diary*, iii. 106.

[60] Ibid. 117.

[61] For a valuable synopsis of the novel's critical reception see Jane Goldman (ed.), *Virginia Woolf: 'To the Lighthouse' 'The Waves'* (Basingstoke and London: Palgrave Macmillan, 1997).

[62] *Diary*, iv. 45.

NOTE ON THE TEXT

The copy text for this new Oxford World's Classics edition of *To the Lighthouse* is the first British edition of the novel, published by Virginia and Leonard Woolf's Hogarth Press on 5 May 1927 (a second impression came out the following month and a third impression in May 1928).

The first American edition of the novel, published by Harcourt Brace, also appeared on 5 May 1927, yet there are a surprising number of textual variants between the two first editions. Some of these variants are substantive (see below), but many more are not and a number are clearly accidental. For a list of all the textual variants between the two first editions, see 'Appendix B: Textual Variants' in the Shakespeare Head Press edition of the novel, edited by Susan Dick (Oxford: Blackwell, 1992), 192–211. Interested readers should also consult J. A. Lavin's account of the textual differences between the first editions: see the Select Bibliography.

Some minor alterations of spelling and punctuation have been made to the base text for this edition on the grounds of consistency and in order to conform with current usage (e.g., 'tonight' for 'tonight' and 'override' for 'over-ride'). More importantly, at the end of the third section of 'Time Passes' (p. 105) the previous Oxford World's Classics edition read: '[Mr Ramsay stumbling along a passage stretched his arms out one dark morning, but, Mrs Ramsay having died rather suddenly the night before, he stretched his arms out. They remained empty.]'. This purported to mirror the English first edition, but that edition reads at this point: '[Mr. Ramsay stumbling along a passage stretched his arms out one dark morning, but Mrs. Ramsay having died rather suddenly the night before he stretched his arms out. They remained empty.]'. The punctuation of the first British edition, therefore, has been reinstated at this important point in the novel, but without the full stops after 'Mr' and 'Mrs'.

On at least three other occasions the text of the previous Oxford World's Classics edition departed from the first British edition but did not make this deviation known to the reader. This new text, on the other hand, like the 1992 edition, retains the word 'it' after 'washing' on page 10 because 'washing' on its own makes little sense, but 'it' does not appear in the first British edition at this point. On page 104 of the OWC edition, the first line of the third paragraph used to read, 'So some random light directing them from an uncovered star' but this has been changed to '. . . from some uncovered star', to exactly follow the wording of the British first edition. And on p. 70 the word 'the' has been introduced so that Lily puts her salt cellar down on a flower in *the* pattern in the table-cloth, and not 'on a flower in pattern in the table-cloth' as it says in the British and American first editions. A small number of typographical errors were also found in the previous Oxford text and these have now been emended.

The holograph manuscript of the novel, which consists of two bound writing books and one loose-leaf folder, is in the Berg Collection in New York Public Library. It has been transcribed and edited, with a commentary, by Susan Dick (1983) and is referred to more than once in the Introduction.

A Selection of the More Substantive Variants between the First British Edition and the First American Edition

The first page reference is to this new Oxford World's Classics edition. Page references to the first British and first American editions are given in parentheses.

First British Edition	*First American Edition*
10 like a Queen's raising from the mud a beggar's dirty foot and washing, when (16–17)	like a Queen's raising from the mud to wash a beggar's dirty foot, when (14)
10 the Isle of Skye (17)	the Isles of Skye (14)
10 disparage them, put them all on edge somehow with his acid way of peeling the flesh and blood off everything, he was not satisfied. (18)	disparage them—he was not satisfied. (16)
14 how he had been to Ibsen with the Ramsays. (25)	how he had gone not to the circus but to Ibsen with the Ramsays. (22)
16 (as she sat in the window), that (29)	(as she sat in the window which opened on the terrace), that (27)

First British Edition	*First American Edition*
19 it was impossible. One could not say what one meant. So now (35)	it was impossible. So now (32)
26 things must spoil. What was the use of flinging a green Cashmere shawl over the edge of a picture frame? In two weeks it would be the colour of pea soup. But it was the doors that annoyed her; every door was left open. (47)	things must spoil. Every door was left open. (44)
27 some freak of idiosyncrasy; or suppose (51)	some freak of idiosyncrasy— she did not like admiration—or suppose—(47)
42 found a glove (79)	found a crumpled glove (76)
61 bringing Prue back into the alliance of family life again, from which she had escaped, throwing catches, asked, (116)	bringing Prue back into throwing catches again, from which she had escaped, asked (112)
85 the thing is made that remains for ever after. This would remain. (163)	the thing is made that endures (158)
100 It's going to be wet to-morrow." She had not said it, but he knew it. And she looked at him smiling. For she had triumphed again. (191)	It's going to be wet tomorrow. You won't be able to go." And she looked at him smiling. For she had triumphed again. She had not said it: yet he knew. (186)
104 directing them from some uncovered star, or wandering ship, or the Lighthouse even, with its pale footfall upon stair and mat, the little airs (197)	directing them with its pale footfall upon stair and mat, from some uncovered star, or wandering ship, or the Lighthouse even, the little airs (191)

First British Edition	*First American Edition*
105 [Mr. Ramsay stumbling along a passage stretched his arms out one dark morning, but Mrs. Ramsay having died rather suddenly the night before he stretched his arms out. They remained empty.] (199–200)	[Mr. Ramsay, stumbling along a passage one dark morning, stretched his arms out, but Mrs. Ramsay having died rather suddenly the night before, his arms, though stretched out, remained empty.] (194)
109 children pelting each other with handfuls of grass, something out of harmony with this jocundity, this serenity. (207)	children making mud pies or pelting each other with handfuls of grass, something out of harmony with this jocundity and this serenity. (201)
116 [Lily Briscoe had her bag carried up to the house late one evening in September. Mr. Carmichael came by the same train.] (219)	(Lily Briscoe had her bag carried up to the house late one evening in September.) (213)
129 seemed to fly back in her face, like a bramble sprung. (242)	seemed to be cast back on her, like a bramble sprung across her face. (233)
132 There must have been a shadow.) Mrs. Ramsay. When she thought (248)	There must have been a shadow.) When she thought (239)
133 She owed this revelation to her. (250)	She owed it all to her. (241)
152 The other was the Lighthouse too. (286)	The other Lighthouse was true too. (277)
153 into her head. "We shall need a big dish to-night. Where is it—the blue dish?" She alone (287–8)	into her head. She alone (278)
159 There was an aloofness about him. (299)	There was an impersonality about him. (290)
160 with them there. She never (301)	with them there in that stuffy little room. She never (291)

First British Edition	*First American Edition*

162–3   on the stairs. They had laughed and laughed, like a couple of children, all because Mr. Ramsay, finding an earwig in his milk at breakfast had sent the whole thing flying through the air on to the terrace outside. "An earwig," Prue murmured, awestruck, "in his milk." Other people might find centipedes. But he had built round him such a fence of sanctity, and occupied the space with such a demeanour of majesty that an earwig in his milk was a monster.
   But it tired Mrs. Ramsay, (306)
	on the stairs. It had been an earwig, apparently. Other people might find centipedes. They had laughed and laughed.
	
	on the stairs. It had been an earwig, apparently. Other people might find centipedes. They had laughed and laughed.
	   But it tired Mrs. Ramsay, (296)

169 He stood there spreading his hands (319)	He stood there as if he were spreading his hands (309)

SELECT BIBLIOGRAPHY

Bibliography

Kirkpatrick, B. J., and Clarke, Stuart N., *A Bibliography of Virginia Woolf* (4th edn., Oxford: Clarendon Press, 1997).

Biography

Bell, Quentin, *Virginia Woolf: A Biography* (1972; London: Pimlico, 1996).

Briggs, Julia, *Virginia Woolf: An Inner Life* (London: Allen Lane, 2005).

Gordon, Lyndall, *Virginia Woolf: A Writer's Life* (Oxford: Oxford University Press, 1984).

Leaska, Mitchell A., *Granite and Rainbow: The Hidden Life of Virginia Woolf* (London: Picador, 1998).

Lee, Hermione, *Virginia Woolf* (London: Chatto and Windus, 1996).

Mepham, John, *Virginia Woolf: A Literary Life* (London and Basingstoke: Macmillan, 1991).

Poole, Roger, *The Unknown Virginia Woolf* (4th edn., Cambridge: Cambridge University Press, 1995).

Editions

The Complete Shorter Fiction of Virginia Woolf, ed. Susan Dick (1985; London: Hogarth Press, rev. edn., 1989).

The Diary of Virginia Woolf, ed. Anne Olivier Bell assisted by Andrew McNeillie (5 vols.; London: Hogarth Press, 1977–84).

The Essays of Virginia Woolf, ed. Andrew McNeillie (6 vols.; London: Hogarth Press, 1986–), 4 vols. published to date.

Hyde Park Gate News: The Stephen Family Newspaper by Virginia Woolf and Vanessa Bell with Thoby Stephen, ed. Gill Lowe (London: Hesperus Press, 2005).

The Letters of Virginia Woolf, ed. Nigel Nicolson and Joanne Trautmann (6 vols.; London: Hogarth Press, 1975–80).

Moments of Being, ed. Jeanne Schulkind, rev. Hermione Lee (1976; London: Pimlico, 2002).

A Passionate Apprentice: The Early Journals and 'Carlyle's House and Other Sketches', ed. Mitchell A. Leaska (1990; London: Pimlico, 2004).

To the Lighthouse: The Original Holograph Draft, transcribed and ed. Susan Dick (London: Hogarth Press, 1983).

General Criticism

Abel, Elizabeth, *Virginia Woolf and the Fictions of Psychoanalysis* (Chicago: University of Chicago Press, 1989).

Banfield, Ann, *The Phantom Table: Woolf, Fry, Russell and the Epistemology of Modernism* (Cambridge: Cambridge University Press, 2000).

Bazin, Nancy Topping, *Virginia Woolf and the Androgynous Vision* (New Brunswick, NJ: Rutgers University Press, 1973).

Beer, Gillian, *Virginia Woolf: The Common Ground* (Edinburgh: Edinburgh University Press, 1996).

Bowlby, Rachel, *Virginia Woolf: Feminist Destinations and Further Essays on Virginia Woolf* (Edinburgh: Edinburgh University Press, 1997).

Briggs, Julia, *Virginia Woolf: Introductions to the Major Works* (London: Virago Press, 1994).

Cuddy-Keane, Melba, *Virginia Woolf, the Intellectual, and the Public Sphere* (Cambridge: Cambridge University Press, 2003).

Dalgarno, Emily, *Virginia Woolf and the Visible World* (Cambridge: Cambridge University Press, 2001).

Dever, Carolyn, *Death and the Mother from Dickens to Freud: Victorian Fiction and the Anxiety of Origins* ((Cambridge: Cambridge University Press, 1998).

DiBattista, Maria, *Virginia Woolf's Major Novels: The Fables of Anon.* (New Haven and London: Yale University Press, 1980).

Dusinberre, Juliet, *Alice to the Lighthouse: Children's Books and Radical Experiments in Art* (1987; Basingstoke and London: Macmillan, 1999)

Fleishman, Avrom, *Virgina Woolf: A Critical Reading* (Baltimore: Johns Hopkins University Press, 1975).

Froula, Christine, *Virginia Woolf and the Bloomsbury Avant-Garde: War, Civilization, Modernity* (New York: Columbia University Press, 2005).

Garrity, Jane, *Step-Daughters of England: British Women Modernists and the National Imaginary* (Manchester: Manchester University Press, 2003).

Gillespie, Diane F., *The Sisters' Arts: The Writing and Painting of Virginia Woolf and Vanessa Bell* (Syracuse, NY: Syracuse University Press, 1988).

Goldman, Jane, *The Feminist Aesthetics of Virginia Woolf: Modernism, Post-Impressionism and the Politics of the Visual* (Cambridge: Cambridge University Press, 1998).

Harper, Howard, *Between Language and Silence: The Novels of Virginia Woolf* (Baton Rouge, La.: Louisiana State University Press, 1982).

Henry, Holly, *Virginia Woolf and the Discourse of Science: The Aesthetics of Astronomy* (Cambridge: Cambridge University Press, 2003).

Hussey, Mark, *The Singing of the Real World: The Philosophy of Virginia Woolf's Fiction* (Columbus, Ohio: Ohio State University Press, 1986).

—— *Virginia Woolf A to Z: A Comprehensive Reference for Students, Teachers, and Common Readers to Her Life, Works, and Critical Reception* (New York: Facts on File, 1995).

—— (ed.), *Virginia Woolf and War: Fiction, Reality and Myth* (Syracuse, NY: Syracuse University Press, 1991).

Leaska, Mitchell A., *The Novels of Virginia Woolf: From Beginning to End* (London: Weidenfeld and Nicolson, 1977).

Lee, Hermione, *The Novels of Virginia Woolf* (London: Methuen, 1977).

McLaurin, Allen, *Virginia Woolf: The Echoes Enslaved* (Cambridge: Cambridge University Press, 1973).

Majumdar, Robin, and McLaurin, Allen (eds.), *Virginia Woolf: The Critical Heritage* (1975; London: Routledge, 1997).

Marcus, Jane, *Art and Anger: Reading Like a Woman* (Columbus: Ohio State University Press, 1988).

—— (ed.), *New Feminist Essays on Virginia Woolf* (Lincoln, Nebr.: University of Nebraska Press, 1981).

—— (ed.), *Virginia Woolf: A Feminist Slant* (Lincoln, Nebr.: University of Nebraska Press, 1983).

—— (ed.), *Virginia Woolf and Bloomsbury: A Centenary Celebration* (Bloomington, Ind.: Indiana University Press, 1987).

—— (ed.), *Virginia Woolf and the Languages of Patriarchy* (Bloomington, Ind.: Indiana University Press, 1987).

Meisel, Perry, *The Absent Father: Virginia Woolf and Walter Pater* (New Haven and London: Yale University Press, 1980).

Minow-Pinkney, Makiko, *Virginia Woolf and the Problem of the Subject: Feminine Writing in the Major Novels* (Brighton: Harvester Wheatsheaf, 1987).

Paul, Janis M., *The Victorian Heritage of Virginia Woolf: The External World in Her Novels* (Norman, Okla.: Pilgrim Books, 1987).

Peach, Linden, *Virginia Woolf* (Basingstoke and London: Macmillan, 2000).

Phillips, Kathy J., *Virginia Woolf Against Empire* (Knoxville, Tenn.: University of Tennessee Press, 1994).

Roe, Sue, and Sellers, Susan (eds.), *The Cambridge Companion to Virginia Woolf* (Cambridge: Cambridge University Press, 2000).

Silver, Brenda R., *Virginia Woolf Icon* (Chicago and London: University of Chicago Press, 1999).

Snaith, Anna, *Virginia Woolf: Public and Private Negotiations* (Basingstoke and London: Palgrave, 2003).

—— (ed.), *Palgrave Advances in Virginia Woolf Studies* (Basingstoke and London: Palgrave Macmillan, 2007)

Wussow, Helen, *The Nightmare of History: The Great War in the Work of Virginia Woolf and D. H. Lawrence* (Bethlehem, Pa. and London: Lehigh University Press, 1998).

Zwerdling, Alex, *Virginia Woolf and the Real World* (Berkeley and Los Angeles: University of California Press, 1986).

Criticism of To the Lighthouse

Abel, Elizabeth, '*To the Lighthouse*: James and Cam' and 'Spatial Relations: Lily Briscoe's Painting', in *Virginia Woolf and the Fictions of Psychoanalysis* (Chicago: University of Chicago Press, 1989), 45–83.

Beer, Gillian, 'Hume, Stephen, and Elegy in *To the Lighthouse*', in *The Common Ground* (Edinburgh: Edinburgh University Press, 1996), 29–47.

Clark, Miriam Marty, 'Consciousness, Stream, and Quanta in *To the Lighthouse*', *Studies in the Novel*, 21 (Winter 1989), 413–23.

Corsa, Helen Storm, 'To the Lighthouse: Death, Mourning, and Transfiguration', *Literature and Psychology*, 21/3 (1971), 115–31.

Davies, Stevie, *Virginia Woolf:* To the Lighthouse (Harmondsworth, Middlesex: Penguin, 1989).

Dell, Marion, and Whybrown, Marion, *Virginia Woolf and Vanessa Bell Remembering St Ives* (Padstow: Tabb House, 2004).

Fisher, Jane, 'The Seduction of the Father: Virginia Woolf and Leslie Stephen', *Women's Studies*, 18 (1990), 31–48.

Flint, Kate, 'Virginia Woolf and the General Strike', *Essays in Criticism*, 36 (1986), 319–34.

Goldman, Jane (ed.), Virginia Woolf: 'To the Lighthouse' 'The Waves' (Basingstoke and London: Palgrave Macmillan, 1997).

Haule, James M., '*To the Lighthouse* and the Great War: The Evidence of Virginia Woolf's Revisions of "Time Passes" ', in Mark Hussey (ed.), *Virginia Woolf and War* (Syracuse, NY: Syracuse University Press, 1991), 164–79.

Hill, Katherine, 'Virginia Woolf and Leslie Stephen: History and Literary Revolution', *PMLA* 96 (1981), 351–62.

Lavin, J. A., 'The First Editions of Virginia Woolf's *To the Lighthouse*', in *Proof: The Yearbook of American Bibliographical and Textual Studies*, ed. Joseph Katz (Columbia: University of South Carolina Press, 1972), 185–211.

Leaska, Mitchell A., *Virginia Woolf's Lighthouse: A Study in Critical Method* (London: Hogarth Press, 1970).

Levenback, Karen L., 'The Language of Memory as Time Passes', in *Virginia Woolf and the Great War* (Syracuse, NY: Syracuse University Press, 1999), 83–113.

Pratt, Annis, 'Sexual Imagery in *To the Lighthouse*: A New Feminist Approach', *Modern Fiction Studies*, 18 (1972), 417–31.

Raitt, Suzanne, *Virginia Woolf's* To the Lighthouse (Hemel Hempstead and London: Harvester Wheatsheaf, 1990).

Rosenbaum, S. P., 'The Philosophical Realism of Virginia Woolf', in S. P. Rosenbaum (ed.), *English Literature and British Philosophy* (Chicago and London: University of Chicago Press, 1971), 316–56.

Sheehan, Paul, 'Woolf's Luminance: Time Out of Mind', in *Modernism, Narrative and Humanism* (Cambridge: Cambridge University Press, 2002), 121–49.

Winston, Janet, ' "Something Out of Harmony": *To the Lighthouse* and the Subject(s) of Empire', *Woolf Studies Annual*, 2 (1996), 39–70.

Further Reading in Oxford World's Classics

Whitworth, Michael, *Virginia Woolf*, Authors in Context.

Woolf, Virginia, *Between the Acts*, ed. Frank Kermode.

—— *Flush*, ed. Kate Flint.

—— *Jacob's Room*, ed. Kate Flint.

—— *The Mark on the Wall and Other Short Fiction*, ed. David Bradshaw.

—— *Mrs Dalloway*, ed. David Bradshaw.

—— *Night and Day*, ed. Suzanne Raitt.

—— *Orlando: A Biography*, ed. Rachel Bowlby.

—— *A Room of One's Own and Three Guineas*, ed. Morag Shiach.

—— *The Voyage Out*, ed. Lorna Sage.

—— *The Waves*, ed. Gillian Beer.

—— *The Years*, ed. Hermione Lee, with notes by Sue Ashbee.

A CHRONOLOGY OF VIRGINIA WOOLF

	Life	*Historical and Cultural Background*
1882	(25 Jan.) Adeline Virginia Stephen (VW) born at 22 Hyde Park Gate, London.	Deaths of Darwin, Trollope, D.G. Rossetti; Joyce born; Stravinsky born; Married Women's Property Act; Society for Psychical Research founded.
1895	(5 May) Death of mother, Julia Stephen; VW's first breakdown occurs soon afterwards.	Death of T. H. Huxley; X-rays discovered; invention of the cinematograph; wireless telegraphy invented; arrest, trials, and conviction of Oscar Wilde. Wilde, *The Importance of Being Earnest* and *An Ideal Husband* Wells, *The Time Machine*
1896	(Nov.) Travels in France with sister Vanessa.	Death of William Morris; *Daily Mail* started. Hardy, *Jude the Obscure* Housman, *A Shropshire Lad*
1897	(10 April) Marriage of half-sister Stella; (19 July) death of Stella; (Nov.) VW learning Greek and history at King's College, London.	Queen Victoria's Diamond Jubilee; Tate Gallery opens. Stoker, *Dracula* James, *What Maisie Knew*
1898		Deaths of Gladstone and Lewis Carroll; radium and plutonium discovered. Wells, *The War of the Worlds*
1899	(30 Oct.) VW's brother Thoby goes up to Trinity College, Cambridge, where he forms friendships with Lytton Strachey, Leonard Woolf, Clive Bell, and others of the future Bloomsbury Group (VW's younger brother Adrian follows him to Trinity in 1902).	Boer War begins. Births of Bowen and Coward. Symons, *The Symbolist Movement in Literature* James, *The Awkward Age* Freud, *The Interpretation of Dreams*
1900		Deaths of Nietzsche, Wilde, and Ruskin; *Daily Express* started; Planck announces quantum theory; Boxer Rising. Conrad, *Lord Jim*

Life	*Historical and Cultural Background*
1901	Death of Queen Victoria; accession of Edward VII; first wireless communication between Europe and USA; 'World's Classics' series begun. Kipling, *Kim*
1902 VW starts private lessons in Greek with Janet Case.	End of Boer War; British Academy founded; *Encyclopaedia Britannica* (10th edn.); *TLS* started Bennett, *Anna of the Five Towns* James, *The Wings of the Dove*
1903	Deaths of Gissing and Spencer; *Daily Mirror* started; Wright brothers make their first aeroplane flight; Emmeline Pankhurst founds Women's Social and Political Union. Butler, *The Way of All Flesh* James, *The Ambassadors* Moore, *Principia Ethica*
1904 (22 Feb.) Death of father, Sir Leslie Stephen. In spring, VW travels to Italy with Vanessa and friend Violet Dickinson. (10 May) VW has second nervous breakdown and is ill for three months. Moves to 46, Gordon Square. (14 Dec.) VW's first publication appears.	Deaths of Christina Rossetti and Chekhov; Russo-Japanese War; *Entente Cordiale* between Britain and France. Chesterton, *The Napoleon of Notting Hill* Conrad, *Nostromo* James, *The Golden Bowl*
1905 (March, April) Travels in Portugal and Spain. Writes reviews and teaches once a week at Morley College, London.	Einstein, *Special Theory of Relativity*; Sartre born Shaw, *Major Barbara* and *Man and Superman* Wells, *Kipps* Forster, *Where Angels Fear to Tread*
1906 (Sept. and Oct.) Travels in Greece. (20 Nov.) Death of Thoby Stephen.	Death of Ibsen; Beckett born; Liberal Government elected; Campbell-Bannerman Prime Minister; launch of HMS *Dreadnought*.
1907 (7 Feb.) Marriage of Vanessa to Clive Bell. VW moves with Adrian to 29 Fitzroy Square. At work on her first novel, 'Melymbrosia' (working title for *The Voyage Out*).	Auden born; Anglo-Russian Entente. Synge, *The Playboy of the Western World* Conrad, *The Secret Agent* Forster, *The Longest Journey*
1908 (Sept.) Visits Italy with the Bells.	Asquith Prime Minister; Old Age Pensions Act; Elgar's First Symphony. Bennett, *The Old Wives' Tale* Forster, *A Room with a View*

Life	*Historical and Cultural Background*
	Chesterton, *The Man Who Was Thursday*
1909 (17 Feb.) Lytton Strachey proposes marriage. (30 March) First meets Lady Ottoline Morrell. (April) Visits Florence. (Aug.) Visits Bayreuth and Dresden.	Death of Meredith; 'People's Budget'; English Channel flown by Blériot. Wells, *Tono-Bungay* Masterman, *The Condition of England* Marinetti, *Futurist Manifesto*
1910 (Jan.) Works for women's suffrage. (June–Aug.) Spends time in a nursing home at Twickenham	Deaths of Edward VII, Tolstoy, and Florence Nightingale; accession of George V; *Encyclopaedia Britannica* (11th edn.); Roger Fry's Post-Impressionist Exhibition. Bennett, *Clayhanger* Forster, *Howards End* Yeats, *The Green Helmet* Wells, *The History of Mr Polly*
1911 (April) Travels to Turkey, where Vanessa is ill. (Nov.) Moves to 38 Brunswick Square, sharing house with Adrian, John Maynard Keynes, Duncan Grant, and Leonard Woolf.	National Insurance Act; Suffragette riots. Conrad, *Under Western Eyes* Wells, *The New Machiavelli* Lawrence, *The White Peacock*
1912 Rents Asheham House. (Feb.) Spends some days in Twickenham nursing home. (10 Aug.) Marriage to Leonard Woolf. Honeymoon in Provence, Spain, and Italy. (Oct.) Moves to 13 Clifford's Inn, London.	Second Post-Impressionist Exhibition; Suffragettes active; strikes by dockers, coal-miners, and transport workers; Irish Home Rule Bill again rejected by Lords; sinking of SS *Titanic*; death of Scott in the Antarctic; *Daily Herald* started. English translations of Chekhov and Dostoevsky begin to appear.
1913 (March) MS of *The Voyage Out* delivered to publisher. Unwell most of summer. (9 Sept.) Suicide attempt. Remains under care of nurses and husband for rest of year.	*New Statesman* started; Suffragettes active. Lawrence, *Sons and Lovers*
1914 (16 Feb.) Last nurse leaves. Moves to Richmond, Surrey.	Irish Home Rule Bill passed by Parliament; First World War begins (4 Aug.); Dylan Thomas born. Lewis, *Blast* Joyce, *Dubliners* Yeats, *Responsibilities* Hardy, *Satires of Circumstance* Bell, *Art*

Life	*Historical and Cultural Background*
1915 Purchase of Hogarth House, Richmond. (26 March) *The Voyage Out* published. (April, May) Bout of violent madness; under care of nurses until November.	Death of Rupert Brooke; Einstein, *General Theory of Relativity*; Second Battle of Ypres; Dardanelles Campaign; sinking of SS *Lusitania*; air attacks on London. Ford, *The Good Soldier* Lawrence, *The Rainbow* Brooke, *1914 and Other Poems* Richardson, *Pointed Roofs*
1916 (17 Oct.) Lectures to Richmond branch of the Women's Co-operative Guild. Regular work for *TLS*.	Death of James; Lloyd George Prime Minister; First Battle of the Somme; Battle of Verdun; Gallipoli Campaign; Easter Rising in Dublin. Joyce, *Portrait of the Artist as a Young Man*
1917 (July) Hogarth Press commences publication with *The Mark on the Wall*. VW begins work on *Night and Day*.	Death of Edward Thomas. Third Battle of Ypres (Passchendaele); T. E. Lawrence's campaigns in Arabia; USA enters the War; Revolution in Russia (Feb., Oct.); Balfour Declaration. Eliot, *Prufrock and Other Observations*
1918 Writes reviews and *Night and Day;* also sets type for the Hogarth Press. (15 Nov.) First meets T. S. Eliot.	Death of Owen; Second Battle of the Somme; final German offensive collapses; Armistice with Germany (11 Nov.); Franchise Act grants vote to women over 30; influenza pandemic kills millions. Lewis, *Tarr* Hopkins, *Poems* Strachey, *Eminent Victorians*
1919 (1 July) Purchase of Monk's House, Rodmell, Sussex. (20 Oct.) *Night and Day* published.	Treaty of Versailles; Alcock and Brown fly the Atlantic; National Socialists founded in Germany. Sinclair, *Mary Olivier* Shaw, *Heartbreak House*
1920 Works on journalism and *Jacob's Room*.	League of Nations established. Pound, *Hugh Selwyn Mauberley* Lawrence, *Women in Love* Eliot, *The Sacred Wood* Fry, *Vision and Design*
1921 Ill for summer months. (4 Nov.) Finishes *Jacob's Room*.	Irish Free State founded. Huxley, *Crome Yellow*

Life	*Historical and Cultural Background*
1922 (Jan. to May) Ill. (24 Oct.) *Jacob's Room* published. (14 Dec.) First meets Vita Sackville-West.	Bonar Law Prime Minister; Mussolini forms Fascist Government in Italy; death of Proust; *Encyclopaedia Britannica* (12th edn.); *Criterion* founded; BBC founded; Irish Free State proclaimed. Eliot, *The Waste Land* Galsworthy, *The Forsyte Saga* Joyce, *Ulysses* Mansfield, *The Garden Party* Wittgenstein, *Tractatus Logico-Philosophicus*
1923 (March, April) Visits Spain. Works on 'The Hours', the first version of *Mrs Dalloway*.	Baldwin Prime Minister; BBC radio begins broadcasting (Nov.); death of K. Mansfield.
1924 Purchase of lease on 52 Tavistock Square, Bloomsbury. Gives lecture that becomes 'Mr Bennett and Mrs Brown'. (8 Oct.) Finishes *Mrs Dalloway*.	First (minority) Labour Government; Ramsay MacDonald Prime Minister; deaths of Lenin, Kafka, and Conrad. Ford, *Some Do Not* Forster, *A Passage to India* O'Casey, *Juno and the Paycock* Coward, *The Vortex*
1925 (23 April) *The Common Reader* published. (14 May) *Mrs Dalloway* published. Ill during summer.	Gerhardie, *The Polyglots* Ford, *No More Parades* Huxley, *Those Barren Leaves* Whitehead, *Science and the Modern World*
1926 (Jan) Unwell with German measles. Writes *To the Lighthouse*.	General Strike (3–12 May); *Encyclopaedia Britannica* (13th edn.); first television demonstration. Ford, *A Man Could Stand Up* Tawney, *Religion and the Rise of Capitalism*
1927 (March, April) Travels in France and Italy. (5 May) *To the Lighthouse* published. (5 Oct.) Begins *Orlando*.	Lindburgh flies solo across the Atlantic; first 'talkie' films.
1928 (11 Oct.) *Orlando* published. Delivers lectures at Cambridge on which she bases *A Room of One's Own*.	Death of Hardy; votes for women over 21. Yeats, *The Tower* Lawrence, *Lady Chatterley's Lover* Waugh, *Decline and Fall* Sherriff, *Journey's End* Ford, *Last Post* Huxley, *Point Counter Point* Bell, *Civilization*

Life	*Historical and Cultural Background*
1929 (Jan.) Travels to Berlin. (24 Oct.) *A Room of One's Own* published.	2nd Labour Government, MacDonald Prime Minister; collapse of New York Stock Exchange; start of world economic depression. Graves, *Goodbye to All That* Aldington, *Death of a Hero* Green, *Living*
1930 (20 Feb.) First meets Ethel Smyth; (29 May) Finishes first version of *The Waves*.	Mass unemployment; television starts in USA; deaths of Lawrence and Conan Doyle. Auden, *Poems* Eliot, *Ash Wednesday* Waugh, *Vile Bodies* Coward, *Private Lives* Lewis, *Apes of God*
1931 (April) Car tour through France. (8 Oct.) *The Waves* published. Writes *Flush*.	Formation of National Government; abandonment of Gold Standard; death of Bennett; Japan invades China.
1932 (21 Jan.) Death of Lytton Strachey. (13 Oct.) *The Common Reader*, 2nd series, published. Begins *The Years*, at this point called 'The Pargiters'.	Roosevelt becomes President of USA; hunger marches start in Britain; *Scrutiny* starts. Huxley, *Brave New World*
1933 (May) Car tour of France and Italy. (5 Oct.) *Flush* published.	Deaths of Galsworthy and George Moore; Hitler becomes Chancellor of Germany. Orwell, *Down and Out in Paris and London* Wells, *The Shape of Things to Come*
1934 Works on *The Years*. (9 Sept.) Death of Roger Fry.	Waugh, *A Handful of Dust* Graves, *I, Claudius* Beckett, *More Pricks than Kicks* Toynbee, *A Study of History*
1935 Rewrites *The Years*. (May) Car tour of Holland, Germany, and Italy.	George V's Silver Jubilee; Baldwin Prime Minister of National Government; Germany re-arms; Italian invasion of Abyssinia (Ethiopia). Isherwood, *Mr Norris Changes Trains* T. S. Eliot, *Murder in the Cathedral*

Life	*Historical and Cultural Background*
1936 (May-Oct.) Ill. Finishes *The Years*. Begins *Three Guineas*.	Death of George V; accession of Edward VIII; abdication crisis; accession of George VI; Civil War breaks out in Spain; first of the Moscow show trials; Germany re-occupies the Rhineland; BBC television begins (2 Nov); deaths of Chesterton, Kipling, and Housman. Orwell, *Keep the Aspidistra Flying*
1937 (15 March) *The Years* published. Begins *Roger Fry: A Biography*. (18 July) Death in Spanish Civil War of Julian Bell, son of Vanessa.	Chamberlain Prime Minister; destruction of Guernica; death of Barrie. Orwell, *The Road to Wigan Pier*
1938 (2 June) *Three Guineas* published. Works on *Roger Fry*, and begins to envisage *Between the Acts*.	German *Anschluss* with Austria; Munich agreement; dismemberment of Czechoslovakia; first jet engine. Beckett, *Murphy* Bowen, *The Death of the Heart* Greene, *Brighton Rock*
1939 VW moves to 37 Mecklenburgh Square, but lives mostly at Monk's House. Works on *Between the Acts*. Meets Freud in London.	End of Civil War in Spain; Russo-German pact; Germany invades Poland (Sept.); Britain and France declare war on Germany (3 Sept.); deaths of Freud, Yeats, and Ford. Joyce, *Finnegans Wake* Isherwood, *Goodbye to Berlin*
1940 (25 July) *Roger Fry* published. (10 Sept.) Mecklenburgh Square house bombed. (18 Oct.) witnesses the ruins of 52 Tavistock Square, destroyed by bombs. (23 Nov.) Finishes *Between the Acts*.	Germany invades north-west Europe; fall of France; evacuation of British troops from Dunkirk; Battle of Britain; beginning of 'the Blitz'; National Government under Churchill.
1941 (26 Feb.) Revises *Between the Acts*. Becomes ill. (28 March) Drowns herself in River Ouse, near Monk's House. (July) *Between the Acts* published.	Germany invades USSR; Japanese destroy US Fleet at Pearl Harbor; USA enters war; death of Joyce.

TO THE LIGHTHOUSE

CONTENTS

Lighthouse- the unattainable self & the failure to keep one's light pervasive enough to mean something beyond one's own existance.

└ Therefore art becomes the sustainable way to exist. Art not only visual but literary as well.

The Confession of the novel is that the world exists in both real and abstract terms. Both these world viewpoints are working towards the same goal, yet is seems their opposition makes it harder for one view to surpass the other, and in the end both are left unresolved.

I

THE WINDOW

1

'YES, of course, if it's fine tomorrow,' said Mrs Ramsay.* 'But you'll have to be up with the lark,' she added.

To her son these words conveyed an extraordinary joy, as if it were settled the expedition were bound to take place, and the wonder to which he had looked forward, for years and years it seemed, was, after a night's darkness and a day's sail, within touch. Since he belonged, even at the age of six, to that great clan which cannot keep this feeling separate from that, but must let future prospects, with their joys and sorrows, cloud what is actually at hand, since to such people even in earliest childhood any turn in the wheel of sensation has the power to crystallize and transfix the moment upon which its gloom or radiance rests, James Ramsay, sitting on the floor cutting out pictures from the illustrated catalogue of the Army and Navy Stores,* endowed the picture of a refrigerator* as his mother spoke with heavenly bliss. It was fringed with joy. The wheelbarrow, the lawn-mower, the sound of poplar trees, leaves whitening before rain, rooks cawing, brooms knocking, dresses rustling—all these were so coloured and distinguished in his mind that he had already his private code, his secret language, though he appeared the image of stark and uncompromising severity, with his high forehead and his fierce blue eyes,* impeccably candid and pure, frowning slightly at the sight of human frailty, so that his mother, watching him guide his scissors neatly round the refrigerator, imagined him all red and ermine on the Bench* or directing a stern and momentous enterprise in some crisis of public affairs.

'But,' said his father, stopping in front of the drawing-room window, 'it won't be fine.'

Had there been an axe handy, a poker, or any weapon that would have gashed a hole in his father's breast and killed him, there and then, James would have seized it. Such were the extremes of emotion that Mr Ramsay excited in his children's breasts by his mere presence; standing, as now, lean as a knife, narrow as the blade of one, grinning sarcastically, not only with the pleasure of disillusioning his son and casting ridicule upon his wife, who was ten thousand times better in every way than he was (James thought), but also with some secret conceit at his own accuracy of judgement. What he said was true. It was always true. He was incapable of untruth; never tampered with a fact; never altered a disagreeable word to suit the pleasure or convenience of any mortal being, least of all of his own children, who, sprung from his loins, should be aware from childhood that life is difficult; facts uncompromising; and the passage to that fabled land where our brightest hopes are extinguished, our frail barks founder in darkness (here Mr Ramsay would straighten his back and narrow his little blue eyes upon the horizon), one that needs, above all, courage, truth, and the power to endure.

'But it may be fine—I expect it will be fine,' said Mrs Ramsay, making some little twist of the reddish-brown stocking she was knitting, impatiently. If she finished it tonight, if they did go to the Lighthouse* after all, it was to be given to the Lighthouse keeper for his little boy, who was threatened with a tuberculous hip; together with a pile of old magazines, and some tobacco, indeed whatever she could find lying about, not really wanted, but only littering the room, to give those poor fellows who must be bored to death sitting all day with nothing to do but polish the lamp and trim the wick and rake about on their scrap of garden, something to amuse them. For how would you like to be shut up for a whole month at a time, and possibly more in stormy weather, upon a rock the size of a tennis lawn? she would ask; and to have no letters or newspapers, and to see nobody; if you were married, not to see your wife, not to know how your children were,—if they were ill, if they had fallen down and broken their legs or arms; to see the same dreary waves breaking week after week, and then a dreadful storm coming, and the windows covered with spray, and birds dashed against the lamp, and the whole place rocking, and not be able to put your nose out of doors for fear of being swept into the sea? How would you like that? she asked, addressing herself particularly to her daughters. So she added, rather differently, one must take them whatever comforts one can.

'It's due west,' said the atheist Tansley, holding his bony fingers spread so that the wind blew through them, for he was sharing Mr Ramsay's evening walk up and down, up and down the terrace.* That is to say, the wind blew from the worst possible direction for landing at the Lighthouse. Yes, he did say disagreeable things, Mrs Ramsay admitted; it was odious of him to rub this in, and make James still more disappointed; but at the same time, she would not let them laugh at him. 'The atheist', they called him; 'the little atheist'. Rose mocked him; Prue mocked him; Andrew, Jasper, Roger mocked him; even old Badger without a tooth in his head had bit him, for being (as Nancy put it) the hundred and tenth young man to chase them all the way up to the Hebrides* when it was ever so much nicer to be alone.

'Nonsense,' said Mrs Ramsay, with great severity. Apart from the habit of exaggeration which they had from her, and from the implication (which was true) that she asked too many people to stay, and had to lodge some in the town, she could not bear incivility to her guests, to young men in particular, who were poor as church mice, 'exceptionally able', her husband said, his great admirers, and come there for a holiday. Indeed, she had the whole of the other sex under her protection; for reasons she could not explain, for their chivalry and valour, for the fact that they negotiated treaties, ruled India,* controlled finance; finally for an attitude towards herself which no woman could fail to feel or to find agreeable, something trustful, childlike, reverential; which an old woman could take from a young man without loss of dignity, and woe betide the girl—pray Heaven it was none of her daughters!—who did not feel the worth of it, and all that it implied, to the marrow of her bones.

She turned with severity upon Nancy. He had not chased them, she said. He had been asked.

They must find a way out of it all. There might be some simpler way, some less laborious way, she sighed. When she looked in the glass and saw her hair grey, her cheek sunk, at fifty,* she thought, possibly she might have managed things better—her husband; money; his books. But for her own part she would never for a single second regret her decision, evade difficulties, or slur over duties. She was now formidable to behold, and it was only in silence, looking up from their plates, after she had spoken so severely about Charles Tansley, that her daughters—Prue, Nancy, Rose—could sport with infidel ideas which they had brewed for themselves of a life different from hers; in Paris, perhaps; a wilder life; not always taking care of some man or other; for there was in all their minds a mute questioning of deference and chivalry, of the Bank of England and the Indian Empire, of ringed fingers and lace, though to them all there was something in this of the essence of beauty, which called out the manliness in their girlish hearts, and made them, as they sat at

table beneath their mother's eyes, honour her strange severity, her
extreme courtesy, like a Queen's raising from the mud a beggar's
dirty foot and washing it, when she thus admonished them so very
severely about that wretched atheist who had chased them to—
or, speaking accurately, been invited to stay with them in—the Isle
of Skye.*

'There'll be no landing at the Lighthouse tomorrow,' said Charles
Tansley, clapping his hands together as he stood at the window with
her husband. Surely, he had said enough. She wished they would
both leave her and James alone and go on talking. She looked at him.
He was such a miserable specimen, the children said, all humps and
hollows. He couldn't play cricket; he poked; he shuffled. He was a
sarcastic brute, Andrew said. They knew what he liked best—to be
for ever walking up and down, up and down, with Mr Ramsay, and
saying who had won this, who had won that, who was a 'first-rate
man' at Latin verses, who was 'brilliant but I think fundamentally
unsound', who was undoubtedly the 'ablest fellow in Balliol',* who
had buried his light temporarily at Bristol or Bedford,* but was
bound to be heard of later when his Prolegomena,* of which
Mr Tansley had the first pages in proof with him if Mr Ramsay
would like to see them, to some branch of mathematics or philosophy saw the light of day. That was what they talked about.

She could not help laughing herself sometimes. She said, the other
day, something about 'waves mountains high'. Yes, said Charles
Tansley, it was a little rough. 'Aren't you drenched to the skin?' she
had said. 'Damp, not wet through,' said Mr Tansley, pinching his
sleeve, feeling his socks.

But it was not that they minded, the children said. It was not his
face; it was not his manners. It was him—his point of view. When
they talked about something interesting, people, music, history, anything, even said it was a fine evening so why not sit out of doors, then
what they complained of about Charles Tansley was that until he
had turned the whole thing round and made it somehow reflect
himself and disparage them, put them all on edge somehow with his
acid way of peeling the flesh and blood off everything, he was not
satisfied. And he would go to picture galleries, they said, and he
would ask one, did one like his tie? God knows, said Rose, one
did not.

Disappearing as stealthily as stags from the dinner-table directly the meal was over, the eight sons and daughters of Mr and Mrs Ramsay sought their bedrooms, their fastnesses in a house where there was no other privacy to debate anything, everything; Tansley's tie; the passing of the Reform Bill;* sea-birds and butterflies; people; while the sun poured into those attics, which a plank alone separated from each other so that every footstep could be plainly heard and the Swiss girl sobbing for her father who was dying of cancer in a valley of the Grisons,* and lit up bats, flannels, straw hats, ink-pots, paint-pots, beetles, and the skulls of small birds, while it drew from the long frilled strips of seaweed pinned to the wall a smell of salt and weeds, which was in the towels too, gritty with sand from bathing.

Strife, divisions, difference of opinion, prejudices twisted into the very fibre of being, oh that they should begin so early, Mrs Ramsay deplored. They were so critical, her children. They talked such nonsense. She went from the dining-room, holding James by the hand, since he would not go with the others. It seemed to her such nonsense—inventing differences, when people, heaven knows, were different enough without that. The real differences, she thought, standing by the drawing-room window, are enough, quite enough. She had in mind at the moment, rich and poor, high and low; the great in birth receiving from her, half grudging, some respect, for had she not in her veins the blood of that very noble, if slightly mythical, Italian house, whose daughters, scattered about English drawing-rooms in the nineteenth century, had lisped so charmingly, had stormed so wildly, and all her wit and her bearing and her temper came from them, and not from the sluggish English, or the cold Scotch; but more profoundly she ruminated the other problem, of rich and poor, and the things she saw with her own eyes, weekly, daily, here or in London, when she visited this widow, or that struggling wife in person with a bag on her arm, and a notebook and pencil with which she wrote down in columns carefully ruled for the purpose wages and spendings, employment and unemployment, in the hope that thus she would cease to be a private woman whose charity was half a sop to her own indignation, half a relief to her own curiosity, and become, what with her untrained mind she greatly admired, an investigator elucidating the social problem.

Insoluble questions they were, it seemed to her, standing there, holding James by the hand. He had followed her into the drawing-room, that young man they laughed at; he was standing by the table, fidgeting with something, awkwardly, feeling himself out of things, as she knew without looking round. They had all gone—the children; Minta Doyle and Paul Rayley; Augustus Carmichael; her husband—they had all gone. So she turned with a sigh and said, 'Would it bore you to come with me, Mr Tansley?'

She had a dull errand in the town;* she had a letter or two to write; she would be ten minutes perhaps; she would put on her hat. And, with her basket and her parasol, there she was again, ten minutes later, giving out a sense of being ready, of being equipped for a jaunt, which, however, she must interrupt for a moment, as they passed the tennis lawn, to ask Mr Carmichael,* who was basking with his yellow cat's eyes ajar, so that like a cat's they seemed to reflect the branches moving or the clouds passing, but to give no inkling of any inner thoughts or emotion whatsoever, if he wanted anything.

For they were making the great expedition, she said, laughing. They were going to the town. 'Stamps, writing-paper, tobacco?' she suggested, stopping by his side. But no, he wanted nothing. His hands clasped themselves over his capacious paunch, his eyes blinked, as if he would have liked to reply kindly to these blandishments (she was seductive but a little nervous) but could not, sunk as he was in a grey-green somnolence which embraced them all, without need of words, in a vast and benevolent lethargy of well-wishing; all the house; all the world; all the people in it, for he had slipped into his glass at lunch a few drops of something;* which accounted, the children thought, for the vivid streak of canary-yellow in moustache and beard that were otherwise milk-white. He wanted nothing, he murmured.

He should have been a great philosopher, said Mrs Ramsay, as they went down the road to the fishing village, but he had made an unfortunate marriage. Holding her black parasol very erect, and moving with an indescribable air of expectation, as if she were going to meet someone round the corner, she told the story; an affair at Oxford with some girl; an early marriage; poverty; going to India; translating a little poetry 'very beautifully, I believe', being willing to teach the boys Persian or Hindustanee,* but what really was the use of that?—and then lying, as they saw him, on the lawn.

It flattered him; snubbed as he had been, it soothed him that

Mrs Ramsay should tell him this. Charles Tansley revived. Insinuating, too, as she did the greatness of man's intellect, even in its decay, the subjection of all wives—not that she blamed the girl, and the marriage had been happy enough, she believed—to their husband's labours, she made him feel better pleased with himself than he had done yet, and he would have liked, had they taken a cab, for example, to have paid the fare. As for her little bag, might he not carry that? No, no, she said, she always carried *that* herself. She did too. Yes, he felt that in her. He felt many things, something in particular that excited him and disturbed him for reasons which he could not give. He would like her to see him, gowned and hooded, walking in a procession.* A fellowship, a professorship,—he felt capable of anything and saw himself—but what was she looking at? At a man pasting a bill. The vast flapping sheet flattened itself out, and each shove of the brush revealed fresh legs, hoops, horses, glistening reds and blues, beautifully smooth, until half the wall was covered with the advertisement of a circus; a hundred horsemen, twenty performing seals, lions, tigers ... Craning forwards, for she was shortsighted, she read out how it ... 'will visit this town'. It was terribly dangerous work for a one-armed man, she exclaimed, to stand on top of a ladder like that—his left arm had been cut off in a reaping machine two years ago.

'Let us all go!' she cried, moving on, as if all those riders and horses had filled her with child-like exultation and made her forget her pity.

'Let's go,' he said, repeating her words, clicking them out, however, with a self-consciousness that made her wince. 'Let us go to the Circus.' No. He could not say it right. He could not feel it right. But why not? she wondered. What was wrong with him then? She liked him warmly, at the moment. Had they not been taken, she asked, to circuses when they were children? Never, he answered, as if she asked the very thing he wanted to reply to; had been longing all these days to say, how they did not go to circuses. It was a large family, nine brothers and sisters, and his father was a working man; 'My father is a chemist, Mrs Ramsay. He keeps a shop.' He himself had paid his own way since he was thirteen. Often he went without a greatcoat in winter. He could never 'return hospitality' (those were his parched stiff words) at college. He had to make things last twice the time other people did; he smoked the cheapest tobacco; shag; the same the old men smoked on the quays. He worked hard—seven hours a day; his subject was now the influence of something upon somebody— they were walking on and Mrs Ramsay did not quite catch the meaning, only the words, here and there . . . dissertation . . . fellow- ship . . . readership* . . . lectureship. She could not follow the ugly academic jargon, that rattled itself off so glibly, but said to herself that she saw now why going to the circus had knocked him off his perch, poor little man, and why he came out, instantly, with all that about his father and mother and brothers and sisters, and she would see to it that they didn't laugh at him any more; she would tell Prue about it. What he would have liked, she supposed, would have been to say how he had been to Ibsen with the Ramsays. He was an awful prig*—oh yes, an insufferable bore. For, though they had reached the town now and were in the main street, with carts grind- ing past on the cobbles, still he went on talking, about settlements, and teaching, and working men, and helping our own class,* and lectures, till she gathered that he had got back entire self-confidence, had recovered from the circus, and was about (and now again she liked him warmly) to tell her—but here, the houses falling away on both sides, they came out on the quay, and the whole bay spread before them and Mrs Ramsay could not help exclaiming, 'Oh, how beautiful!' For the great plateful of blue water was before her; the hoary Lighthouse, distant, austere, in the midst; and on the right, as far as the eye could see, fading and falling, in soft low pleats, the green sand dunes with the wild flowing grasses on them, which always seemed to be running away into some moon country, uninhabited of men.

That was the view, she said, stopping, growing greyer-eyed, that her husband loved.

She paused a moment. But now, she said, artists had come here.* There indeed, only a few paces off, stood one of them, in Panama hat and yellow boots, seriously, softly, absorbedly, for all that he was watched by ten little boys, with an air of profound contentment on his round red face, gazing, and then, when he had gazed, dipping; imbuing the tip of his brush in some soft mound of green or pink. Since Mr Paunceforte had been there, three years before, all the pictures were like that she said, green and grey, with lemon-coloured sailing-boats, and pink women on the beach.*

But her grandmother's friends, she said, glancing discreetly as they passed, took the greatest pains; first they mixed their own colours, and then they ground them, and then they put damp cloths on them to keep them moist.

So Mr Tansley supposed she meant him to see that that man's picture was skimpy, was that what one said? The colours weren't solid? Was that what one said? Under the influence of that extraordinary emotion which had been growing all the walk, had begun in the garden when he had wanted to take her bag, had increased in the town when he had wanted to tell her everything about himself, he was coming to see himself and everything he had ever known gone crooked a little. It was awfully strange.

There he stood in the parlour of the poky little house where she had taken him, waiting for her, while she went upstairs a moment to see a woman. He heard her quick step above; heard her voice cheerful, then low; looked at the mats, tea-caddies, glass shades; waited quite impatiently; looked forward eagerly to the walk home, determined to carry her bag; then heard her come out; shut a door; say they must keep the windows open and the doors shut,* ask at the house for anything they wanted (she must be talking to a child), when, suddenly, in she came, stood for a moment silent (as if she had been pretending up there, and for a moment let herself be now), stood quite motionless for a moment against a picture of Queen Victoria wearing the blue ribbon of the Garter;* and all at once he realized that it was this: it was this:—she was the most beautiful person he had ever seen.

With stars in her eyes and veils in her hair, with cyclamen and wild violets—what nonsense was he thinking? She was fifty at least; she had eight children. Stepping through fields of flowers and taking to her breast buds that had broken and lambs that had fallen; with the stars in her eyes and the wind in her hair—He took her bag.

'Good-bye, Elsie,' she said, and they walked up the street, she holding her parasol erect and walking as if she expected to meet someone round the corner, while for the first time in his life Charles Tansley felt an extraordinary pride; a man digging in a drain stopped digging and looked at her; let his arm fall down and looked at her; Charles Tansley felt an extraordinary pride; felt the wind and the cyclamen and the violets for he was walking with a beautiful woman for the first time in his life. He had hold of her bag.

2

'No going to the Lighthouse, James,' he said, as he stood by the window, speaking awkwardly, but trying in deference to Mrs Ramsay to soften his voice into some semblance of geniality at least.

Odious little man, thought Mrs Ramsay, why go on saying that?

3

'Perhaps you will wake up and find the sun shining and the birds singing,' she said compassionately, smoothing the little boy's hair, for her husband, with his caustic saying that it would not be fine, had dashed his spirits she could see. This going to the Lighthouse was a passion of his, she saw, and then, as if her husband had not said enough, with his caustic saying that it would not be fine tomorrow, this odious little man went and rubbed it in all over again.

'Perhaps it will be fine tomorrow,' she said, smoothing his hair.

All she could do now was to admire the refrigerator, and turn the pages of the Stores list in the hope that she might come upon something like a rake, or a mowing-machine, which, with its prongs and its handles, would need the greatest skill and care in cutting out. All these young men parodied her husband, she reflected; he said it would rain; they said it would be a positive tornado.

But here, as she turned the page, suddenly her search for the picture of a rake or a mowing-machine was interrupted. The gruff murmur, irregularly broken by the taking out of pipes and the putting in of pipes which had kept on assuring her, though she could not hear what was said (as she sat in the window), that the men were happily talking; this sound which had lasted now half an hour and had taken its place soothingly in the scale of sounds pressing on top of her, such as the tap of balls upon bats, the sharp, sudden bark now and then, 'How's that? How's that?' of the children playing cricket,* had ceased; so that the monotonous fall of the waves on the beach, which for the most part beat a measured and soothing tattoo to her thoughts and seemed consolingly to repeat over and over again as she sat with the children the words of some old cradle song, murmured by nature, 'I am guarding you—I am your support', but at other times suddenly and unexpectedly, especially when her mind raised itself slightly from the task actually in hand, had no such kindly meaning, but like a ghostly roll of drums remorselessly beat the measure of life, made one think of the destruction of the island and its engulfment in the sea, and warned her whose day had slipped past in one quick doing after another that it was all ephemeral as a rainbow—this sound which had been obscured and concealed under the other sounds suddenly thundered hollow in her ears and made her look up with an impulse of terror.

They had ceased to talk; that was the explanation. Falling in one second from the tension which had gripped her to the other extreme which, as if to recoup her for her unnecessary expense of emotion, was cool, amused, and even faintly malicious, she concluded that poor Charles Tansley had been shed. That was of little account to her. If her husband required sacrifices (and indeed he did) she cheerfully offered up to him Charles Tansley, who had snubbed her little boy.

One moment more, with her head raised, she listened, as if she waited for some habitual sound, some regular mechanical sound; and then, hearing something rhythmical, half said, half chanted, beginning in the garden, as her husband beat up and down the terrace, something between a croak and a song,* she was soothed once more, assured again that all was well, and looking down at the book on her knee found the picture of a pocket knife with six blades* which could only be cut out if James was very careful.

Suddenly a loud cry, as of a sleep-walker, half roused, something about

Stormed at with shot and shell*

sung out with the utmost intensity in her ear, made her turn apprehensively to see if anyone heard him. Only Lily Briscoe, she was glad to find; and that did not matter. But the sight of the girl standing on the edge of the lawn painting reminded her; she was supposed to be keeping her head as much in the same position as possible for Lily's picture. Lily's picture! Mrs Ramsay smiled. With her little Chinese eyes* and her puckered-up face she would never marry; one could not take her painting very seriously; but she was an independent little creature, Mrs Ramsay liked her for it, and so remembering her promise, she bent her head.

4

INDEED, he almost knocked her easel over, coming down upon her with his hands waving, shouting out 'Boldly we rode and well', but, mercifully, he turned sharp, and rode off, to die gloriously she supposed upon the heights of Balaclava.* Never was anybody at once so ridiculous and so alarming. But so long as he kept like that, waving, shouting, she was safe; he would not stand still and look at her picture. And that was what Lily Briscoe could not have endured. Even while she looked at the mass, at the line, at the colour, at Mrs Ramsay sitting in the window with James, she kept a feeler on her surroundings lest someone should creep up, and suddenly she should find her picture looked at. But now, with all her senses quickened as they were, looking, straining, till the colour of the wall and the jacmanna* beyond burnt into her eyes, she was aware of someone coming out of the house, coming towards her; but somehow divined, from the footfall, William Bankes, so that though her brush quivered, she did not, as she would have done had it been Mr Tansley, Paul Rayley, Minta Doyle, or practically anybody else, turn her canvas upon the grass, but let it stand. William Bankes stood beside her.

They had rooms in the village, and so, walking in, walking out, parting late on door-mats, had said little things about the soup, about the children, about one thing and another which made them allies; so that when he stood beside her now in his judicial way (he was old enough to be her father too, a botanist, a widower, smelling of soap, very scrupulous and clean) she just stood there. He just stood there. Her shoes were excellent, he observed. They allowed the toes their natural expansion.* Lodging in the same house with her, he had noticed too, how orderly she was, up before breakfast and off to paint, he believed, alone: poor, presumably, and without the complexion or the allurement of Miss Doyle certainly, but with a good sense which made her in his eyes superior to that young lady. Now, for instance, when Ramsay bore down on them, shouting, gesticulating, Miss Briscoe, he felt certain, understood.

Someone had blundered.

Mr Ramsay glared at them. He glared at them without seeming to see them. That did make them both vaguely uncomfortable. Together they had seen a thing they had not been meant to see. They had encroached upon a privacy. So, Lily thought, it was probably an excuse of his for moving, for getting out of earshot, that made Mr Bankes almost immediately say something about its being chilly and suggest taking a stroll. She would come, yes. But it was with difficulty that she took her eyes off her picture.

The jacmanna was bright violet; the wall staring white. She would not have considered it honest to tamper with the bright violet and the staring white, since she saw them like that, fashionable though it was, since Mr Paunceforte's visit, to see everything pale, elegant, semi-transparent. Then beneath the colour there was the shape. She could see it all so clearly, so commandingly, when she looked: it was when she took her brush in hand that the whole thing changed. It was in that moment's flight between the picture and her canvas that the demons set on her who often brought her to the verge of tears and made this passage from conception to work as dreadful as any down a dark passage for a child. Such she often felt herself— struggling against terrific odds to maintain her courage; to say: 'But this is what I see; this is what I see', and so to clasp some miserable remnant of her vision to her breast, which a thousand forces did their best to pluck from her. And it was then too, in that chill and windy way, as she began to paint, that there forced themselves upon her other things, her own inadequacy, her insignificance, keeping house for her father off the Brompton Road,* and had much ado to control her impulse to fling herself (thank Heaven she had always resisted so far) at Mrs Ramsay's knee and say to her—but what could one say to her? 'I'm in love with you'? No, that was not true. 'I'm in love with this all', waving her hand at the hedge, at the house, at the children? It was absurd, it was impossible. One could not say what one meant. So now she laid her brushes neatly in the box, side by side, and said to William Bankes:

'It suddenly gets cold. The sun seems to give less heat,' she said, looking about her, for it was bright enough, the grass still a soft deep green, the house starred in its greenery with purple passion flowers, and rooks dropping cool cries from the high blue. But something moved, flashed, turned a silver wing in the air. It was September after all, the middle of September, and past six in the evening. So off they strolled down the garden in the usual direction, past the tennis lawn, past the pampas grass, to that break in the thick hedge, guarded by red-hot pokers* like brasiers of clear burning coal, between which the blue waters of the bay looked bluer than ever.

They came there regularly every evening drawn by some need. It was as if the water floated off and set sailing thoughts which had grown stagnant on dry land, and gave to their bodies even some sort of physical relief. First, the pulse of colour flooded the bay with blue, and the heart expanded with it and the body swam, only the next instant to be checked and chilled by the prickly blackness on the ruffled waves. Then, up behind the great black rock, almost every evening spurted irregularly, so that one had to watch for it and it was a delight when it came, a fountain of white water; and then, while one waited for that, one watched, on the pale semicircular beach, wave after wave shedding again and again smoothly a film of mother-of-pearl.

They both smiled, standing there. They both felt a common hilarity, excited by the moving waves; and then by the swift cutting race of a sailing boat, which, having sliced a curve in the bay, stopped; shivered; let its sail drop down; and then, with a natural instinct to complete the picture, after this swift movement, both of them looked at the dunes far away, and instead of merriment felt come over them some sadness—because the thing was completed partly, and partly because distant views seem to outlast by a million years (Lily thought) the gazer and to be communing already with a sky which beholds an earth entirely at rest.

Looking at the far sand-hills, William Bankes thought of Ramsay: thought of a road in Westmorland,* thought of Ramsay striding along a road by himself hung round with that solitude which seemed to be his natural air. But this was suddenly interrupted, William Bankes remembered (and this must refer to some actual incident), by a hen, straddling her wings out in protection of a covey of little chicks, upon which Ramsay, stopping, pointed his stick and said 'Pretty—pretty', an odd illumination into his heart, Bankes had thought it, which showed his simplicity, his sympathy with humble things; but it seemed to him as if their friendship had ceased, there, on that stretch of road. After that, Ramsay had married. After that, what with one thing and another, the pulp had gone out of their friendship. Whose fault it was he could not say, only, after a time, repetition had taken the place of newness. It was to repeat that they met. But in this dumb colloquy with the sand dunes he maintained that his affection for Ramsay had in no way diminished; but there, like the body of a young man laid up in peat for a century, with the red fresh on his lips, was his friendship, in its acuteness and reality laid up across the bay among the sand-hills.

He was anxious for the sake of this friendship and perhaps too in order to clear himself in his own mind from the imputation of having dried and shrunk—for Ramsay lived in a welter of children, whereas Bankes was childless and a widower—he was anxious that Lily Briscoe should not disparage Ramsay (a great man in his own way) yet should understand how things stood between them. Begun long years ago, their friendship had petered out on a Westmorland road, where the hen spread her wings before her chicks; after which Ramsay had married, and their paths lying different ways, there had been, certainly for no one's fault, some tendency, when they met, to repeat.

Yes. That was it. He finished. He turned from the view. And, turning to walk back the other way, up the drive, Mr Bankes was alive to things which would not have struck him had not those sand-hills revealed to him the body of his friendship lying with the red on its lips laid up in peat—for instance, Cam,* the little girl, Ramsay's youngest daughter. She was picking Sweet Alice on the bank. She was wild and fierce. She would not 'give a flower to the gentleman' as the nursemaid told her. No! no! no! she would not! She clenched her fist. She stamped. And Mr Bankes felt aged and saddened and somehow put into the wrong by her about his friendship. He must have dried and shrunk.

The Ramsays were not rich, and it was a wonder how they managed to contrive it all. Eight children! To feed eight children on philosophy! Here was another of them, Jasper this time, strolling past, to have a shot at a bird, he said, nonchalantly, swinging Lily's hand like a pump-handle as he passed, which caused Mr Bankes to say, bitterly, how *she* was a favourite. There was education now to be considered (true, Mrs Ramsay had something of her own perhaps) let alone the daily wear and tear of shoes and stockings which those 'great fellows', all well grown, angular, ruthless youngsters, must require. As for being sure which was which, or in what order they came, that was beyond him. He called them privately after the Kings and Queens of England; Cam the Wicked, James the Ruthless, Andrew the Just, Prue the Fair*—for Prue would have beauty, he thought, how could she help it?—and Andrew brains. While he walked up the drive and Lily Briscoe said yes and no and capped his comments (for she was in love with them all, in love with this world) he weighed Ramsay's case, commiserated him, envied him, as if he had seen him divest himself of all those glories of isolation and austerity which crowned him in youth to cumber himself definitely with fluttering wings and clucking domesticities. They gave him something—William Bankes acknowledged that; it would have been pleasant if Cam had stuck a flower in his coat or clambered over his shoulder, as over her father's, to look at a picture of Vesuvius in eruption,* but they had also, his old friends could not but feel, destroyed something. What would a stranger think now? What did this Lily Briscoe think? Could one help noticing that habits grew on him? eccentricities, weaknesses perhaps? It was astonishing that a man of his intellect could stoop so low as he did—but that was too harsh a phrase—could depend so much as he did upon people's praise.

'Oh but', said Lily, 'think of his work!'

Whenever she 'thought of his work' she always saw clearly before her a large kitchen table. It was Andrew's doing. She asked him what his father's books were about. 'Subject and object and the nature of reality',* Andrew had said. And when she said Heavens, she had no notion what that meant. 'Think of a kitchen table then', he told her, 'when you're not there'.

So she always saw, when she thought of Mr Ramsay's work, a scrubbed kitchen table. It lodged now in the fork of a pear tree, for they had reached the orchard. And with a painful effort of concentration, she focused her mind, not upon the silver-bossed bark of the tree, or upon its fish-shaped leaves, but upon a phantom kitchen table, one of those scrubbed board tables, grained and knotted, whose virtue seems to have been laid bare by years of muscular integrity, which stuck there, its four legs in air. Naturally, if one's days were passed in this seeing of angular essences, this reducing of lovely evenings, with all their flamingo clouds and blue and silver to a white deal four-legged table (and it was a mark of the finest minds so to do), naturally one could not be judged like an ordinary person.

Mr Bankes liked her for bidding him 'think of his work'. He had thought of it, often and often. Times without number, he had said, 'Ramsay is one of those men who do their best work before they are forty.' He had made a definite contribution to philosophy in one little book when he was only five and twenty; what came after was more or less amplification, repetition. But the number of men who make a definite contribution to anything whatsoever is very small, he said, pausing by the pear tree, well brushed, scrupulously exact, exquisitely judicial. Suddenly, as if the movement of his hand had released it, the load of her accumulated impressions of him tilted up, and down poured in a ponderous avalanche all she felt about him. That was one sensation. Then up rose in a fume the essence of his being. That was another. She felt herself transfixed by the intensity of her perception; it was his severity; his goodness. I respect you (she addressed him silently) in every atom; you are not vain; you are entirely impersonal; you are finer than Mr Ramsay; you are the finest human being that I know; you have neither wife nor child (without any sexual feeling, she longed to cherish that loneliness), you live for science (involuntarily, sections of potatoes* rose before her eyes); praise would be an insult to you; generous, pure-hearted, heroic man! But simultaneously, she remembered how he had brought a valet all the way up here; objected to dogs on chairs; would prose for hours (until Mr Ramsay slammed out of the room) about salt in vegetables* and the iniquity of English cooks.

How then did it work out, all this? How did one judge people, think of them? How did one add up this and that and conclude that it was liking one felt, or disliking? And to those words, what meaning attached, after all? Standing now, apparently transfixed, by the pear tree, impressions poured in upon her of those two men, and to follow her thought was like following a voice which speaks too quickly to be taken down by one's pencil, and the voice was her own voice saying without prompting undeniable, everlasting, contradictory things, so that even the fissures and humps on the bark of the pear tree were irrevocably fixed there for eternity. You have greatness, she continued, but Mr Ramsay has none of it. He is petty, selfish, vain, egotistical; he is spoilt; he is a tyrant; he wears Mrs Ramsay to death; but he has what you (she addressed Mr Bankes) have not; a fiery unworldliness; he knows nothing about trifles; he loves dogs and his children. He has eight. You have none. Did he not come down in two coats the other night and let Mrs Ramsay trim his hair into a pudding basin? All of this danced up and down, like a company of gnats, each separate, but all marvellously controlled in an invisible elastic net—danced up and down in Lily's mind, in and about the branches of the pear tree, where still hung in effigy the scrubbed kitchen table, symbol of her profound respect for Mr Ramsay's mind, until her thought which had spun quicker and quicker exploded of its own intensity; she felt released; a shot went off close at hand, and there came, flying from its fragments, frightened, effusive, tumultuous, a flock of starlings.

'Jasper!' said Mr Bankes. They turned the way the starlings flew, over the terrace. Following the scatter of swift-flying birds in the sky they stepped through the gap in the high hedge straight into Mr Ramsay, who boomed tragically at them, 'Someone had blundered!'

His eyes, glazed with emotion, defiant with tragic intensity, met theirs for a second, and trembled on the verge of recognition; but then, raising his hand half-way to his face as if to avert, to brush off, in an agony of peevish shame, their normal gaze, as if he begged them to withhold for a moment what he knew to be inevitable, as if he impressed upon them his own child-like resentment of interruption, yet even in the moment of discovery was not to be routed utterly, but was determined to hold fast to something of this delicious emotion, this impure rhapsody of which he was ashamed, but in which he revelled—he turned abruptly, slammed his private door on them; and, Lily Briscoe and Mr Bankes, looking uneasily up into the sky, observed that the flock of starlings which Jasper had routed with his gun had settled on the tops of the elm trees.

5

'AND even if it isn't fine tomorrow,' said Mrs Ramsay, raising her eyes to glance at William Bankes and Lily Briscoe as they passed, 'it will be another day. And now,' she said, thinking that Lily's charm was her Chinese eyes, aslant in her white, puckered little face, but it would take a clever man to see it, 'and now stand up, and let me measure your leg,' for they might go to the Lighthouse after all, and she must see if the stocking did not need to be an inch or two longer in the leg.

Smiling, for an admirable idea had flashed upon her this very second—William and Lily should marry—she took the heather mixture stocking, with its criss-cross of steel needles at the mouth of it, and measured it against James's leg.

'My dear, stand still,' she said, for in his jealousy, not liking to serve as measuring-block for the Lighthouse keeper's little boy, James fidgeted purposely; and if he did that, how could she see, was it too long, was it too short? she asked.

She looked up—what demon possessed him, her youngest, her cherished?—and saw the room, saw the chairs, thought them fearfully shabby. Their entrails, as Andrew said the other day, were all over the floor; but then what was the point, she asked herself, of buying good chairs to let them spoil up here all through the winter when the house, with only one old woman* to see to it, positively dripped with wet? Never mind: the rent was precisely twopence halfpenny;* the children loved it; it did her husband good to be three thousand, or if she must be accurate, three hundred miles* from his library and his lectures and his disciples; and there was room for visitors. Mats, camp beds, crazy ghosts of chairs and tables whose London life of service was done—they did well enough here; and a photograph or two, and books. Books, she thought, grew of themselves. She never had time to read them. Alas! even the books that had been given her, and inscribed by the hand of the poet himself: 'For her whose wishes must be obeyed' . . . 'The happier Helen of our days'* . . . disgraceful to say, she had never read them. And Croom on the Mind and Bates on the Savage Customs of Polynesia* ('My dear, stand still,' she said)—neither of those could one send to the Lighthouse. At a certain moment, she supposed, the house would become so shabby that something must be done. If they could be taught to wipe their feet and not bring the beach in with them—that would be something. Crabs, she had to allow, if Andrew really wished to dissect them, or if Jasper believed that one could make soup from seaweed, one could not prevent it; or Rose's objects—shells, reeds, stones; for they were gifted, her children, but all in quite different ways. And the result of it was, she sighed, taking in the whole room from floor to ceiling, as she held the stocking against James's leg, that things got shabbier and got shabbier summer after summer. The mat was fading; the wallpaper was flapping. You couldn't tell any more that those were roses on it. Still, if every door

in a house is left perpetually open, and no lockmaker in the whole of
Scotland can mend a bolt, things must spoil. What was the use of
flinging a green Cashmere shawl* over the edge of a picture frame?
In two weeks it would be the colour of pea soup. But it was the
doors that annoyed her; every door was left open. She listened. The
drawing-room door was open; the hall door was open; it sounded as
if the bedroom doors were open; and certainly the window on the
landing was open, for that she had opened herself. That windows
should be open, and doors shut—simple as it was, could none of
them remember it? She would go into the maids' bedrooms at night
and find them sealed like ovens, except for Marie's, the Swiss girl,
who would rather go without a bath than without fresh air, but then
at home, she had said, 'the mountains are so beautiful'. She had said
that last night looking out of the window with tears in her eyes. 'The
mountains are so beautiful.' Her father was dying there, Mrs Ramsay
knew. He was leaving them fatherless. Scolding and demonstrating
(how to make a bed, how to open a window, with hands that shut and
spread like a Frenchwoman's) all had folded itself quietly about her,
when the girl spoke, as, after a flight through the sunshine the wings
of a bird fold themselves quietly and the blue of its plumage changes
from bright steel to soft purple. She had stood there silent for there
was nothing to be said. He had cancer of the throat. At the recollection—how she had stood there, how the girl had said, 'At home
the mountains are so beautiful', and there was no hope, no hope
whatever, she had a spasm of irritation, and speaking sharply, said to
James:

  'Stand still. Don't be tiresome,' so that he knew instantly that her
severity was real, and straightened his leg and she measured it.

  The stocking was too short by half an inch at least, making allow-
ance for the fact that Sorley's little boy would be less well grown
than James.

  'It's too short,' she said, 'ever so much too short.'

  Never did anybody look so sad.* Bitter and black, halfway down, in
the darkness, in the shaft which ran from the sunlight to the depths,
perhaps a tear formed; a tear fell; the waters swayed this way and
that, received it, and were at rest. Never did anybody look so sad.

  But was it nothing but looks? people said. What was there behind
it—her beauty, her splendour? Had he blown his brains out, they
asked, had he died the week before they were married—some other,

earlier lover, of whom rumours reached one? Or was there nothing? nothing but an incomparable beauty which she lived behind, and could do nothing to disturb? For easily though she might have said at some moment of intimacy when stories of great passion, of love foiled, of ambition thwarted came her way how she too had known or felt or been through it herself, she never spoke. She was silent always. She knew then—she knew without having learnt. Her simplicity fathomed what clever people falsified. Her singleness of mind made her drop plumb like a stone, alight exact as a bird, gave her, naturally, this swoop and fall of the spirit upon truth which delighted, eased, sustained—falsely perhaps.

('Nature has but little clay,' said Mr Bankes once, hearing her voice on the telephone, and much moved by it though she was only telling him a fact about a train, 'like that of which she moulded you'. He saw her at the end of the line, Greek, blue-eyed, straight-nosed. How incongruous it seemed to be telephoning to a woman like that. The Graces assembling seemed to have joined hands in meadows of asphodel* to compose that face. Yes, he would catch the 10.30 at Euston.*

'But she's no more aware of her beauty than a child,' said Mr Bankes, replacing the receiver and crossing the room to see what progress the workmen were making with an hotel which they were building at the back of his house. And he thought of Mrs Ramsay as he looked at that stir among the unfinished walls. For always, he thought, there was something incongruous to be worked into the harmony of her face. She clapped a deer-stalker's hat on her head; she ran across the lawn in goloshes to snatch a child from mischief. So that if it was her beauty merely that one thought of, one must remember the quivering thing, the living thing (they were carrying bricks up a little plank as he watched them), and work it into the picture; or if one thought of her simply as a woman, one must endow her with some freak of idiosyncrasy; or suppose some latent desire to doff her royalty of form as if her beauty bored her and all that men say of beauty, and she wanted only to be like other people, insignificant. He did not know. He did not know. He must go to his work.)

Knitting her reddish-brown hairy stocking,* with her head outlined absurdly by the gilt frame, the green shawl which she had tossed over the edge of the frame, and the authenticated masterpiece

by Michael Angelo,* Mrs Ramsay smoothed out what had been harsh
in her manner a moment before, raised his head, and kissed her little
boy on the forehead. 'Let's find another picture to cut out,' she said.

6

BUT what had happened?

Someone had blundered.

Starting from her musing she gave meaning to words which
she had held meaningless in her mind for a long stretch of time.
'Someone had blundered'—Fixing her short-sighted eyes upon her
husband, who was now bearing down upon her, she gazed steadily
until his closeness revealed to her (the jingle mated itself in her head)
that something had happened, someone had blundered. But she
could not for the life of her think what.

He shivered; he quivered. All his vanity, all his satisfaction in his
own splendour, riding fell as a thunderbolt, fierce as a hawk at the
head of his men through the valley of death, had been shattered,
destroyed. Stormed at by shot and shell, boldly we rode and well,
flashed through the valley of death, volleyed and thundered—straight
into Lily Briscoe and William Bankes. He quivered; he shivered.

Not for the world would she have spoken to him, realizing, from
the familiar signs, his eyes averted, and some curious gathering
together of his person, as if he wrapped himself about and needed
privacy into which to regain his equilibrium, that he was outraged
and anguished. She stroked James's head; she transferred to him
what she felt for her husband, and, as she watched him chalk yellow
the white dress shirt of a gentleman in the Army and Navy Stores
catalogue, thought what a delight it would be to her should he turn
out a great artist; and why should he not? He had a splendid forehead. Then, looking up, as her husband passed her once more, she
was relieved to find that the ruin was veiled; domesticity triumphed;
custom crooned its soothing rhythm, so that when stopping deliberately, as his turn came round again, at the window he bent quizzically and whimsically to tickle James's bare calf with a sprig of
something, she twitted him for having dispatched 'that poor young
man', Charles Tansley. Tansley had had to go in and write his
dissertation, he said.

Art w words

'James will have to write *his* dissertation one of these days,' he added ironically, flicking his sprig.

Hating his father, James brushed away the tickling spray with which in a manner peculiar to him, compound of severity and humour, he teased his youngest son's bare leg.

She was trying to get these tiresome stockings finished to send to Sorley's little boy tomorrow, said Mrs Ramsay.

There wasn't the slightest possible chance that they could go to the Lighthouse tomorrow, Mr Ramsay snapped out irascibly.

How did he know? she asked. The wind often changed.

The extraordinary irrationality of her remark, the folly of women's minds enraged him. He had ridden through the valley of death, been shattered and shivered; and now she flew in the face of facts, made his children hope what was utterly out of the question, in effect, told lies. He stamped his foot on the stone step. 'Damn you,' he said. But what had she said? Simply that it might be fine tomorrow. So it might.

Not with the barometer falling and the wind due west.

To pursue truth with such astonishing lack of consideration for other people's feelings, to rend the thin veils of civilization so wantonly, so brutally, was to her so horrible an outrage of human decency that, without replying, dazed and blinded, she bent her head as if to let the pelt of jagged hail, the drench of dirty water, bespatter her unrebuked. There was nothing to be said.

He stood by her in silence. Very humbly, at length, he said that he would step over and ask the Coastguards if she liked.

There was nobody whom she reverenced as she reverenced him.

She was quite ready to take his word for it, she said. Only then they need not cut sandwiches—that was all. They came to her, naturally, since she was a woman, all day long with this and that; one wanting this, another that; the children were growing up; she often felt she was nothing but a sponge sopped full of human emotions. 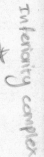 Then he said, Damn you. He said, It must rain. He said, It won't rain; and instantly a Heaven of security opened before her. There was nobody she reverenced more. She was not good enough to tie his shoe strings, she felt.

Already ashamed of that petulance, of that gesticulation of the hands when charging at the head of his troops, Mr Ramsay rather sheepishly prodded his son's bare legs once more, and then, as if he had her leave for it, with a movement which oddly reminded his wife of the great sea lion at the Zoo* tumbling backwards after swallowing his fish and walloping off so that the water in the tank washes from side to side, he dived into the evening air which already thinner was taking the substance from leaves and hedges but, as if in return, restoring to roses and pinks a lustre which they had not had by day.

'Someone had blundered,' he said again, striding off, up and down the terrace.

But how extraordinarily his note had changed! It was like the cuckoo; 'in June he gets out of tune';* as if he were trying over, tentatively seeking, some phrase for a new mood, and having only this at hand, used it, cracked though it was. But it sounded ridiculous—'Someone had blundered'—said like that, almost as a question, without any conviction, melodiously. Mrs Ramsay could not help smiling, and soon, sure enough, walking up and down, he hummed it, dropped it, fell silent.

He was safe, he was restored to his privacy. He stopped to light his pipe, looked once at his wife and son in the window, and as one raises one's eyes from a page in an express train and sees a farm, a tree, a cluster of cottages as an illustration, a confirmation of something on the printed page to which one returns, fortified, and satisfied, so without his distinguishing either his son or his wife, the sight of them fortified him and satisfied him and consecrated his effort to arrive at a perfectly clear understanding of the problem which now engaged the energies of his splendid mind.

It was a splendid mind. For if thought is like the keyboard of a piano, divided into so many notes, or like the alphabet is ranged in twenty-six letters all in order, then his splendid mind had no sort of difficulty in running over those letters one by one, firmly and accurately, until it had reached, say, the letter Q.* He reached Q. Very few people in the whole of England ever reach Q. Here, stopping for one moment by the stone urn* which held the geraniums, he saw, but now far far away, like children picking up shells, divinely innocent and occupied with little trifles at their feet and somehow entirely defenceless against a doom which he perceived, his wife and son, together, in the window. They needed his protection; he gave it them. But after Q? What comes next? After Q there are a number of letters the last of which is scarcely visible to mortal eyes, but glimmers red in the distance. Z is only reached once by one man in a generation.

Still, if he could reach R it would be something. Here at least was Q.
He dug his heels in at Q. Q he was sure of. Q he could demonstrate.
If Q then is Q—R—Here he knocked his pipe out, with two or three
resonant taps on the ram's horn which made the handle of the urn,
and proceeded. 'Then R . . .' He braced himself. He clenched
himself.

Qualities that would have saved a ship's company exposed on a
broiling sea with six biscuits and a flask of water—endurance and
justice, foresight, devotion, skill, came to his help. R is then—
what is R?

A shutter, like the leathern eyelid of a lizard, flickered over the
intensity of his gaze and obscured the letter R. In that flash of
darkness he heard people saying—he was a failure*—that R was
beyond him. He would never reach R. On to R, once more. R——

Qualities that in a desolate expedition across the icy solitudes
of the Polar region* would have made him the leader, the guide,
the counsellor, whose temper, neither sanguine nor despondent, sur-
veys with equanimity what is to be and faces it, came to his help
again. R——

The lizard's eye flickered once more. The veins on his forehead
bulged. The geranium in the urn became startlingly visible and, displayed among its leaves, he could see, without wishing it, that old, that
obvious distinction between the two classes of men; on the one hand
the steady goers of superhuman strength who, plodding and per-
severing, repeat the whole alphabet in order, twenty-six letters in all,
from start to finish; on the other the gifted, the inspired who, miraculously, lump all the letters together in one flash—the way of genius.
He had not genius; he laid no claim to that: but he had, or might have
had, the power to repeat every letter of the alphabet from A to Z
accurately in order. Meanwhile, he stuck at Q. On, then, on to R.

Feelings that would not have disgraced a leader who, now that the
snow has begun to fall and the mountain-top is covered in mist,
knows that he must lay himself down and die before morning comes,
stole upon him, paling the colour of his eyes, giving him, even in the
two minutes of his turn on the terrace, the bleached look of withered
old age. Yet he would not die lying down; he would find some crag of
rock, and there, his eyes fixed on the storm, trying to the end to
pierce the darkness, he would die standing. He would never reach R.

He stood stock still, by the urn, with the geranium flowing over it.

How many men in a thousand million, he asked himself, reach Z after all? Surely the leader of a forlorn hope* may ask himself that, and answer, without treachery to the expedition behind him, 'One perhaps'. One in a generation. Is he to be blamed then if he is not that one? provided he has toiled honestly, given to the best of his power, till he has no more left to give? And his fame lasts how long? It is permissible even for a dying hero to think before he dies how men will speak of him hereafter. His fame lasts perhaps two thousand years. And what are two thousand years? (asked Mr Ramsay ironically, staring at the hedge). What, indeed, if you look from a mountain-top down the long wastes of the ages? The very stone one kicks with one's boot will outlast Shakespeare. His own little light would shine, not very brightly, for a year or two, and would then be merged in some bigger light, and that in a bigger still. (He looked into the darkness, into the intricacy of the twigs.) Who then could blame the leader of that forlorn party which after all has climbed high enough to see the waste of the years and the perishing of stars, if before death stiffens his limbs beyond the power of movement he does a little consciously raise his numbed fingers to his brow, and square his shoulders, so that when the search party comes they will find him dead at his post, the fine figure of a soldier? Mr Ramsay squared his shoulders and stood very upright by the urn.

Who shall blame him, if, so standing for a moment, he dwells upon fame, upon search parties, upon cairns raised by grateful followers over his bones? Finally, who shall blame the leader of the doomed expedition, if, having adventured to the uttermost, and used his strength wholly to the last ounce and fallen asleep not much caring if he wakes or not, he now perceives by some pricking in his toes that he lives, and does not on the whole object to live, but requires sympathy, and whisky, and someone to tell the story of his suffering to at once? Who shall blame him? Who will not secretly rejoice when the hero puts his armour off, and halts by the window and gazes at his wife and son, who very distant at first, gradually come closer and closer, till lips and book and head are clearly before him, though still lovely and unfamiliar from the intensity of his isolation and the waste of ages and the perishing of the stars, and finally putting his pipe in his pocket and bending his magnificent head before her—who will blame him if he does homage to the beauty of the world?

7

But his son hated him. He hated him for coming up to them, for stopping and looking down on them; he hated him for interrupting them; he hated him for the exaltation and sublimity of his gestures; for the magnificence of his head; for his exactingness and egotism (for there he stood, commanding them to attend to him); but most of all he hated the twang and twitter of his father's emotion which, vibrating round them, disturbed the perfect simplicity and good sense of his relations with his mother. By looking fixedly at the page, he hoped to make him move on; by pointing his finger at a word, he hoped to recall his mother's attention, which, he knew angrily, wavered instantly his father stopped. But no. Nothing would make Mr Ramsay move on. There he stood, demanding sympathy.

Mrs Ramsay, who had been sitting loosely, folding her son in her arm, braced herself, and, half turning, seemed to raise herself with an effort, and at once to pour erect into the air a rain of energy, a column of spray, looking at the same time animated and alive as if all her energies were being fused into force, burning and illuminating (quietly though she sat, taking up her stocking again), and into this delicious fecundity, this fountain and spray of life, the fatal sterility of the male plunged itself, like a beak of brass, barren and bare. He wanted sympathy. He was a failure, he said. Mrs Ramsay flashed her needles. Mr Ramsay repeated, never taking his eyes from her face, that he was a failure. She blew the words back at him. 'Charles Tansley . . .' she said. But he must have more than that. It was sympathy he wanted, to be assured of his genius, first of all, and then to be taken within the circle of life, warmed and soothed, to have his senses restored to him, his barrenness made fertile, and all the rooms of the house made full of life—the drawing-room; behind the drawing-room the kitchen; above the kitchen the bedrooms; and beyond them the nurseries; they must be furnished, they must be filled with life.

Charles Tansley thought him the greatest metaphysician of the time, she said. But he must have more than that. He must have sympathy. He must be assured that he too lived in the heart of life; was needed; not here only, but all over the world. Flashing her needles, confident, upright, she created drawing-room and kitchen, set them all aglow; bade him take his ease there, go in and out, enjoy himself. She laughed, she knitted. Standing between her knees, very stiff, James felt all her strength flaring up to be drunk and quenched by the beak of brass, the arid scimitar of the male, which smote mercilessly, again and again, demanding sympathy.

He was a failure, he repeated. Well, look then, feel then. Flashing her needles, glancing round about her, out of the window, into the room, at James himself, she assured him, beyond a shadow of a doubt, by her laugh, her poise, her competence (as a nurse carrying a light across a dark room assures a fractious child), that it was real; the house was full; the garden blowing. If he put implicit faith in her, nothing should hurt him; however deep he buried himself or climbed high, not for a second should he find himself without her. So boasting of her capacity to surround and protect, there was scarcely a shell of herself left for her to know herself by; all was so lavished and spent; and James, as he stood stiff between her knees, felt her rise in a rosy-flowered fruit tree laid with leaves and dancing boughs into which the beak of brass, the arid scimitar of his father, the egotistical man, plunged and smote, demanding sympathy.

Filled with her words, like a child who drops off satisfied, he said, at last, looking at her with humble gratitude, restored, renewed, that he would take a turn; he would watch the children playing cricket. He went.

Immediately, Mrs Ramsay seemed to fold herself together, one petal closed in another, and the whole fabric fell in exhaustion upon itself, so that she had only strength enough to move her finger, in exquisite abandonment to exhaustion, across the page of Grimm's fairy story,* while there throbbed through her, like the pulse in a spring which has expanded to its full width and now gently ceases to beat, the rapture of successful creation.

Every throb of this pulse seemed, as he walked away, to enclose her and her husband, and to give to each that solace which two different notes, one high, one low, struck together, seem to give each other as they combine. Yet, as the resonance died, and she turned to the Fairy Tale again, Mrs Ramsay felt not only exhausted in body (afterwards, not at the time, she always felt this) but also there tinged her physical fatigue some faintly disagreeable sensation with another origin. Not that, as she read aloud the story of the Fisherman's Wife she knew precisely what it came from; nor did she let herself put into words her dissatisfaction when she realized, at the turn of the page when she stopped and heard dully, ominously, a wave fall, how it came from this: she did not like, even for a second, to feel finer than her husband; and further, could not bear not being entirely sure, when she spoke to him, of the truth of what she said. Universities and people wanting him, lectures and books and their being of the highest importance— all that she did not doubt for a moment; but it was their relation, and his coming to her like that, openly, so that anyone could see, that discomposed her; for then people said he depended on her, when they must know that of the two he was infinitely the more important, and what she gave the world, in comparison with what he gave, negligible. But then again, it was the other thing too—not being able to tell him the truth, being afraid, for instance, about the greenhouse roof and the expense it would be, fifty pounds perhaps, to mend it,* and then about his books, to be afraid that he might guess, what she a little suspected, that his last book was not quite his best book (she gathered that from William Bankes); and then to hide small daily things, and the children seeing it, and the burden it laid on them—all this diminished the entire joy, the pure joy, of the two notes sounding together, and let the sound die on her ear now with a dismal flatness.

A shadow was on the page; she looked up. It was Augustus Carmichael shuffling past, precisely now, at the very moment when it was painful to be reminded of the inadequacy of human relationships, that the most perfect was flawed, and could not bear the examination which, loving her husband, with her instinct for truth, she turned upon it; when it was painful to feel herself convicted of unworthiness, and impeded in her proper function by these lies, these exaggerations,—it was at this moment when she was fretted thus ignobly in the wake of her exaltation, that Mr Carmichael shuffled past, in his yellow slippers, and some demon in her made it necessary for her to call out, as he passed,

'Going indoors, Mr Carmichael?'

8

HE said nothing. He took opium. The children said he had stained his beard yellow with it. Perhaps. What was obvious to her was that the poor man was unhappy, came to them every year as an escape;

and yet every year, she felt the same thing; he did not trust her. She said, 'I am going to the town. Shall I get you stamps, paper, tobacco?' and she felt him wince. He did not trust her. It was his wife's doing. She remembered that iniquity of his wife's towards him, which had made her turn to steel and adamant there, in the horrid little room in St John's Wood,* when with her own eyes she had seen that odious woman turn him out of the house. He was unkempt; he dropped things on his coat; he had the tiresomeness of an old man with nothing in the world to do; and she turned him out of the room. She said, in her odious way, 'Now, Mrs Ramsay and I want to have a little talk together,' and Mrs Ramsay could see, as if before her eyes, the innumerable miseries of his life. Had he money enough to buy tobacco? Did he have to ask her for it? half a crown? eighteenpence? Oh, she could not bear to think of the little indignities she made him suffer. And always now (why, she could not guess, except that it came probably from that woman somehow) he shrank from her. He never told her anything. But what more could she have done? There was a sunny room given up to him. The children were good to him. Never did she show a sign of not wanting him. She went out of her way indeed to be friendly. Do you want stamps, do you want tobacco? Here's a book you might like and so on. And after all—after all (here insensibly she drew herself together, physically, the sense of her own beauty becoming, as it did so seldom, present to her)—after all, she had not generally any difficulty in making people like her; for instance, George Manning; Mr Wallace; famous as they were, they would come to her of an evening, quietly, and talk alone over her fire. She bore about with her, she could not help knowing it, the torch of her beauty; she carried it erect into any room that she entered; and after all, veil it as she might, and shrink from the monotony of bearing that it imposed on her, her beauty was apparent. She had been admired. She had been loved. She had entered rooms where mourners sat. Tears had flown in her presence. Men, and women too, letting go the multiplicity of things, had allowed themselves with her the relief of simplicity. It injured her that he should shrink. It hurt her. And yet not cleanly, not rightly. That was what she minded, coming as it did on top of her discontent with her husband; the sense she had now when Mr Carmichael shuffled past, just nodding to her question, with a book beneath his arm, in his yellow slippers, that she was suspected; and that all this desire of hers to give, to help, was vanity. For her own self-satisfaction was it that she wished so instinctively to help, to give, that people might say of her, 'O Mrs Ramsay! dear Mrs Ramsay . . . Mrs Ramsay, of course!' and need her and send for her and admire her? Was it not secretly this that she wanted, and therefore when Mr Carmichael shrank away from her, as he did at this moment, making off to some corner where he did acrostics endlessly, she did not feel merely snubbed back in her instinct, but made aware of the pettiness of some part of her, and of human relations how flawed they are, how despicable, how self-seeking, at their best. Shabby and worn out, and not presumably (her cheeks were hollow, her hair was white) any longer a sight that filled the eyes with joy, she had better devote her mind to the story of the Fisherman and his Wife and so pacify that bundle of sensitiveness (none of her children was as sensitive as he was) her son James.

'The man's heart grew heavy,' she read aloud, 'and he would not go. He said to himself, "It is not right," and yet he went. And when he came to the sea the water was quite purple and dark blue, and grey and thick, and no longer so green and yellow, but it was still quiet. And he stood there and said——'

Mrs Ramsay could have wished that her husband had not chosen that moment to stop. Why had he not gone as he said to watch the children playing cricket? But he did not speak; he looked; he nodded; he approved; he went on. He slipped seeing before him that hedge which had over and over again rounded some pause, signified some conclusion, seeing his wife and child, seeing again the urns with the trailing red geraniums which had so often decorated processes of thought, and bore, written up among their leaves, as if they were scraps of paper on which one scribbles notes in the rush of reading —he slipped, seeing all this, smoothly into speculation suggested by an article in *The Times* about the number of Americans who visit Shakespeare's house every year. If Shakespeare had never existed, he asked, would the world have differed much from what it is today? Does the progress of civilization depend upon great men? Is the lot of the average human being better now than in the time of the Pharaohs? Is the lot of the average human being, however, he asked himself, the criterion by which we judge the measure of civilization? Possibly not. Possibly the greatest good requires the existence of a slave class. The liftman in the Tube* is an eternal necessity. The thought was distasteful to him. He tossed his head. To avoid it, he would find some way of snubbing the predominance of the arts. He would argue that the world exists for the average human being; that the arts are merely a decoration imposed on the top of human life; they do not express it. Nor is Shakespeare necessary to it. Not knowing precisely why it was that he wanted to disparage Shakespeare and come to the rescue of the man who stands eternally in the door of the lift, he picked a leaf sharply from the hedge. All this would have to be dished up for the young men at Cardiff* next month, he thought; here, on his terrace, he was merely foraging and picnicking (he threw away the leaf that he had picked so peevishly) like a man who reaches from his horse to pick a bunch of roses, or stuffs his pockets with nuts as he ambles at his ease through the lanes and fields of a country known to him from boyhood. It was all familiar; this turning, that stile, that cut across the fields. Hours he would spend thus, with his pipe, of an evening, thinking up and down and in and out of the old familiar lanes and commons, which were all stuck about with the history of that campaign there, the life of this statesman here, with poems and with anecdotes, with figures too, this thinker, that soldier; all very brisk and clear; but at length the lane, the field, the common, the fruitful nut-tree and the flowering hedge led him on to that further turn of the road where he dismounted always, tied his horse to a tree, and proceeded on foot alone. He reached the edge of the lawn and looked out on the bay beneath.

It was his fate, his peculiarity, whether he wished it or not, to come out thus on a spit of land which the sea is slowly eating away, and there to stand, like a desolate seabird, alone. It was his power, his gift, suddenly to shed all superfluities, to shrink and diminish so that he looked barer and felt sparer, even physically, yet lost none of his intensity of mind, and so to stand on his little ledge facing the dark of human ignorance, how we know nothing and the sea eats away the ground we stand on—that was his fate, his gift. But having thrown away, when he dismounted, all gestures and fripperies, all trophies of nuts and roses, and shrunk so that not only fame but even his own name was forgotten by him, he kept even in that desolation a vigilance which spared no phantom and luxuriated in no vision, and it was in this guise that he inspired in William Bankes (intermittently) and in Charles Tansley (obsequiously) and in his wife now, when she looked up and saw him standing at the edge of the lawn, profound reverence, and pity, and gratitude too, as a stake driven into the bed of a channel upon which the gulls perch and the waves beat inspires in merry boatloads a feeling of gratitude for the duty it has taken upon itself of marking the channel out there in the floods alone.

'But the father of eight children has no choice . . .' Muttering half aloud, so he broke off, turned, sighed, raised his eyes, sought the figure of his wife reading stories to the little boy; filled his pipe. He turned from the sight of human ignorance and human fate and the sea eating the ground we stand on, which, had he been able to contemplate it fixedly might have led to something; and found consolation in trifles so slight compared with the august theme just now before him that he was disposed to slur that comfort over, to deprecate it, as if to be caught happy in a world of misery was for an honest man the most despicable of crimes. It was true; he was for the most part happy; he had his wife; he had his children; he had promised in six weeks' time to talk 'some nonsense' to the young men of Cardiff about Locke, Hume, Berkeley, and the causes of the French Revolution.* But this and his pleasure in it, in the phrases he made, in the ardour of youth, in his wife's beauty, in the tributes that reached him from Swansea, Cardiff, Exeter, Southampton, Kidderminster,* Oxford, Cambridge—all had to be deprecated and concealed under the phrase 'talking nonsense', because, in effect, he had not done the thing he might have done. It was a disguise; it was the refuge of a man afraid to own his own feelings, who could not say, This is what I like—this is what I am; and rather pitiable and distasteful to William Bankes and Lily Briscoe, who wondered why such concealments should be necessary; why he needed always praise; why so brave a man in thought should be so timid in life; how strangely he was venerable and laughable at one and the same time.

Teaching and preaching is beyond human power, Lily suspected. (She was putting away her things.) If you are exalted you must somehow come a cropper. Mrs Ramsay gave him what he asked too easily. Then the change must be so upsetting, Lily said. He comes in from his books and finds us all playing games and talking nonsense. Imagine what a change from the things he thinks about, she said.

He was bearing down upon them. Now he stopped dead and stood looking in silence at the sea. Now he had turned away again.

9

YES, Mr Bankes said, watching him go. It was a thousand pities. (Lily had said something about his frightening her—he changed from one mood to another so suddenly.) Yes, said Mr Bankes, it was a thousand pities that Ramsay could not behave a little more like other people. (For he liked Lily Briscoe; he could discuss Ramsay with her quite openly.) It was for that reason, he said, that the young don't read Carlyle.* A crusty old grumbler who lost his temper if the porridge was cold, why should he preach to us? was what Mr Bankes understood that young people said nowadays. It was a thousand pities if you thought, as he did, that Carlyle was one of the great teachers of mankind. Lily was ashamed to say that she had not read Carlyle since she was at school. But in her opinion one liked Mr Ramsay all the better for thinking that if his little finger ached the whole world must come to an end. It was not *that* she minded. For who could be deceived by him? He asked you quite openly to flatter him, to admire him, his little dodges deceived nobody. What she disliked was his narrowness, his blindness, she said, looking after him.

'A bit of a hypocrite?' Mr Bankes suggested, looking, too, at Mr Ramsay's back, for was he not thinking of his friendship, and of Cam refusing to give him a flower, and of all those boys and girls, and his own house, full of comfort, but, since his wife's death, quiet rather? Of course, he had his work . . . All the same, he rather wished Lily to agree that Ramsay was, as he said, 'a bit of a hypocrite'.

Lily Briscoe went on putting away her brushes, looking up, looking down. Looking up, there he was—Mr Ramsay—advancing towards them, swinging, careless, oblivious, remote. A bit of a hypocrite? she repeated. Oh no—the most sincere of men, the truest (here he was), the best; but, looking down, she thought, he is absorbed in himself, he is tyrannical, he is unjust; and kept looking down, purposely, for only so could she keep steady, staying with the Ramsays. Directly one looked up and saw them, what she called 'being in love' flooded them. They became part of that unreal but penetrating and exciting universe which is the world seen through the eyes of love. The sky stuck to them; the birds sang through them.

And, what was even more exciting, she felt, too, as she saw Mr Ramsay bearing down and retreating, and Mrs Ramsay sitting with James in the window and the cloud moving and the tree bending, how life, from being made up of little separate incidents which one lived one by one, became curled and whole like a wave which bore one up with it and threw one down with it, there, with a dash on the beach.

Mr Bankes expected her to answer. And she was about to say something criticizing Mrs Ramsay, how she was alarming, too, in her way, high-handed, or words to that effect, when Mr Bankes made it entirely unnecessary for her to speak by his rapture. For such it was considering his age, turned sixty, and his cleanliness and his impersonality, and the white scientific coat which seemed to clothe him. For him to gaze as Lily saw him gazing at Mrs Ramsay was a rapture, equivalent, Lily felt, to the loves of dozens of young men (and perhaps Mrs Ramsay had never excited the loves of dozens of young men). It was love, she thought, pretending to move her canvas, distilled and filtered; love that never attempted to clutch its object; but, like the love which mathematicians bear their symbols, or poets their phrases, was meant to be spread over the world and become part of the human gain. So it was indeed. The world by all means should have shared it, could Mr Bankes have said why that woman pleased him so; why the sight of her reading a fairy tale to her boy had upon him precisely the same effect as the solution of a scientific problem, so that he rested in contemplation of it, and felt, as he felt when he had proved something absolute about the digestive system of plants, that barbarity was tamed, the reign of chaos subdued.

Such a rapture—for by what other name could one call it?—made Lily Briscoe forget entirely what she had been about to say. It was nothing of importance; something about Mrs Ramsay. It paled beside this 'rapture', this silent stare, for which she felt intense gratitude; for nothing so solaced her, eased her of the perplexity of life, and miraculously raised its burdens, as this sublime power, this heavenly gift, and one would no more disturb it, while it lasted, than break up the shaft of sunlight lying level across the floor.

That people should love like this, that Mr Bankes should feel this for Mrs Ramsay (she glanced at him musing) was helpful, was exalting. She wiped one brush after another upon a piece of old rag, menially, on purpose. She took shelter from the reverence which covered all women; she felt herself praised. Let him gaze; she would steal a look at her picture.

She could have wept. It was bad, it was bad, it was infinitely bad! She could have done it differently of course; the colour could have been thinned and faded; the shapes etherealized; that was how Paunceforte would have seen it. But then she did not see it like that. She saw the colour burning on a framework of steel; the light of a butterfly's wing lying upon the arches of a cathedral. Of all that only a few random marks scrawled upon the canvas remained. And it would never be seen; never be hung even, and there was Mr Tansley whispering in her ear, 'Women can't paint, women can't write . . .'

She now remembered what she had been going to say about Mrs Ramsay. She did not know how she would have put it; but it would have been something critical. She had been annoyed the other night by some high-handedness. Looking along the level of Mr Bankes's glance at her, she thought that no woman could worship another woman in the way he worshipped; they could only seek shelter under the shade which Mr Bankes extended over them both. Looking along his beam she added to it her different ray, thinking that she was unquestionably the loveliest of people (bowed over her book); the best perhaps; but also, different too from the perfect shape which one saw there. But why different, and how different? she asked herself, scraping her palette of all those mounds of blue and green which seemed to her like clods with no life in them now, yet she vowed, she would inspire them, force them to move, flow, do her bidding tomorrow. How did she differ? What was the spirit in her, the essential thing, by which, had you found a glove in the corner of a sofa, you would have known it, from its twisted finger, hers indisputably? She was like a bird for speed, an arrow for directness. She was wilful; she was commanding (of course, Lily reminded herself, I am thinking of her relations with women, and I am much younger, an insignificant person, living off the Brompton Road). She opened bedroom windows. She shut doors. (So she tried to start the tune of Mrs Ramsay in her head.) Arriving late at night, with a light tap on one's bedroom door, wrapped in an old fur coat (for the setting of her beauty was always that—hasty, but apt), she would enact again whatever it might be—Charles Tansley losing his umbrella; Mr Carmichael snuffling and sniffing; Mr Bankes saying, 'the vegetable salts are lost'. All this she would adroitly shape; even maliciously twist; and, moving over to the window, in pretence that she must go,—it was dawn, she could see the sun rising,—half turn back, more intimately, but still always laughing, insist that she must, Minta must, they all must marry, since in the whole world, whatever laurels might be tossed to her (but Mrs Ramsay cared not a fig for her painting), or triumphs won by her (probably Mrs Ramsay had had her share of those), and here she saddened, darkened, and came back to her chair, there could be no disputing this: an unmarried woman (she lightly took her hand for a moment), an unmarried woman has missed the best of life. The house seemed full of children sleeping and Mrs Ramsay listening; of shaded lights and regular breathing.

Oh but, Lily would say, there was her father; her home; even, had she dared to say it, her painting. But all this seemed so little, so virginal, against the other. Yet, as the night wore on, and white lights parted the curtains, and even now and then some bird chirped in the garden, gathering a desperate courage she would urge her own exemption from the universal law; plead for it; she liked to be alone; she liked to be herself; she was not made for that; and so have to meet a serious stare from eyes of unparalleled depth, and confront Mrs Ramsay's simple certainty (and she was childlike now) that her dear Lily, her little Brisk, was a fool. Then, she remembered, she had laid her head on Mrs Ramsay's lap and laughed and laughed and laughed, laughed almost hysterically at the thought of Mrs Ramsay presiding with immutable calm over destinies which she completely failed to understand. There she sat, simple, serious. She had recovered her sense of her now—this was the glove's twisted finger. But into what sanctuary had one penetrated? Lily Briscoe had looked up at last, and there was Mrs Ramsay, unwitting entirely what had caused her laughter, still presiding, but now with every trace of wilfulness abolished, and in its stead, something clear as the space which the clouds at last uncover—the little space of sky which sleeps beside the moon.

Was it wisdom? Was it knowledge? Was it, once more, the decep- tiveness of beauty, so that all one's perceptions, half-way to truth, were tangled in a golden mesh? or did she lock up within her some secret which certainly Lily Briscoe believed people must have for the world to go on at all? Every one could not be as helter skelter, hand to mouth as she was. But if they knew, could they tell one what they knew? Sitting on the floor with her arms round Mrs Ramsay's knees, close as she could get, smiling to think that Mrs Ramsay would never know the reason of that pressure, she imagined how in the chambers of the mind and heart of the woman who was, physically, touching her, were stood, like the treasures in the tombs of kings, tablets bearing sacred inscriptions,* which if one could spell them out would teach one everything, but they would never be offered openly, never made public. What art was there, known to love or cunning, by which one pressed through into those secret chambers? What device for becoming, like waters poured into one jar, inextricably the same, one with the object one adored? Could the body achieve it, or the mind, subtly mingling in the intricate passages of the brain? or the heart? Could loving, as people called it, make her and Mrs Ramsay one? for it was not knowledge but unity that she desired, not inscriptions on tablets, nothing that could be written in any language known to men, but intimacy itself, which is knowledge, she had thought, leaning her head on Mrs Ramsay's knee.

Nothing happened. Nothing! Nothing! as she leant her head against Mrs Ramsay's knee. And yet, she knew knowledge and wisdom were stored in Mrs Ramsay's heart. How then, she had asked herself, did one know one thing or another thing about people, sealed as they were? Only like a bee, drawn by some sweetness or sharpness in the air intangible to touch or taste, one haunted the dome-shaped hive,* ranged the wastes of the air over the countries of the world alone, and then haunted the hives with their murmurs and their stirrings; the hives which were people. Mrs Ramsay rose. Lily rose. Mrs Ramsay went. For days there hung about her, as after a dream some subtle change is felt in the person one has dreamt of, more vividly than anything she said, the sound of murmuring and, as she sat in the wicker armchair in the drawing-room window she wore, to Lily's eyes, an august shape; the shape of a dome.

This ray passed level with Mr Bankes's ray straight to Mrs Ramsay sitting reading there with James at her knee. But now while she still looked, Mr Bankes had done. He had put on his spectacles. He had stepped back. He had raised his hand. He had slightly narrowed his clear blue eyes, when Lily, rousing herself, saw what he was at, and winced like a dog who sees a hand raised to strike it. She would have snatched her picture off the easel, but she said to herself, One must.

If her inner jumbled self must be seen by the outside world.

She braced herself to stand the awful trial of someone looking at her picture. One must, she said, one must. And if it must be seen, Mr Bankes was less alarming than another. But that any other eyes should see the residue of her thirty-three years, the deposit of each day's living, mixed with something more secret than she had ever spoken or shown in the course of all those days was an agony. At the same time it was immensely exciting.

Nothing could be cooler and quieter. Taking out a penknife, Mr Bankes tapped the canvas with the bone handle. What did she wish to indicate by the triangular purple shape, 'just there?' he asked.

It was Mrs Ramsay reading to James, she said. She knew his objection—that no one could tell it for a human shape. But she had made no attempt at likeness,* she said. For what reason had she introduced them then? he asked. Why indeed?—except that if there, in that corner, it was bright, here, in this, she felt the need of darkness. Simple, obvious, commonplace, as it was, Mr Bankes was interested. Mother and child then—objects of universal veneration, and in this case the mother was famous for her beauty—might be reduced, he pondered, to a purple shadow without irreverence.

But the picture was not of them, she said. Or, not in his sense. There were other senses, too, in which one might reverence them. By a shadow here and a light there, for instance. Her tribute took that form, if, as she vaguely supposed, a picture must be a tribute. A mother and child might be reduced to a shadow without irreverence. A light here required a shadow there. He considered. He was interested. He took it scientifically in complete good faith. The truth was that all his prejudices were on the other side, he explained. The largest picture in his drawing-room, which painters had praised, and valued at a higher price than he had given for it, was of the cherry trees in blossom on the banks of the Kennet.* He had spent his honeymoon on the banks of the Kennet, he said. Lily must come and see that picture, he said. But now—he turned, with his glasses raised to the scientific examination of her canvas. The question being one of the relations of masses, of lights and shadows, which, to be honest, he had never considered before, he would like to have it explained—what then did she wish to make of it? And he indicated the scene before them. She looked. She could not show him what she wished to make of it, could not see it even herself, without a brush in her hand. She took up once more her old painting position with the dim eyes and the absent-minded manner, subduing all her impressions as a woman to something much more general; becoming once more under the power of that vision which she had seen clearly once and must now grope for among hedges and houses and mothers and children—her picture. It was a question, she remembered, how to connect this mass on the right hand with that on the left. She might do it by bringing the line of the branch across so; or break the vacancy in the foreground by an object (James perhaps) so. But the danger was that by doing that the unity of the whole might be broken. She stopped; she did not want to bore him; she took the canvas lightly off the easel.

But it had been seen; it had been taken from her. This man had shared with her something profoundly intimate. And, thanking Mr Ramsay for it and Mrs Ramsay for it and the hour and the place, crediting the world with a power which she had not suspected, that one could walk away down that long gallery not alone any more but arm in arm with somebody—the strangest feeling in the world, and the most exhilarating—she nicked the catch of her paint-box to, more firmly than was necessary, and the nick seemed to surround in a circle for ever the paint-box, the lawn, Mr Bankes, and that wild villain, Cam, dashing past.

10

FOR Cam grazed the easel by an inch; she would not stop for Mr Bankes and Lily Briscoe; though Mr Bankes, who would have liked a daughter of his own, held out his hand; she would not stop for her father, whom she grazed also by an inch; nor for her mother, who called 'Cam! I want you a moment!' as she dashed past. She was off like a bird, bullet, or arrow, impelled by what desire, shot by whom, at what directed, who could say? What, what? Mrs Ramsay pondered, watching her. It might be a vision—of a shell, of a wheelbarrow, of a fairy kingdom on the far side of the hedge; or it might be the glory of speed; no one knew. But when Mrs Ramsay called 'Cam!' a second time, the projectile dropped in mid-career, and Cam came lagging back, pulling a leaf by the way, to her mother.

What was she dreaming about, Mrs Ramsay wondered, seeing her engrossed, as she stood there, with some thought of her own, so that she had to repeat the message twice—ask Mildred if Andrew, Miss Doyle, and Mr Rayley have come back?—The words seemed to be dropped into a well, where, if the waters were clear, they were also so extraordinarily distorting that, even as they descended, one saw them twisting about to make Heaven knows what pattern on the floor of the child's mind. What message would Cam give the cook? Mrs Ramsay wondered. And indeed it was only by waiting patiently, and hearing that there was an old woman in the kitchen with very red cheeks, drinking soup out of a basin,* that Mrs Ramsay at last prompted that parrot-like instinct which had picked up Mildred's words quite accurately and could now produce them, if one waited, in a colourless singsong. Shifting from foot to foot, Cam repeated the words, 'No, they haven't, and I've told Ellen to clear away tea.'

Minta Doyle and Paul Rayley had not come back then. That could only mean, Mrs Ramsay thought, one thing. She must accept him, or she must refuse him. This going off after luncheon for a walk, even though Andrew was with them—what could it mean? except that she had decided, rightly, Mrs Ramsay thought (and she was very, very fond of Minta), to accept that good fellow, who might not be brilliant, but then, thought Mrs Ramsay, realizing that James was tugging at her to make her go on reading aloud the Fisherman and his Wife, she did in her own heart infinitely prefer boobies to clever men who wrote dissertations; Charles Tansley for instance. Anyhow it must have happened, one way or the other, by now.

But she read, 'Next morning the wife awoke first, and it was just daybreak, and from her bed she saw the beautiful country lying before her. Her husband was still stretching himself . . .'

But how could Minta say now that she would not have him? Not if she agreed to spend whole afternoons trapesing about the country alone—for Andrew would be off after his crabs—but possibly Nancy was with them. She tried to recall the sight of them standing at the hall door after lunch. There they stood, looking at the sky, wondering about the weather, and she had said, thinking partly to cover their shyness, partly to encourage them to be off (for her sympathies were with Paul),

'There isn't a cloud anywhere within miles,' at which she could feel little Charles Tansley, who had followed them out, snigger. But she did it on purpose. Whether Nancy was there or not, she could not be certain, looking from one to the other in her mind's eye.

She read on: 'Ah, wife,' said the man, 'why should we be King?
I do not want to be King.' 'Well,' said the wife, 'if you won't be King,
I will; go to the Flounder, for I will be King.'

'Come in or go out, Cam,' she said, knowing that Cam was
attracted only by the word 'Flounder' and that in a moment she
would fidget and fight with James as usual. Cam shot off. Mrs Ramsay
went on reading, relieved, for she and James shared the same tastes
and were comfortable together.

'And when he came to the sea, it was quite dark grey, and the
water heaved up from below, and smelt putrid. Then he went and
stood by it and said,

> "Flounder, flounder, in the sea,
> Come, I pray thee, here to me;
> For my wife, good Ilsabil,
> Wills not as I'd have her will."

"Well, what does she want then?" said the Flounder.' And where
were they now? Mrs Ramsay wondered, reading and thinking, quite
easily, both at the same time; for the story of the Fisherman and his
Wife was like the bass gently accompanying a tune, which now and
then ran up unexpectedly into the melody. And when should she be
told? If nothing happened, she would have to speak seriously to
Minta. For she could not go trapesing about all over the country,
even if Nancy were with them (she tried again, unsuccessfully, to
visualize their backs going down the path, and to count them). She
was responsible to Minta's parents—the Owl and the Poker. Her
nicknames for them shot into her mind as she read. The Owl and the
Poker—yes, they would be annoyed if they heard—and they were
certain to hear—that Minta, staying with the Ramsays, had been
seen etcetera, etcetera, etcetera. 'He wore a wig in the House of
Commons and she ably assisted him at the head of the stairs,' she
repeated, fishing them up out of her mind by a phrase which, coming back from some party, she had made to amuse her husband.
Dear, dear, Mrs Ramsay said to herself, how did they produce this
incongruous daughter? this tomboy Minta, with a hole in her stocking? How did she exist in that portentous atmosphere where the
maid was always removing in a dust-pan the sand that the parrot had
scattered, and conversation was almost entirely reduced to the
exploits—interesting perhaps, but limited after all—of that bird?

Naturally, one had asked her to lunch, tea, dinner, finally to stay with them up at Finlay,* which had resulted in some friction with the Owl, her mother, and more calling, and more conversation, and more sand, and really at the end of it, she had told enough lies about parrots to last her a lifetime (so she had said to her husband that night, coming back from the party). However, Minta came . . . Yes, she came, Mrs Ramsay thought, suspecting some thorn in the tangle of this thought; and disengaging it found it to be this: a woman had once accused her of 'robbing her of her daughter's affections'; something Mrs Doyle had said made her remember that charge again. Wishing to dominate, wishing to interfere, making people do what she wished—that was the charge against her, and she thought it most unjust. How could she help being 'like that' to look at? No one could accuse her of taking pains to impress. She was often ashamed of her own shabbiness. Nor was she domineering, nor was she tyrannical. It was more true about hospitals and drains and the dairy.* About things like that she did feel passionately, and would, if she had had the chance, have liked to take people by the scruff of their necks and make them see. No hospital on the whole island. It was a disgrace. Milk delivered at your door in London positively brown with dirt. It should be made illegal. A model dairy and a hospital up here—those two things she would have liked to do, herself. But how? With all these children? When they were older, then perhaps she would have time; when they were all at school.

Oh, but she never wanted James to grow a day older or Cam either. These two she would have liked to keep for ever just as they were, demons of wickedness, angels of delight, never to see them grow up into long-legged monsters. Nothing made up for the loss. When she read just now to James, 'and there were numbers of soldiers with kettle-drums and trumpets', and his eyes darkened, she thought, why should they grow up, and lose all that? He was the most gifted, the most sensitive of her children. But all, she thought, were full of promise. Prue, a perfect angel with the others, and sometimes now, at night especially, she took one's breath away with her beauty. Andrew—even her husband admitted that his gift for mathematics was extraordinary. And Nancy and Roger, they were both wild creatures now, scampering about over the country all day long. As for Rose, her mouth was too big, but she had a wonderful gift with her hands. If they had charades, Rose made the dresses;

made everything; liked best arranging tables, flowers, anything. She did not like it that Jasper should shoot birds; but it was only a stage; they all went through stages. Why, she asked, pressing her chin on James's head, should they grow up so fast? Why should they go to school? She would have liked always to have had a baby. She was happiest carrying one in her arms. Then people might say she was tyrannical, domineering, masterful, if they chose; she did not mind. And, touching his hair with her lips, she thought, he will never be so happy again, but stopped herself, remembering how it angered her husband that she should say that. Still, it was true. They were happier now than they would ever be again. A tenpenny tea set made Cam happy for days. She heard them stamping and crowing on the floor above her head the moment they woke. They came bustling along the passage. Then the door sprang open and in they came, fresh as roses, staring, wide awake, as if this coming into the dining-room after breakfast, which they did every day of their lives was a positive event to them; and so on, with one thing after another, all day long, until she went up to say good-night to them, and found them netted in their cots like birds among cherries and raspberries still making up stories about some little bit of rubbish—something they had heard, something they had picked up in the garden. They had all their little treasures . . . And so she went down and said to her husband, Why must they grow up and lose it all? Never will they be so happy again. And he was angry. Why take such a gloomy view of life? he said. It is not sensible. For it was odd; and she believed it to be true; that with all his gloom and desperation he was happier, more hopeful on the whole, than she was. Less exposed to human worries—perhaps that was it. He had always his work to fall back on. Not that she herself was 'pessimistic', as he accused her of being. Only she thought life—and a little strip of time presented itself to her eyes, her fifty years. There it was before her—life. Life: she thought but she did not finish her thought. She took a look at life, for she had a clear sense of it there, something real, something private, which she shared neither with her children nor with her husband. A sort of transaction went on between them, in which she was on one side, and life was on another, and she was always trying to get the better of it, as it was of her; and sometimes they parleyed (when she sat alone); there were, she remembered, great reconciliation scenes; but for the most part, oddly enough, she must admit that she felt this thing that she called life terrible, hostile, and quick to pounce on you if you gave it a chance. There were the eternal problems: suffering; death; the poor. There was always a woman dying of cancer even here. And yet she had said to all these children, You shall go through with it. To eight people she had said relentlessly that (and the bill for the greenhouse would be fifty pounds). For that reason, knowing what was before them—love and ambition and being wretched alone in dreary places—she had often the feeling, why must they grow up and lose it all? And then she said to herself, brandishing her sword at life, nonsense. They will be perfectly happy. And here she was, she reflected, feeling life rather sinister again, making Minta marry Paul Rayley; because whatever she might feel about her own transaction and she had had experiences which need not happen to everyone (she did not name them to herself); she was driven on, too quickly she knew, almost as if it were an escape for her too, to say that people must marry; people must have children.

Was she wrong in this, she asked herself, reviewing her conduct for the past week or two, and wondering if she had indeed put any pressure upon Minta, who was only twenty-four, to make up her mind. She was uneasy. Had she not laughed about it? Was she not forgetting again how strongly she influenced people? Marriage needed—oh all sorts of qualities (the bill for the greenhouse would be fifty pounds); one—she need not name it—*that* was essential; the thing she had with her husband. Had they that?

'Then he put on his trousers and ran away like a madman,' she read. 'But outside a great storm was raging and blowing so hard that he could scarcely keep his feet; houses and trees toppled over, the mountains trembled, rocks rolled into the sea, the sky was pitch black, and it thundered and lightened, and the sea came in with black waves as high as church towers and mountains, and all with white foam at the top.'

She turned the page; there were only a few lines more, so that she would finish the story, though it was past bedtime. It was getting late. The light in the garden told her that; and the whitening of the flowers and something grey in the leaves conspired together to rouse in her a feeling of anxiety. What it was about she could not think at first. Then she remembered; Paul and Minta and Andrew had not come back. She summoned before her again the little group on the terrace in front of the hall door, standing looking up into the sky.

Andrew had his net and basket. That meant he was going to catch crabs and things. That meant he would climb out on to a rock; he would be cut off. Or coming back single file on one of those little paths above the cliff one of them might slip. He would roll and then crash. It was growing quite dark.

But she did not let her voice change in the least as she finished the story, and added, shutting the book, and speaking the last words as if she had made them up herself, looking into James's eyes: 'And there they are living still at this very time.'

'And that's the end,' she said, and she saw in his eyes, as the interest of the story died away in them, something else take its place; something wondering, pale, like the reflection of a light, which at once made him gaze and marvel. Turning, she looked across the bay, and there, sure enough, coming regularly across the waves first two quick strokes and then one long steady stroke, was the light of the Lighthouse. It had been lit.

In a moment he would ask her, 'Are we going to the Lighthouse?' And she would have to say, 'No: not tomorrow; your father says not.' Happily, Mildred came in to fetch them, and the bustle distracted them. But he kept looking back over his shoulder as Mildred carried him out, and she was certain that he was thinking, we are not going to the Lighthouse tomorrow; and she thought, he will remember that all his life.

11

No, she thought, putting together some of the pictures he had cut out—a refrigerator, a mowing-machine, a gentleman in evening dress—children never forget. For this reason, it was so important what one said, and what one did, and it was a relief when they went to bed. For now she need not think about anybody. She could be herself, by herself. And that was what now she often felt the need of—to think; well not even to think. To be silent; to be alone. All the being and the doing, expansive, glittering, vocal, evaporated; and one shrunk, with a sense of solemnity, to being oneself, a wedge-shaped core of darkness, something invisible to others. Although she continued to knit, and sat upright, it was thus that she felt herself; and this self having shed its attachments was free for the strangest adventures. When life sank down for a moment, the range of experience seemed limitless. And to everybody there was always this sense of unlimited resources, she supposed; one after another, she, Lily, Augustus Carmichael, must feel our apparitions, the things you know us by, are simply childish. Beneath it is all dark, it is all spreading, it is unfathomably deep; but now and again we rise to the surface and that is what you see us by. Her horizon seemed to her limitless. There were all the places she had not seen; the Indian plains;* she felt herself pushing aside the thick leather curtain of a church in Rome.* This core of darkness could go anywhere, for no one saw it. They could not stop it, she thought, exulting. There was freedom, there was peace, there was, most welcome of all, a summoning together, a resting on a platform of stability. Not as oneself did one find rest ever, in her experience (she accomplished here something dexterous with her needles), but as a wedge of darkness. Losing personality, one lost the fret, the hurry, the stir; and there rose to her lips always some exclamation of triumph over life when things came together in this peace, this rest, this eternity; and pausing there she looked out to meet that stroke of the Lighthouse, the long steady stroke, the last of the three, which was her stroke, for watching them in this mood always at this hour one could not help attaching oneself to one thing especially of the things one saw; and this thing, the long steady stroke, was her stroke. Often she found herself sitting and looking, sitting and looking, with her work in her hands until she became the thing she looked at—that light for example. And it would lift up on it some little phrase or other which had been lying in her mind like that—'Children don't forget, children don't forget'—which she would repeat and begin adding to it, It will end, It will end, she said. It will come, it will come, when suddenly she added, We are in the hands of the Lord.*

But instantly she was annoyed with herself for saying that. Who had said it? not she; she had been trapped into saying something she did not mean. She looked up over her knitting and met the third stroke and it seemed to her like her own eyes meeting her own eyes, searching as she alone could search into her mind and her heart, purifying out of existence that lie, any lie. She praised herself in praising the light, without vanity, for she was stern, she was searching, she was beautiful like that light. It was odd, she thought, how if one was alone, one leant to things, inanimate things; trees, streams, flowers; felt they expressed one; felt they became one; felt they knew one, in a sense were one; felt an irrational tenderness thus (she looked at that long steady light) as for oneself. There rose, and she looked and looked with her needles suspended, there curled up off the floor of the mind, rose from the lake of one's being, a mist, a bride to meet her lover.

What brought her to say that: 'We are in the hands of the Lord?' she wondered. The insincerity slipping in among the truths roused her, annoyed her. She returned to her knitting again. How could any Lord have made this world? she asked. With her mind she had always seized the fact that there is no reason, order, justice: but suffering, death, the poor. There was no treachery too base for the world to commit; she knew that. No happiness lasted; she knew that. She knitted with firm composure, slightly pursing her lips and, without being aware of it, so stiffened and composed the lines of her face in a habit of sternness that when her husband passed, though he was chuckling at the thought that Hume, the philosopher, grown enormously fat, had stuck in a bog,* he could not help noting, as he passed, the sternness at the heart of her beauty. It saddened him, and her remoteness pained him, and he felt, as he passed, that he could not protect her, and, when he reached the hedge, he was sad. He could do nothing to help her. He must stand by and watch her. Indeed, the infernal truth was, he made things worse for her. He was irritable—he was touchy. He had lost his temper over the Lighthouse. He looked into the hedge, into its intricacy, its darkness.

Always, Mrs Ramsay felt, one helped oneself out of solitude reluctantly by laying hold of some little odd or end, some sound, some sight. She listened, but it was all very still; cricket was over; the children were in their baths; there was only the sound of the sea. She stopped knitting; she held the long reddish-brown stocking dangling in her hands a moment. She saw the light again. With some irony in her interrogation, for when one woke at all, one's relations changed, she looked at the steady light, the pitiless, the remorseless, which was so much her, yet so little her, which had her at its beck and call (she woke in the night and saw it bent across their bed, stroking the floor), but for all that she thought, watching it with fascination, hypnotized, as if it were stroking with its silver fingers some sealed vessel in her brain whose bursting would flood her with delight, she had known happiness, exquisite happiness, intense happiness, and it silvered the rough waves a little more brightly, as daylight faded, and the blue went out of the sea and it rolled in waves of pure lemon which curved and swelled and broke upon the beach and the ecstasy burst in her eyes and waves of pure delight raced over the floor of her mind and she felt, It is enough! It is enough!

He turned and saw her. Ah! She was lovely, lovelier now than ever he thought. But he could not speak to her. He could not interrupt her. He wanted urgently to speak to her now that James was gone and she was alone at last. But he resolved, no; he would not interrupt her. She was aloof from him now in her beauty, in her sadness. He would let her be, and he passed her without a word, though it hurt him that she should look so distant, and he could not reach her, he could do nothing to help her. And again he would have passed her without a word had she not, at that very moment, given him of her own free will what she knew he would never ask, and called to him and taken the green shawl off the picture frame, and gone to him. For he wished, she knew, to protect her.

12

SHE folded the green shawl about her shoulders. She took his arm. His beauty was so great, she said, beginning to speak of Kennedy the gardener at once; he was so awfully handsome, that she couldn't dismiss him. There was a ladder against the greenhouse, and little lumps of putty stuck about, for they were beginning to mend the greenhouse roof. Yes, but as she strolled along with her husband, she felt that that particular source of worry had been placed. She had it on the tip of her tongue to say, as they strolled, 'It'll cost fifty pounds,' but instead, for her heart failed her about money, she talked about Jasper shooting birds, and he said, at once, soothing her instantly, that it was natural in a boy, and he trusted he would find better ways of amusing himself before long. Her husband was so sensible, so just. And so she said, 'Yes; all children go through stages,' and began considering the dahlias in the big bed, and wondering what about next year's flowers, and had he heard the children's nickname for Charles Tansley, she asked. The atheist, they called him, the little atheist. 'He's not a polished specimen,' said Mr Ramsay. 'Far from it,' said Mrs Ramsay.

She supposed it was all right leaving him to his own devices, Mrs Ramsay said, wondering whether it was any use sending down bulbs; did they plant them? 'Oh, he has his dissertation to write,' said Mr Ramsay. She knew all about *that*, said Mrs Ramsay. He talked of nothing else. It was about the influence of somebody upon something. 'Well, it's all he has to count on,' said Mr Ramsay. 'Pray Heaven he won't fall in love with Prue,' said Mrs Ramsay. He'd disinherit her if she married him, said Mr Ramsay. He did not look at the flowers, which his wife was considering, but at a spot about a foot or so above them. There was no harm in him, he added, and was just about to say that anyhow he was the only young man in England who admired his——when he choked it back. He would not bother her again about his books. These flowers seemed creditable, Mr Ramsay said, lowering his gaze and noticing something red, something brown. Yes, but then these she had put in with her own hands, said Mrs Ramsay. The question was, what happened if she sent bulbs down; did Kennedy plant them? It was his incurable laziness; she added, moving on. If she stood over him all day long with a spade in her hand, he did sometimes do a stroke of work. So they strolled along, towards the red-hot pokers. 'You're teaching your daughters to exaggerate,' said Mr Ramsay, reproving her. Her Aunt Camilla was far worse than she was, Mrs Ramsay remarked. 'Nobody ever held up your Aunt Camilla as a model of virtue that I'm aware of,' said Mr Ramsay. 'She was the most beautiful woman I ever saw,' said Mrs Ramsay. 'Somebody else was that,' said Mr Ramsay. Prue was going to be far more beautiful than she was, said Mrs Ramsay. He saw no trace of it, said Mr Ramsay. 'Well, then, look tonight,' said Mrs Ramsay. They paused. He wished Andrew could be induced to work harder. He would lose every chance of a scholarship* if he didn't. 'Oh scholarships!' she said. Mr Ramsay thought her foolish for saying that, about a serious thing, like a scholarship. He should be very proud of Andrew if he got a scholarship, he said. She would be just as proud of him if he didn't, she answered. They disagreed always about this, but it did not matter. She liked him to believe in scholarships, and he liked her to be proud of Andrew whatever he did. Suddenly she remembered those little paths on the edge of the cliffs.

Wasn't it late? she asked. They hadn't come home yet. He flicked his watch carelessly open. But it was only just past seven. He held his watch open for a moment, deciding that he would tell her what he had felt on the terrace. To begin with, it was not reasonable to be so nervous. Andrew could look after himself. Then, he wanted to tell her that when he was walking on the terrace just now—here he became uncomfortable, as if he were breaking into that solitude, that aloofness, that remoteness of hers ... But she pressed him. What had he wanted to tell her, she asked, thinking it was about going to the Lighthouse; and that he was sorry he had said 'Damn you'. But no. He did not like to see her look so sad, he said. Only wool-gathering, she protested, flushing a little. They both felt uncomfortable, as if they did not know whether to go on or go back. She had been reading fairy tales to James, she said. No, they could not share that; they could not say that.

They had reached the gap between the two clumps of red-hot pokers, and there was the Lighthouse again, but she would not let herself look at it. Had she known that he was looking at her, she thought, she would not have let herself sit there, thinking. She dis- liked anything that reminded her that she had been seen sitting thinking. So she looked over her shoulder, at the town. The lights were rippling and running as if they were drops of silver water held firm in a wind. And all the poverty, all the suffering had turned to that, Mrs Ramsay thought. The lights of the town and of the har- bour and of the boats seemed like a phantom net floating there to mark something which had sunk. Well, if he could not share her thoughts, Mr Ramsay said to himself, he would be off, then, on his own. He wanted to go on thinking, telling himself the story how Hume was stuck in a bog;* he wanted to laugh. But first it was nonsense to be anxious about Andrew. When he was Andrew's age he used to walk about the country all day long, with nothing but a biscuit in his pocket and nobody bothered about him, or thought that he had fallen over a cliff. He said aloud he thought he would be off for a day's walk if the weather held.* He had had about enough of Bankes and of Carmichael. He would like a little solitude. Yes, she said. It annoyed him that she did not protest. She knew that he would never do it. He was too old now to walk all day long with a biscuit in his pocket. She worried about the boys, but not about him. Years ago, before he had married, he thought, looking across the bay, as they stood between the clumps of red-hot pokers, he had walked all day. He had made a meal off bread and cheese in a public house. He had worked ten hours at a stretch; an old woman just popped her

Failure

head in now and again and saw to the fire. That was the country he liked best, over there; those sand-hills dwindling away into darkness. One could walk all day without meeting a soul. There was not a house scarcely, not a single village for miles on end. One could worry things out alone. There were little sandy beaches where no one had been since the beginning of time. The seals sat up and looked at you. It sometimes seemed to him that in a little house out there, alone— he broke off, sighing. He had no right. The father of eight children— he reminded himself. And he would have been a beast and a cur to wish a single thing altered. Andrew would be a better man than he had been. Prue would be a beauty, her mother said. They would stem the flood a bit. That was a good bit of work on the whole—his eight children. They showed he did not damn the poor little universe entirely, for on an evening like this, he thought, looking at the land dwindling away, the little island seemed pathetically small, half swallowed up in the sea.

'Poor little place,' he murmured with a sigh.

She heard him. He said the most melancholy things, but she noticed that directly he had said them he always seemed more cheerful than usual. All this phrase-making was a game, she thought, for if she had said half what he said, she would have blown her brains out by now.

It annoyed her, this phrase-making, and she said to him, in a matter-of-fact way, that it was a perfectly lovely evening. And what was he groaning about, she asked, half laughing, half complaining, for she guessed what he was thinking—he would have written better books if he had not married.

He was not complaining, he said. She knew that he did not complain. She knew that he had nothing whatever to complain of. And he seized her hand and raised it to his lips and kissed it with an intensity that brought the tears to her eyes, and quickly he dropped it.

They turned away from the view and began to walk up the path where the silver-green spear-like plants grew, arm in arm. His arm was almost like a young man's arm, Mrs Ramsay thought, thin and hard, and she thought with delight how strong he still was, though he was over sixty, and how untamed and optimistic, and how strange it was that being convinced, as he was, of all sorts of horrors, seemed not to depress him, but to cheer him. Was it not odd, she reflected? Indeed he seemed to her sometimes made differently from other people, born blind, deaf, and dumb, to the ordinary things, but to the extraordinary things, with an eye like an eagle's. His understanding often astonished her. But did he notice the flowers? No. Did he notice the view? No. Did he even notice his own daughter's beauty, or whether there was pudding on his plate or roast beef? He would sit at table with them like a person in a dream. And his habit of talking aloud, or saying poetry aloud, was growing on him, she was afraid; for sometimes it was awkward—

Best and brightest, come away!*

poor Miss Giddings, when he shouted that at her, almost jumped out of her skin. But then, Mrs Ramsay, though instantly taking his side against all the silly Giddingses in the world, then, she thought, intimating by a little pressure on his arm that he walked up hill too fast for her, and she must stop for a moment to see whether those were fresh mole-hills on the bank, then, she thought, stooping down to look, a great mind like his must be different in every way from ours. All the great men she had ever known, she thought, deciding that a rabbit must have got in, were like that, and it was good for young men (though the atmosphere of lecture-rooms was stuffy and depressing to her beyond endurance almost) simply to hear him, simply to look at him. But without shooting rabbits, how was one to keep them down? she wondered. It might be a rabbit; it might be a mole. Some creature anyhow was ruining her Evening Primroses. And looking up, she saw above the thin trees the first pulse of the full-throbbing star, and wanted to make her husband look at it; for the sight gave her such keen pleasure. But she stopped herself. He never looked at things. If he did, all he would say would be, Poor little world, with one of his sighs.

At that moment, he said, 'Very fine,' to please her, and pretended to admire the flowers. But she knew quite well that he did not admire them, or even realize that they were there. It was only to please her ... Ah, but was that not Lily Briscoe strolling along with William Bankes? She focused her short-sighted eyes upon the backs of a retreating couple. Yes, indeed it was. Did that not mean that they would marry? Yes, it must! What an admirable idea! They must marry!*

13

HE had been to Amsterdam, Mr Bankes was saying as he strolled across the lawn with Lily Briscoe. He had seen the Rembrandts. He had been to Madrid. Unfortunately, it was Good Friday and the Prado* was shut. He had been to Rome. Had Miss Briscoe never been to Rome? Oh, she should—It would be a wonderful experience for her—the Sistine Chapel; Michael Angelo; and Padua, with its Giottos.* His wife had been in bad health for many years, so that their sight-seeing had been on a modest scale.

She had been to Brussels; she had been to Paris, but only for a flying visit to see an aunt who was ill. She had been to Dresden; there were masses of pictures she had not seen; however, Lily Briscoe reflected, perhaps it was better not to see pictures: they only made one hopelessly discontented with one's own work. Mr Bankes thought one could carry that point of view too far. We can't all be Titians and we can't all be Darwins,* he said; at the same time he doubted whether you could have your Darwin and your Titian if it weren't for humble people like ourselves. Lily would have liked to pay him a compliment; you're not humble, Mr Bankes, she would have liked to have said. But he did not want compliments (most men do, she thought), and she was a little ashamed of her impulse and said nothing while he remarked that perhaps what he was saying did not apply to pictures. Anyhow, said Lily, tossing off her little insincerity, she would always go on painting, because it interested her. Yes, said Mr Bankes, he was sure she would, and as they reached the end of the lawn he was asking her whether she had difficulty in finding subjects in London when they turned and saw the Ramsays. So that is marriage, Lily thought, a man and a woman looking at a girl throwing a ball. That is what Mrs Ramsay tried to tell me the other night, she thought. For she was wearing a green shawl, and they were standing close together watching Prue and Jasper throwing catches. And suddenly the meaning which, for no reason at all, as perhaps they are stepping out of the Tube or ringing a doorbell, descends on people, making them symbolical, making them representative, came upon them, and made them in the dusk standing, looking, the symbols of marriage, husband and wife. Then, after an instant, the symbolical outline which transcended the real figures sank down again and they became, as they met them, Mr and Mrs Ramsay watching the children throwing catches. But still for a moment, though Mrs Ramsay greeted them with her usual smile (oh, she's thinking we're going to get married, Lily thought) and said, 'I have triumphed tonight,' meaning that for once Mr Bankes had agreed to dine with them and not run off to his own lodging where his man cooked vegetables properly; still, for one moment, there was a sense of things having been blown apart, of space, of irresponsibility as the ball soared high, and they followed it and lost it and saw the one star and the draped branches. In the failing light they all looked sharp-edged and ethereal and divided by great distances. Then, darting backwards over the vast space (for it seemed as if solidity had vanished altogether), Prue ran full tilt into them and caught the ball brilliantly high up in her left hand, and her mother said, 'Haven't they come back yet?' whereupon the spell was broken. Mr Ramsay felt free now to laugh out loud at Hume, who had stuck in a bog and an old woman rescued him on condition he said the Lord's Prayer, and chuckling to himself he strolled off to his study. Mrs Ramsay, bringing Prue back into the alliance of family life again, from which she had escaped, throwing catches, asked,

'Did Nancy go with them?'

14

(CERTAINLY, Nancy had gone with them, since Minta Doyle had asked it with her dumb look, holding out her hand, as Nancy made off, after lunch, to her attic, to escape the horror of family life. She supposed she must go then. She did not want to go. She did not want to be drawn into it all. For as they walked along the road to the cliff Minta kept on taking her hand. Then she would let it go. Then she would take it again. What was it she wanted? Nancy asked herself. There was something, of course, that people wanted; for when Minta took her hand and held it, Nancy, reluctantly, saw the whole world spread out beneath her, as if it were Constantinople seen through a mist, and then, however heavy-eyed one might be, one must needs ask, 'Is that Santa Sofia?' 'Is that the Golden Horn?'* So Nancy asked, when Minta took her hand, 'What is it that she wants?

Is it that?' And what was that? Here and there emerged from the mist (as Nancy looked down upon life spread beneath her) a pinnacle, a dome; prominent things, without names. But when Minta dropped her hand, as she did when they ran down the hillside, all that, the dome, the pinnacle, whatever it was that had protruded through the mist, sank down into it and disappeared.

Minta, Andrew observed, was rather a good walker. She wore more sensible clothes than most women. She wore very short skirts and black knickerbockers. She would jump straight into a stream and flounder across. He liked her rashness, but he saw that it would not do—she would kill herself in some idiotic way one of these days. She seemed to be afraid of nothing—except bulls. At the mere sight of a bull in a field she would throw up her arms and fly screaming, which was the very thing to enrage a bull of course. But she did not mind owning up to it in the least; one must admit that. She knew she was an awful coward about bulls, she said. She thought she must have been tossed in her perambulator when she was a baby. She didn't seem to mind what she said or did. Suddenly now she pitched down on the edge of the cliff and began to sing some song about

Damn your eyes, damn your eyes.*

They all had to join in and sing the chorus, and shout out together:

Damn your eyes, damn your eyes,

but it would be fatal to let the tide come in and cover up all the good hunting-grounds before they got on to the beach.

'Fatal,' Paul agreed, springing up, and as they went slithering down, he kept quoting the guide-book about 'these islands being justly celebrated for their park-like prospects and the extent and variety of their marine curiosities'. But it would not do altogether, this shouting and damning your eyes, Andrew felt, picking his way down the cliff, this clapping him on the back, and calling him 'old fellow' and all that; it would not altogether do. It was the worst of taking women on walks. Once on the beach they separated, he going out on to the Pope's Nose,* taking his shoes off, and rolling his socks in them and letting that couple look after themselves; Nancy waded out to her own rocks and searched her own pools and let that couple look after themselves. She crouched low down and touched the smooth rubber-like sea anemones, who were stuck like lumps of jelly to the side of the rock. Brooding, she changed the pool into the sea, and made the minnows into sharks and whales, and cast vast clouds over this tiny world by holding her hand against the sun, and so brought darkness and desolation, like God himself, to millions of ignorant and innocent creatures, and then took her hand away suddenly and let the sun stream down. Out on the pale criss-crossed sand, high-stepping, fringed, gauntletted, stalked some fantastic leviathan (she was still enlarging the pool), and slipped into the vast fissures of the mountainside. And then, letting her eyes slide imperceptibly above the pool and rest on that wavering line of sea and sky, on the tree trunks which the smoke of steamers made waver upon the horizon, she became with all that power sweeping savagely in and inevitably withdrawing, hypnotized, and the two senses of that vastness and this tininess (the pool had diminished again) flowering within it made her feel that she was bound hand and foot and unable to move by the intensity of feelings which reduced her own body, her own life, and the lives of all the people in the world, for ever, to nothingness. So listening to the waves, crouched over the pool, she brooded.

And Andrew shouted that the sea was coming in, so she leapt splashing through the shallow waves on to the shore and ran up the beach and was carried by her own impetuosity and her desire for rapid movement right behind a rock and there oh heavens! in each other's arms were Paul and Minta! kissing probably. She was outraged, indignant. She and Andrew put on their shoes and stockings in dead silence without saying a thing about it. Indeed they were rather sharp with each other. She might have called him when she saw the crayfish or whatever it was, Andrew grumbled. However, they both felt, it's not our fault. They had not wanted this horried nuisance to happen. All the same it irritated Andrew that Nancy should be a woman, and Nancy that Andrew should be a man, and they tied their shoes very neatly and drew the bows rather tight.

It was not until they had climbed right up on to the top of the cliff again that Minta cried out that she had lost her grandmother's brooch*—her grandmother's brooch, the sole ornament she possessed—a weeping willow, it was (they must remember it) set in pearls. They must have seen it, she said, with the tears running down her cheeks, the brooch which her grandmother had fastened her cap with till the last day of her life. Now she had lost it. She would rather

have lost anything than that! She would go back and look for it. They
all went back. They poked and peered and looked. They kept their
heads very low, and said things shortly and gruffly. Paul Rayley
searched like a madman all about the rock where they had been
sitting. All this pother about a brooch really didn't do at all, Andrew
thought, as Paul told him to make a 'thorough search between this
point and that'. The tide was coming in fast. The sea would cover
the place where they had sat in a minute. There was not a ghost of a
chance of their finding it now. 'We shall be cut off!' Minta shrieked,
suddenly terrified. As if there were any danger of that! It was the
same as the bulls all over again—she had no control over her emotions, Andrew thought. Women hadn't. The wretched Paul had to
pacify her. The men (Andrew and Paul at once became manly, and
different from usual) took counsel briefly and decided that they
would plant Rayley's stick where they had sat and come back at low
tide again. There was nothing more that could be done now. If the
brooch was there, it would still be there in the morning, they assured
her, but Minta still sobbed, all the way up to the top of the cliff. It
was her grandmother's brooch; she would rather have lost anything
but that, and yet Nancy felt, though it might be true that she minded
losing her brooch, she wasn't crying only for that. She was crying for
something else. We might all sit down and cry, she felt. But she did
not know what for.

They drew ahead together, Paul and Minta, and he comforted her,
and said how famous he was for finding things. Once when he was a
little boy he had found a gold watch. He would get up at daybreak
and he was positive he would find it. It seemed to him that it would
be almost dark, and he would be alone on the beach, and somehow it
would be rather dangerous. He began telling her, however, that he
would certainly find it, and she said that she would not hear of his
getting up at dawn: it was lost: she knew that: she had had a pre-
sentiment when she put it on that afternoon. And secretly he
resolved that he would not tell her, but he would slip out of the house
at dawn when they were all asleep and if he could not find it he
would go to Edinburgh and buy her another, just like it but more
beautiful. He would prove what he could do. And as they came out
on the hill and saw the lights of the town beneath them, the lights
coming out suddenly one by one seemed like things that were going
to happen to him—his marriage, his children, his house; and again

he thought, as they came out on to the high road, which was shaded with high bushes, how they would retreat into solitude together, and walk on and on, he always leading her, and she pressing close to his side (as she did now). As they turned by the crossroads he thought what an appalling experience he had been through, and he must tell someone—Mrs Ramsay of course, for it took his breath away to think what he had been and done. It had been far and away the worst moment of his life when he asked Minta to marry him. He would go straight to Mrs Ramsay, because he felt somehow that she was the person who had made him do it. She had made him think he could do anything. Nobody else took him seriously. But she made him believe that he could do whatever he wanted. He had felt her eyes on him all day today, following him about (though she never said a word) as if she were saying, 'Yes, you can do it. I believe in you. I expect it of you.' She had made him feel all that, and directly they got back (he looked for the lights of the house above the bay) he would go to her and say, 'I've done it, Mrs Ramsay; thanks to you.' And so turning into the lane that led to the house he could see lights moving about in the upper windows. They must be awfully late then. People were getting ready for dinner.* The house was all lit up, and the lights after the darkness made his eyes feel full, and he said to himself, childishly, as he walked up the drive, Lights, lights, lights,* and repeated in a dazed way, Lights, lights, lights, as they came into the house, staring about him with his face quite stiff. But, good heavens, he said to himself, putting his hand to his tie, I must not make a fool of myself.

15

'YES,' said Prue, in her considering way, answering her mother's question, 'I think Nancy did go with them.'

16

WELL then, Nancy had gone with them, Mrs Ramsay supposed, wondering, as she put down a brush, took up a comb, and said 'Come in' to a tap at the door (Jasper and Rose came in), whether the fact that Nancy was with them made it less likely or more likely that anything would happen; it made it less likely, somehow, Mrs Ramsay felt, very irrationally, except that after all holocaust on such a scale was not probable. They could not all be drowned. And again she felt alone in the presence of her old antagonist, life.

Jasper and Rose said that Mildred wanted to know whether she should wait dinner.

'Not for the Queen of England,' said Mrs Ramsay emphatically.

'Not for the Empress of Mexico,* she added, laughing at Jasper; for he shared his mother's vice: he, too, exaggerated.

And if Rose liked, she said, while Jasper took the message, she might choose which jewels she was to wear.* When there are fifteen people sitting down to dinner,* one cannot keep things waiting for ever. She was now beginning to feel annoyed with them for being so late; it was inconsiderate of them, and it annoyed her on top of her anxiety about them, that they should choose this very night to be out late, when, in fact, she wished the dinner to be particularly nice, since William Bankes had at last consented to dine with them; and they were having Mildred's masterpiece—Bœuf en Daube.* Everything depended upon things being served up the precise moment they were ready. The beef, the bayleaf, and the wine—all must be done to a turn. To keep it waiting was out of the question. Yet of course tonight, of all nights, out they went, and they came in late, and things had to be sent out, things had to be kept hot; the Bœuf en Daube would be entirely spoilt.

Jasper offered her an opal necklace; Rose a gold necklace. Which looked best against her black dress? Which did indeed? said Mrs Ramsay absent-mindedly, looking at her neck and shoulders (but avoiding her face), in the glass. And then, while the children rummaged among her things, she looked out of the window at a sight which always amused her—the rooks trying to decide which tree to settle on. Every time, they seemed to change their minds and rose up into the air again, because, she thought, the old rook, the father rook, old Joseph was her name for him, was a bird of a very trying and difficult disposition. He was a disreputable old bird, with half his wing feathers missing. He was like some seedy old gentleman in a top hat she had seen playing the horn in front of a public house.

'Look!' she said, laughing. They were actually fighting. Joseph and Mary were fighting. Anyhow they all went up again, and the air was shoved aside by their black wings and cut into exquisite scimitar shapes. The movement of the wings beating out, out, out—she could never describe it accurately enough to please herself—was one of the loveliest of all to her. Look at that, she said to Rose, hoping that Rose would see it more clearly than she could. For one's children so often gave one's own perceptions a little thrust forwards.

But which was it to be? They had all the trays of her jewel-case open. The gold necklace, which was Italian, or the opal necklace, which Uncle James had brought her from India;* or should she wear her amethysts?

'Choose, dearests, choose,' she said, hoping that they would make haste.

But she let them take their time to choose: she let Rose, particularly, take up this and then that, and hold her jewels against the black dress, for this little ceremony of choosing jewels, which was gone through every night, was what Rose liked best, she knew. She had some hidden reason of her own for attaching great importance to this choosing what her mother was to wear. What was the reason, Mrs Ramsay wondered, standing still to let her clasp the necklace she had chosen, divining, through her own past, some deep, some buried, some quite speechless feeling that one had for one's mother at Rose's age. Like all feelings felt for oneself, Mrs Ramsay thought, it made one sad. It was so inadequate, what one could give in return; and what Rose felt was quite out of proportion to anything she actually was. And Rose would grow up; and Rose would suffer, she supposed, with these deep feelings, and she said she was ready now, and they would go down, and Jasper, because he was the gentleman, should give her his arm, and Rose, as she was the lady, should carry her handkerchief (she gave her the handkerchief), and what else? oh, yes, it might be cold: a shawl. Choose me a shawl, she said, for that would please Rose, who was bound to suffer so. 'There,' she said, stopping by the window on the landing, 'there they are again.' Joseph had settled on another tree-top. 'Don't you think they mind', she said to Jasper, 'having their wings broken?' Why did he want to shoot poor old Joseph and Mary? He shuffled a little on the stairs, and felt rebuked, but not seriously, for she did not understand the fun of shooting birds; that they did not feel; and being his mother she lived away in another division of the world, but he rather liked her stories about Mary and Joseph. She made him laugh. But how

did she know that those were Mary and Joseph? Did she think the
same birds came to the same trees every night? he asked. But here,
suddenly, like all grown-up people, she ceased to pay him the least
attention. She was listening to a clatter in the hall.

'They've come back!' she exclaimed, and at once she felt much
more annoyed with them than relieved. Then she wondered, had it
happened? She would go down and they would tell her—but no.
They could not tell her anything, with all these people about. So she
must go down and begin dinner and wait. And, like some queen who,
finding her people gathered in the hall, looks down upon them, and
descends among them, and acknowledges their tributes silently, and
accepts their devotion and their prostration before her (Paul did not
move a muscle but looked straight before him as she passed), she
went down, and crossed the hall and bowed her head very slightly, as
if she accepted what they could not say: their tribute to her beauty.

But she stopped. There was a smell of burning. Could they have
let the Bœuf en Daube overboil, she wondered? pray heaven not!
when the great clangour of the gong announced solemnly, authori-
tatively, that all those scattered about, in attics, in bedrooms, on little
perches of their own, reading, writing, putting the last smooth to
their hair, or fastening dresses, must leave all that, and the little
odds and ends on their washing-tables and dressing-tables, and the
novels on the bed-tables, and the diaries which were so private, and
assemble in the dining-room for dinner.

17

But what have I done with my life? thought Mrs Ramsay, taking her
place at the head of the table, and looking at all the plates making
white circles on it. 'William, sit by me,' she said. 'Lily,' she said,
wearily, 'over there.' They had that—Paul Rayley and Minta Doyle—
she, only this—an infinitely long table and plates and knives. At the
far end, was her husband, sitting down, all in a heap, frowning. What
at? She did not know. She did not mind. She could not understand
how she had ever felt any emotion or any affection for him. She had a
sense of being past everything, through everything, out of everything, as she helped the soup, as if there was an eddy—there—and
one could be in it, or one could be out of it, and she was out of it. It's

all come to an end, she thought, while they came in one after another, Charles Tansley—'Sit there, please,' she said—Augustus Carmichael—and sat down. And meanwhile she waited, passively, for someone to answer her, for something to happen. But this is not a thing, she thought, ladling out soup, that one says.

Raising her eyebrows at the discrepancy—that was what she was thinking, this was what she was doing—ladling out soup—she felt, more and more strongly, outside that eddy; or as if a shade had fallen, and, robbed of colour, she saw things truly. The room (she looked round it) was very shabby. There was no beauty anywhere. *Mod. thought* She forbore to look at Mr Tansley. Nothing seemed to have merged. They all sat separate. And the whole of the effort of merging and flowing and creating rested on her. Again she felt, as a fact without hostility, the sterility of men, for if she did not do it nobody would do it, and so, giving herself the little shake that one gives a watch that has stopped, the old familiar pulse began beating, as the watch begins ticking—one, two, three, one, two, three. And so on and so on, she repeated, listening to it, sheltering and fostering the still feeble pulse as one might guard a weak flame with a newspaper.* And so then, she concluded, addressing herself by bending silently in his direction to William Bankes—poor man! who had no wife and no children, and dined alone in lodgings except for tonight; and in pity for him, life being now strong enough to bear her on again, she began all this business, as a sailor not without weariness sees the wind fill his sail and yet hardly wants to be off again and thinks how, had the ship sunk, he would have whirled round and round and found rest on the floor of the sea.

'Did you find your letters? I told them to put them in the hall for you,' she said to William Bankes.

Lily Briscoe watched her drifting into that strange no-man's land where to follow people is impossible and yet their going inflicts such a chill on those who watch them that they always try at least to follow them with their eyes as one follows a fading ship until the sails have sunk beneath the horizon.

How old she looks, how worn she looks, Lily thought, and how remote. Then when she turned to William Bankes, smiling, it was as if the ship had turned and the sun had struck its sails again, and Lily thought with some amusement because she was relieved, Why does she pity him? For that was the impression she gave, when she told him that his letters were in the hall. Poor William Bankes, she seemed to be saying, as if her own weariness had been partly pitying people, and the life in her, her resolve to live again, had been stirred by pity. And it was not true, Lily thought; it was one of those misjudgements of hers that seemed to be instinctive and to arise from some need of her own rather than of other people's. He is not in the least pitiable. He has his work, Lily said to herself. She remembered, all of a sudden as if she had found a treasure, that she too had her work. In a flash she saw her picture, and thought, Yes, I shall put the tree further in the middle; then I shall avoid that awkward space. That's what I shall do. That's what has been puzzling me. She took up the salt cellar and put it down again on a flower in the pattern in the table-cloth, so as to remind herself to move the tree.

'It's odd that one scarcely gets anything worth having by post, yet one always wants one's letters,' said Mr Bankes.

What damned rot they talk, thought Charles Tansley, laying down his spoon precisely in the middle of his plate, which he had swept clean, as if, Lily thought (he sat opposite to her with his back to the window precisely in the middle of view), he were determined to make sure of his meals. Everything about him had that meagre fixity, that bare unloveliness. But nevertheless, the fact remained, it was almost impossible to dislike anyone if one looked at them. She liked his eyes; they were blue, deep set, frightening.

'Do you write many letters, Mr Tansley?' asked Mrs Ramsay, pitying him too, Lily supposed; for that was true of Mrs Ramsay—she pitied men always as if they lacked—something—women never, as if they had something. He wrote to his mother; otherwise he did not suppose he wrote one letter a month, said Mr Tansley, shortly.

For he was not going to talk the sort of rot these people wanted him to talk. He was not going to be condescended to by these silly women. He had been reading in his room, and now he came down and it all seemed to him silly, superficial, flimsy. Why did they dress? He had come down in his ordinary clothes. He had not got any dress clothes. 'One never gets anything worth having by post'—that was the sort of thing they were always saying. They made men say that sort of thing. Yes, it was pretty well true, he thought. They never got anything worth having from one year's end to another. They did nothing but talk, talk, talk, eat, eat, eat. It was the women's fault. Women made civilization impossible with all their 'charm', all their silliness.

'No going to the Lighthouse tomorrow, Mrs Ramsay,' he said asserting himself. He liked her; he admired her; he still thought of the man in the drain-pipe looking up at her; but he felt it necessary to assert himself.

He was really, Lily Briscoe thought, in spite of his eyes, but then look at his nose, look at his hands, the most uncharming human being she had ever met. Then why did she mind what he said? Women can't write, women can't paint—what did that matter coming from him, since clearly it was not true to him but for some reason helpful to him, and that was why he said it? Why did her whole being bow, like corn under a wind, and erect itself again from this abasement only with a great and rather painful effort? She must make it once more. There's the sprig on the table-cloth; there's my painting; I must move the tree to the middle; that matters—nothing else. Could she not hold fast to that, she asked herself, and not lose her temper, and not argue; and if she wanted a little revenge take it by laughing at him?

'Oh, Mr Tansley,' she said, 'do take me to the Lighthouse with you. I should so love it.'

She was telling lies he could see. She was saying what she did not mean to annoy him, for some reason. She was laughing at him. He was in his old flannel trousers. He had no others. He felt very rough and isolated and lonely. He knew that she was trying to tease him for some reason; she didn't want to go to the Lighthouse with him; she despised him: so did Prue Ramsay; so did they all. But he was not going to be made a fool of by women, so he turned deliberately in his chair and looked out of the window and said, all in a jerk, very rudely, it would be too rough for her tomorrow. She would be sick.

It annoyed him that she should have made him speak like that, with Mrs Ramsay listening. If only he could be alone in his room working, he thought, among his books. That was where he felt at his ease. And he had never run a penny into debt; he had never cost his father a penny since he was fifteen; he had helped them at home out of his savings; he was educating his sister. Still, he wished he had known how to answer Miss Briscoe properly; he wished it had not come out all in a jerk like that. 'You'd be sick.' He wished he could think of something to say to Mrs Ramsay, something which would show her that he was not just a dry prig. That was what they all thought him. He turned to her. But Mrs Ramsay was talking about people he had never heard of to William Bankes.

'Yes, take it away,' she said briefly, interrupting what she was saying to Mr Bankes to speak to the maid. 'It must have been fifteen—no, twenty years ago—that I last saw her,' she was saying, turning back to him again as if she could not lose a moment of their talk, for she was absorbed by what they were saying. So he had actually heard from her this evening! And was Carrie still living at Marlow,* and was everything still the same? Oh she could remember it as if it were yesterday—going on the river, feeling very cold. But if the Mannings made a plan they stuck to it. Never should she forget Herbert killing a wasp with a teaspoon on the bank! And it was still going on, Mrs Ramsay mused, gliding like a ghost among the chairs and tables of that drawing-room on the banks of the Thames where she had been so very, very cold twenty years ago; but now she went among them like a ghost; and it fascinated her, as if, while she had changed, that particular day, now become very still and beautiful, had remained there, all these years. Had Carrie written to him herself? she asked.

'Yes. She says they're building a new billiard room,' he said. No! No! That was out of the question! Building a billiard room! It seemed to her impossible.

Mr Bankes could not see that there was anything very odd about it. They were very well off now. Should he give her love to Carrie?

'Oh,' said Mrs Ramsay with a little start, 'No,' she added, reflecting that she did not know this Carrie who built a new billiard room. But how strange, she repeated, to Mr Bankes's amusement, that they should be going on there still. For it was extraordinary to think that they had been capable of going on living all these years when she had not thought of them more than once all that time. How eventful her own life had been, during those same years. Yet perhaps Carrie Manning had not thought about her either. The thought was strange and distasteful.

'People soon drift apart,' said Mr Bankes, feeling, however, some satisfaction when he thought that after all he knew both the Mannings and the Ramsays. He had not drifted apart, he thought, laying down his spoon and wiping his clean shaven lips punctiliously. But perhaps he was rather unusual, he thought, in this; he never let himself get into a groove. He had friends in all circles . . . Mrs Ramsay had to break off here to tell the maid something about keeping food hot. That was why he preferred dining alone. All these interruptions annoyed him. Well, thought William Bankes, preserving a demeanour of exquisite courtesy and merely spreading the fingers of his left hand on the table-cloth as a mechanic examines a tool beautifully polished and ready for use in an interval of leisure, such are the sacrifices one's friends ask of one. It would have hurt her if he had refused to come. But it was not worth it for him. Looking at his hand he thought that if he had been alone dinner would have been almost over now; he would have been free to work. Yes, he thought, it is a terrible waste of time. The children were dropping in still. 'I wish one of you would run up to Roger's room,' Mrs Ramsay was saying. How trifling it all is, how boring it all is, he thought, compared with the other thing—work. Here he sat drumming his fingers on the table-cloth when he might have been—he took a flashing bird's-eye view of his work. What a waste of time it all was to be sure! Yet, he thought, she is one of my oldest friends. I am by way of being devoted to her. Yet now, at this moment her presence meant absolutely nothing to him: her beauty meant nothing to him; her sitting with her little boy at the window—nothing, nothing. He wished only to be alone and to take up that book. He felt uncomfortable; he felt treacherous, that he could sit by her side and feel nothing for her. The truth was that he did not enjoy family life. It was in this sort of state that one asked oneself, What does one live for? Why, one asked oneself, does one take all these pains for the human race to go on? Is it so very desirable? Are we attractive as a species? Not so very, he thought, looking at those rather untidy boys. His favourite, Cam, was in bed, he supposed. Foolish questions, vain questions, questions one never asked if one was occupied. Is human life this? Is human life that? One never had time to think about it. But here he was asking himself that sort of question, because Mrs Ramsay was giving orders to servants, and also because it had struck him, thinking how surprised Mrs Ramsay was that Carrie Manning should still exist, that friendships, even the best of them, are frail things. One drifts apart. He reproached himself again. He was sitting beside Mrs Ramsay and he had nothing in the world to say to her.

'I'm so sorry,' said Mrs Ramsay, turning to him at last. He felt rigid and barren, like a pair of boots that has been soaked and gone dry so that you can hardly force your feet into them. Yet he must

force his feet into them. He must make himself talk. Unless he were
very careful, she would find out this treachery of his; that he did not
care a straw for her, and that would not be at all pleasant, he thought.
So he bent his head courteously in her direction.

'How you must detest dining in this bear garden,' she said, making use, as she did when she was distracted, of her social manner. So,
when there is a strife of tongues at some meeting, the chairman, to
obtain unity, suggests that every one shall speak in French. Perhaps
it is bad French; French may not contain the words that express the
speaker's thoughts; nevertheless speaking French imposes some
order, some uniformity. Replying to her in the same language,
Mr Bankes said, 'No, not at all,' and Mr Tansley, who had no knowledge of this language, even spoken thus in words of one syllable, at
once suspected its insincerity. They did talk nonsense, he thought,
the Ramsays; and he pounced on this fresh instance with joy, making
a note which, one of these days, he would read aloud, to one or two
friends. There, in a society where one could say what one liked he
would sarcastically describe 'staying with the Ramsays' and what
nonsense they talked. It was worth while doing it once, he would say;
but not again. The women bored one so, he would say. Of course
Ramsay had dished himself by marrying a beautiful woman and
having eight children. It would shape itself something like that, but
now, at this moment, sitting stuck there with an empty seat beside
him nothing had shaped itself at all. It was all in scraps and fragments. He felt extremely, even physically, uncomfortable. He wanted
somebody to give him a chance of asserting himself. He wanted it so
urgently that he fidgeted in his chair, looked at this person, then at
that person, tried to break into their talk, opened his mouth and shut
it again. They were talking about the fishing industry. Why did no
one ask him his opinion? What did they know about the fishing
industry?

Lily Briscoe knew all that. Sitting opposite him could she not see,
as in an X-ray photograph,* the ribs and thigh bones of the young
man's desire to impress himself lying dark in the mist of his flesh—
that thin mist which convention had laid over his burning desire
to break into the conversation? But, she thought, screwing up her
Chinese eyes, and remembering how he sneered at women, 'can't
paint, can't write', why should I help him to relieve himself?

There is a code of behaviour she knew, whose seventh article (it may be) says that on occasions of this sort it behoves the woman, whatever her own occupation may be, to go to the help of the young man opposite so that he may expose and relieve the thigh bones, the ribs, of his vanity, of his urgent desire to assert himself; as indeed it is their duty, she reflected, in her old maidenly fairness, to help us, suppose the Tube were to burst into flames. Then, she thought, I should certainly expect Mr Tansley to get me out. But how would it be, she thought, if neither of us did either of these things? So she sat there smiling.

'You're not planning to go to the Lighthouse, are you, Lily?' said Mrs Ramsay. 'Remember poor Mr Langley; he had been round the world dozens of times, but he told me he never suffered as he did when my husband took him there. Are you a good sailor, Mr Tansley?' she asked.

Mr Tansley raised a hammer: swung it high in air; but realizing, as it descended, that he could not smite that butterfly with such an instrument as this, said only that he had never been sick in his life. But in that one sentence lay compact, like gunpowder, that his grandfather was a fisherman; his father a chemist; that he had worked his way up entirely himself; that he was proud of it; that he was Charles Tansley—a fact that nobody there seemed to realize; but one of these days every single person would know it. He scowled ahead of him. He could almost pity these mild cultivated people, who would be blown sky high, like bales of wool and barrels of apples, one of these days by the gunpowder that was in him.

'Will you take me, Mr Tansley?' said Lily, quickly, kindly, for, of course, if Mrs Ramsay said to her, as in effect she did, 'I am drowning, my dear, in seas of fire. Unless you apply some balm to the anguish of this hour and say something nice to that young man there, life will run upon the rocks—indeed I hear the grating and the growling at this minute. My nerves are taut as fiddle strings. Another touch and they will snap'—when Mrs Ramsay said all this, as the glance in her eyes said it, of course for the hundred and fiftieth time Lily Briscoe had to renounce the experiment—what happens if one is not nice to that young man there—and be nice.

Judging the turn in her mood correctly—that she was friendly to him now—he was relieved of his egotism, and told her how he had been thrown out of a boat when he was a baby; how his father used to fish him out with a boat-hook; that was how he had learnt to swim.

One of his uncles kept the light on some rock or other off the Scottish coast, he said. He had been there with him in a storm. This was said loudly in a pause. They had to listen to him when he said that he had been with his uncle in a lighthouse in a storm. Ah, thought Lily Briscoe, as the conversation took this auspicious turn, and she felt Mrs Ramsay's gratitude (for Mrs Ramsay was free now to talk for a moment herself), ah, she thought, but what haven't I paid to get it for you? She had not been sincere.

She had done the usual trick—been nice. She would never know him. He would never know her. Human relations were all like that, she thought, and the worst (if it had not been for Mr Bankes) were between men and women. Inevitably these were extremely insincere. Then her eye caught the salt cellar, which she had placed there to remind her, and she remembered that next morning she would move the tree further towards the middle, and her spirits rose so high at the thought of painting tomorrow that she laughed out loud at what Mr Tansley was saying. Let him talk all night if he liked it.

'But how long do they leave men on a Lighthouse?' she asked. He told her. He was amazingly well informed. And as he was grateful, and as he liked her, and as he was beginning to enjoy himself, so now, Mrs Ramsay thought, she could return to that dream land, that unreal but fascinating place, the Mannings' drawing-room at Marlow twenty years ago; where one moved about without haste or anxiety, for there was no future to worry about. She knew what had happened to them, what to her. It was like reading a good book again, for she knew the end of that story, since it had happened twenty years ago, and life, which shot down even from this dining-room table in cascades, heaven knows where, was sealed up there, and lay, like a lake, placidly between its banks. He said they had built a billiard room—was it possible? Would William go on talking about the Mannings? She wanted him to. But no—for some reason he was no longer in the mood. She tried. He did not respond. She could not force him. She was disappointed.

'The children are disgraceful,' she said, sighing. He said something about punctuality being one of the minor virtues which we do not acquire until later in life.

'If at all,' said Mrs Ramsay merely to fill up space, thinking what an old maid William was becoming. Conscious of his treachery, conscious of her wish to talk about something more intimate, yet out of mood for it at present, he felt come over him the disagreeableness of life, sitting there, waiting. Perhaps the others were saying something interesting? What were they saying?

That the fishing season was bad; that the men were emigrating. They were talking about wages and unemployment. The young man was abusing the government. William Bankes, thinking what a relief it was to catch on to something of this sort when private life was disagreeable, heard him say something about 'one of the most scandalous acts of the present government'. Lily was listening; Mrs Ramsay was listening; they were all listening. But already bored, Lily felt that something was lacking; Mr Bankes felt that something was lacking. Pulling her shawl round her, Mrs Ramsay felt that something was lacking. All of them bending themselves to listen thought, 'Pray heaven that the inside of my mind may not be exposed,' for each thought, 'The others are feeling this. They are outraged and indignant with the government about the fishermen. Whereas, I feel nothing at all.' But perhaps, thought Mr Bankes, as he looked at Mr Tansley, here is the man. One was always waiting for the man. There was always a chance. At any moment the leader might arise; the man of genius, in politics as in anything else. Probably he will be extremely disagreeable to us old fogies, thought Mr Bankes, doing his best to make allowances, for he knew by some curious physical sensation, as of nerves erect in his spine, that he was jealous, for himself partly, partly more probably for his work, for his point of view, for his science; and therefore he was not entirely open-minded or altogether fair, for Mr Tansley seemed to be saying, You have wasted your lives. You are all of you wrong. Poor old fogies, you're hopelessly behind the times. He seemed to be rather cocksure, this young man; and his manners were bad. But Mr Bankes bade himself observe, he had courage; he had ability; he was extremely well up in the facts. Probably, Mr Bankes thought, as Tansley abused the government, there is a good deal in what he says.

'Tell me now . . .' he said. So they argued about politics, and Lily looked at the leaf on the table-cloth; and Mrs Ramsay, leaving the argument entirely in the hands of the two men, wondered why she was so bored by this talk, and wished, looking at her husband at the other end of the table, that he would say something. One word, she said to herself. For if he said a thing, it would make all the difference. He went to the heart of things. He cared about fishermen and their wages. He could not sleep for thinking of them. It was altogether different when he spoke; one did not feel then, pray heaven you don't see how little I care, because one did care. Then, realizing that it was because she admired him so much that she was waiting for him to speak, she felt as if somebody had been praising her husband to her and their marriage, and she glowed all over without realizing that it was she herself who had praised him. She looked at him thinking to find this shown in his face; he would be looking magnificent . . . But not in the least! He was screwing his face up, he was scowling and frowning, and flushing with anger. What on earth was it about? she wondered. What could be the matter? Only that poor old Augustus had asked for another plate of soup—that was all. It was unthinkable, it was detestable (so he signalled to her across the table) that Augustus should be beginning his soup over again. He loathed people eating when he had finished. She saw his anger fly like a pack of hounds into his eyes, his brow, and she knew that in a moment something violent would explode, and then—but thank goodness! she saw him clutch himself and clap a brake on the wheel, and the whole of his body seemed to emit sparks but not words. He sat there scowling. He had said nothing, he would have her observe. Let her give him the credit for that! But why after all should poor Augustus not ask for another plate of soup? He had merely touched Ellen's arm and said:

'Ellen, please, another plate of soup,' and then Mr Ramsay scowled like that.

And why not? Mrs Ramsay demanded. Surely they could let Augustus have his soup if he wanted it. He hated people wallowing in food, Mr Ramsay frowned at her. He hated everything dragging on for hours like this. But he had controlled himself, Mr Ramsay would have her observe, disgusting though the sight was. But why show it so plainly, Mrs Ramsay demanded (they looked at each other down the long table sending these questions and answers across, each knowing exactly what the other felt). Everybody could see, Mrs Ramsay thought. There was Rose gazing at her father, there was Roger gazing at his father; both would be off in spasms of laughter in another second, she knew, and so she said promptly (indeed it was time):

'Light the candles,' and they jumped up instantly and went and fumbled at the sideboard.

Why could he never conceal his feelings? Mrs Ramsay wondered, and she wondered if Augustus Carmichael had noticed. Perhaps he had; perhaps he had not. She could not help respecting the composure with which he sat there, drinking his soup. If he wanted soup, he asked for soup. Whether people laughed at him or were angry with him he was the same. He did not like her, she knew that; but partly for that very reason she respected him, and looking at him, drinking soup, very large and calm in the failing light, and monumental, and contemplative, she wondered what he did feel then, and why he was always content and dignified; and she thought how devoted he was to Andrew, and would call him into his room, and, Andrew said, 'show him things'. And there he would lie all day long on the lawn brooding presumably over his poetry, till he reminded one of a cat watching birds, and then he clapped his paws together when he had found the word, and her husband said, 'Poor old Augustus—he's a true poet,' which was high praise from her husband.

Now eight candles were stood down the table, and after the first stoop the flames stood upright and drew with them into visibility the long table entire, and in the middle a yellow and purple dish of fruit. What had she done with it, Mrs Ramsay wondered, for Rose's arrangement of the grapes and pears, of the horny pink-lined shell, of the bananas, made her think of a trophy fetched from the bottom of the sea, of Neptune's banquet, of the bunch that hangs with vine leaves over the shoulder of Bacchus (in some picture), among the leopard skins and the torches lolloping red and gold* . . . Thus brought up suddenly into the light it seemed possessed of great size and depth, was like a world in which one could take one's staff and climb up hills, she thought, and go down into valleys, and to her pleasure (for it brought them into sympathy momentarily) she saw that Augustus too feasted his eyes on the same plate of fruit, plunged in, broke off a bloom there, a tassel here, and returned, after feasting, to his hive. That was his way of looking, different from hers. But looking together united them.

Now all the candles were lit, and the faces on both sides of the table were brought nearer by the candle light, and composed, as they had not been in the twilight, into a party round a table, for the night was now shut off by panes of glass, which, far from giving any accurate view of the outside world, rippled it so strangely that here, inside the room, seemed to be order and dry land; there, outside, a reflection in which things wavered and vanished, waterily.

Some change at once went through them all, as if this had really happened, and they were all conscious of making a party together in a hollow, on an island; had their common cause against the fluidity out there. Mrs Ramsay who had been uneasy, waiting for Paul and Minta to come in, and unable, she felt, to settle to things, now felt her uneasiness changed to expectation. For now they must come, and Lily Briscoe, trying to analyse the cause of the sudden exhilaration, compared it with that moment on the tennis lawn, when solidity suddenly vanished, and such vast spaces lay between them; and now the same effect was got by the many candles in the sparely furnished room, and the uncurtained windows, and the bright mask-like look of faces seen by candlelight. Some weight was taken off them; anything might happen, she felt. They must come now, Mrs Ramsay thought, looking at the door, and at that instant, Minta Doyle, Paul Rayley, and a maid carrying a great dish in her hands came in together. They were awfully late; they were horribly late, Minta said, as they found their way to different ends of the table.

'I lost my brooch—my grandmother's brooch,' said Minta with a sound of lamentation in her voice, and a suffusion in her large brown eyes, looking down, looking up, as she sat by Mr Ramsay, which roused his chivalry so that he bantered her.

How could she be such a goose, he asked, as to scramble about the rocks in jewels?

She was by way of being terrified of him—he was so fearfully clever, and the first night when she had sat by him, and he talked about George Eliot, she had been really frightened, for she had left the third volume of *Middlemarch** in the train and she never knew what happened in the end; but afterwards she got on perfectly, and made herself out even more ignorant than she was, because he liked telling her she was a fool. And so tonight, directly he laughed at her, she was not frightened. Besides, she knew, directly she came into the room, that the miracle had happened; she wore her golden haze. Sometimes she had it; sometimes not. She never knew why it came or why it went, or if she had it until she came into the room and then she knew instantly by the way some man looked at her. Yes, tonight she had it, tremendously; she knew that by the way Mr Ramsay told her not to be a fool. She sat beside him, smiling.

It must have happened then, thought Mrs Ramsay; they are engaged. And for a moment she felt what she had never expected to feel again—jealousy. For he, her husband, felt it too—Minta's glow; he liked these girls, these golden-reddish girls, with something fly-ing, something a little wild and harum-scarum about them, who didn't 'scrape their hair off', weren't, as he said about poor Lily Briscoe, 'skimpy'. There was some quality which she herself had not, some lustre, some richness, which attracted him, amused him, led him to make favourites of girls like Minta. They might cut his hair for him, plait him watch-chains, or interrupt him at his work, hailing him (she heard them), 'Come along, Mr Ramsay; it's our turn to beat them now,' and out he came to play tennis.

But indeed she was not jealous, only, now and then, when she made herself look in her glass a little resentful that she had grown old, perhaps, by her own fault. (The bill for the greenhouse and all the rest of it.) She was grateful to them for laughing at him. ('How many pipes have you smoked today, Mr Ramsay?' and so on), till he seemed a young man; a man very attractive to women, not burdened, not weighed down with the greatness of his labours and the sorrows of the world and his fame or his failure, but again as she had first known him, gaunt but gallant; helping her out of a boat, she remem-bered; with delightful ways, like that (she looked at him, and he looked astonishingly young, teasing Minta). For herself—'Put it down there,' she said, helping the Swiss girl to place gently before her the huge brown pot in which was the Bœuf en Daube—for her own part she liked her boobies. Paul must sit by her. She had kept a place for him. Really, she sometimes thought she liked the boobies best. They did not bother one with their dissertations. How much they missed, after all, these very clever men! How dried up they did become, to be sure. There was something, she thought as he sat down, very charming about Paul. His manners were delightful to her, and his sharp cut nose and his bright blue eyes. He was so considerate. Would he tell her—now that they were all talking again—what had happened?

'We went back to look for Minta's brooch,' he said, sitting down by her. 'We'—that was enough. She knew from the effort, the rise in his voice to surmount a difficult word that it was the first time he had said 'we'. 'We' did this, 'we' did that. They'll say that all their lives, she thought, and an exquisite scent of olives and oil and juice rose from the great brown dish as Marthe, with a little flourish, took the cover off. The cook had spent three days over that dish. And she must take great care, Mrs Ramsay thought, diving into the soft mass, to choose a specially tender piece for William Bankes. And she peered into the dish, with its shiny walls and its confusion of savoury brown and yellow meats, and its bay leaves and its wine, and thought, This will celebrate the occasion—a curious sense rising in her, at once freakish and tender, of celebrating a festival, as if two emotions were called up in her, one profound—for what could be more serious than the love of man for woman, what more commanding, more impressive, bearing in its bosom the seeds of death; at the same time these lovers, these people entering into illusion glittering eyed, must be danced round with mockery, decorated with garlands.

'It is a triumph,' said Mr Bankes, laying his knife down for a moment. He had eaten attentively. It was rich; it was tender. It was perfectly cooked. How did she manage these things in the depths of the country? he asked her. She was a wonderful woman. All his love, all his reverence had returned; and she knew it.

'It is a French recipe of my grandmother's,' said Mrs Ramsay, speaking with a ring of great pleasure in her voice. Of course it was French. What passes for cookery in England is an abomination (they agreed). It is putting cabbages in water. It is roasting meat till it is like leather. It is cutting off the delicious skins of vegetables. 'In which,' said Mr Bankes, 'all the virtue of the vegetable is contained.' And the waste, said Mrs Ramsay. A whole French family could live on what an English cook throws away. Spurred on by her sense that William's affection had come back to her, and that everything was all right again, and that her suspense was over, and that now she was free both to triumph and to mock, she laughed, she gesticulated, till Lily thought, How childlike, how absurd she was, sitting up there with all her beauty opened again in her, talking about the skins of vegetables. There was something frightening about her. She was irresistible. Always she got her own way in the end, Lily thought. Now she had brought this off—Paul and Minta, one might suppose, were engaged. Mr Bankes was dining here. She put a spell on them all, by wishing, so simply, so directly; and Lily contrasted that abundance with her own poverty of spirit, and supposed that it was partly that belief (for her face was all lit up—without looking young, she looked radiant) in this strange, this terrifying thing, which made

Paul Rayley, the centre of it, all of a tremor, yet abstract, absorbed, silent. Mrs Ramsay, Lily felt, as she talked about the skins of vege-tables, exalted that, worshipped that; held her hands over it to warm them, to protect it, and yet, having brought it all about, somehow laughed, led her victims, Lily felt, to the altar. It came over her too now—the emotion, the vibration of love. How inconspicuous she felt herself by Paul's side! He, glowing, burning; she, aloof, satirical; he, bound for adventure; she, moored to the shore; he, launched, incautious; she solitary, left out—and, ready to implore a share, if it were disaster, in his disaster, she said shyly:

'When did Minta lose her brooch?'

He smiled the most exquisite smile, veiled by memory, tinged by dreams. He shook his head. 'On the beach,' he said.

'I'm going to find it,' he said, 'I'm getting up early.' This being kept secret from Minta, he lowered his voice, and turned his eyes to where she sat, laughing, beside Mr Ramsay.

Lily wanted to protest violently and outrageously her desire to help him, envisaging how in the dawn on the beach she would be the one to pounce on the brooch half-hidden by some stone, and thus herself be included among the sailors and adventurers. But what did he reply to her offer? She actually said with an emotion that she seldom let appear, 'Let me come with you'; and he laughed. He meant yes or no—either perhaps. But it was not his meaning—it was the odd chuckle he gave, as if he had said, Throw yourself over the cliff if you like, I don't care. He turned on her cheek the heat of love, its horror, its cruelty, its unscrupulosity. It scorched her, and Lily, looking at Minta being charming to Mr Ramsay at the other end of the table, flinched for her exposed to those fangs, and was thankful. For at any rate, she said to herself, catching sight of the salt cellar on the pattern, she need not marry, thank Heaven: she need not undergo that degradation. She was saved from that dilution. She would move the tree rather more to the middle.

Such was the complexity of things. For what happened to her, especially staying with the Ramsays, was to be made to feel violently two opposite things at the same time; that's what you feel, was one; that's what I feel was the other, and then they fought together in her mind, as now. It is so beautiful, so exciting, this love, that I tremble on the verge of it, and offer, quite out of my own habit, to look for a brooch on a beach; also it is the stupidest, the most barbaric of human passions, and turns a nice young man with a profile like a gem (Paul's was exquisite) into a bully with a crowbar (he was swaggering, he was insolent) in the Mile End Road.* Yet she said to herself, from the dawn of time odes have been sung to love; wreaths heaped and roses; and if you asked nine people out of ten they would say they wanted nothing but this; while the women, judging from her own experience, would all the time be feeling, This is not what we want; there is nothing more tedious, puerile, and inhumane than love; yet it is also beautiful and necessary. Well then, well then? she asked, somehow expecting the others to go on with the argument, as if in an argument like this one threw one's own little bolt which fell short obviously and left the others to carry it on. So she listened again to what they were saying in case they should throw any light upon the question of love.

'Then,' said Mr Bankes, 'there is that liquid the English call coffee.'

'Oh coffee!' said Mrs Ramsay. But it was much rather a question (she was thoroughly roused, Lily could see, and talked very emphatically) of real butter and clean milk. Speaking with warmth and eloquence she described the iniquity of the English dairy system, and in what state milk was delivered at the door, and was about to prove her charges, for she had gone into the matter, when all round the table, beginning with Andrew in the middle, like a fire leaping from tuft to tuft of furze, her children laughed; her husband laughed; she was laughed at, fire-encircled, and forced to vail her crest, dismount her batteries, and only retaliate by displaying the raillery and ridicule of the table to Mr Bankes as an example of what one suffered if one attacked the prejudices of the British Public.

Purposely, however, for she had it on her mind that Lily, who had helped her with Mr Tansley, was out of things, she exempted her from the rest; said 'Lily anyhow agrees with me,' and so drew her in, a little fluttered, a little startled. (For she was thinking about love.) They were both out of things, Mrs Ramsay had been thinking, both Lily and Charles Tansley. Both suffered from the glow of the other two. He, it was clear, felt himself utterly in the cold; no woman would look at him with Paul Rayley in the room. Poor fellow! Still, he had his dissertation, the influence of somebody upon something: he could take care of himself. With Lily it was different. She faded, under Minta's glow; became more inconspicuous than ever, in her little grey dress with her little puckered face and her little Chinese eyes. Everything about her was so small. Yet, thought Mrs Ramsay, comparing her with Minta, as she claimed her help (for Lily should bear her out she talked no more about her dairies than her husband did about his boots—he would talk by the hour about his boots), of the two Lily at forty will be the better. There was in Lily a thread of something; a flare of something; something of her own which Mrs Ramsay liked very much indeed, but no man would, she feared. Obviously, not, unless it were a much older man, like William Bankes. But then he cared, well, Mrs Ramsay sometimes thought that he cared, since his wife's death, perhaps for her. He was not 'in love' of course; it was one of those unclassified affections of which there are so many. Oh but nonsense, she thought; William must marry Lily. They have so many things in common. Lily is so fond of flowers. They are both cold and aloof and rather self-sufficing. She must arrange for them to take a long walk together.

Foolishly, she had set them opposite each other. That could be remedied tomorrow. If it were fine, they should go for a picnic. Everything seemed possible. Everything seemed right. Just now (but this cannot last, she thought, dissociating herself from the moment while they were all talking about boots) just now she had reached security; she hovered like a hawk suspended; like a flag floated in an element of joy which filled every nerve of her body fully and sweetly, not noisily, solemnly rather, for it arose, she thought, looking at them all eating there, from husband and children and friends; all of which rising in this profound stillness (she was helping William Bankes to one very small piece more and peered into the depths of the earth-enware pot) seemed now for no special reason to stay there like a smoke, like a fume rising upwards, holding them safe together. Nothing need be said; nothing could be said. There it was, all round them. It partook, she felt, carefully helping Mr Bankes to a specially tender piece, of eternity; as she had already felt about something different once before that afternoon; there is a coherence in things, a stability; something, she meant, is immune from change, and shines out (she glanced at the window with its ripple of reflected lights) in the face of the flowing, the fleeting, the spectral, like a ruby; so that again tonight she had the feeling she had had once today already, of peace, of rest. Of such moments, she thought, the thing is made that remains for ever after. This would remain.

'Yes,' she assured William Bankes, 'there is plenty for everybody.'

'Andrew,' she said, 'hold your plate lower, or I shall spill it.' (The Bœuf en Daube was a perfect triumph.) Here, she felt, putting the spoon down, was the still space that lies about the heart of things, where one could move or rest; could wait now (they were all helped) listening; could then, like a hawk which lapses suddenly from its high station, flaunt and sink on laughter easily, resting her whole weight upon what at the other end of the table her husband was saying about the square root of one thousand two hundred and fifty-three,* which happened to be the number on his railway ticket.

What did it all mean? To this day she had no notion. A square root? What was that? Her sons knew. She leant on them; on cubes and square roots; that was what they were talking about now; on Voltaire and Madame de Staël; on the character of Napoleon; on the French system of land tenure; on Lord Rosebery; on Creevey's Memoirs:* she let it uphold her and sustain her, this admirable fabric of the masculine intelligence, which ran up and down, crossed this way and that, like iron girders spanning the swaying fabric, upholding the world, so that she could trust herself to it utterly, even shut her eyes, or flicker them for a moment, as a child staring up from its pillow winks at the myriad layers of the leaves of a tree. Then she woke up. It was still being fabricated. William Bankes was praising the Waverley novels.*

He read one of them every six months, he said. And why should that make Charles Tansley angry? He rushed in (all, thought Mrs Ramsay, because Prue will not be nice to him) and denounced the Waverley novels when he knew nothing about it, nothing about it whatsoever, Mrs Ramsay thought, observing him rather than listening to what he said. She could see how it was from his manner—he wanted to assert himself, and so it would always be with him till he got his Professorship or married his wife, and so need not be always saying, 'I—I—I.' For that was what his criticism of poor Sir Walter, or perhaps it was Jane Austen, amounted to. 'I—I—I.'* He was thinking of himself and the impression he was making, as she could tell by the sound of his voice, and his emphasis and his uneasiness. Success would be good for him. At any rate they were off again. Now she need not listen. It could not last she knew, but at the moment her eyes were so clear that they seemed to go round the table unveiling each of these people, and their thoughts and their feelings, without effort like a light stealing under water so that its ripples and the reeds in it and the minnows balancing themselves, and the sudden silent trout are all lit up hanging, trembling. So she saw them; she heard them; but whatever they said had also this quality, as if what they said was like the movement of a trout when, at the same time, one can see the ripple and the gravel, something to the right, something to the left; and the whole is held together; for whereas in active life she would be netting and separating one thing from another; she would be saying she liked the Waverley novels or had not read them; she would be urging herself forward; now she said nothing. For the moment she hung suspended.

'Ah, but how long do you think it'll last?' said somebody. It was as if she had antennae trembling out from her, which, intercepting certain sentences, forced them upon her attention. This was one of them. She scented danger for her husband. A question like that would lead, almost certainly, to something being said which reminded him of his own failure. How long would he be read—he would think at once. William Bankes (who was entirely free from all such vanity) laughed, and said he attached no importance to changes in fashion. Who could tell what was going to last—in literature or indeed in anything else?

'Let us enjoy what we do enjoy,' he said. His integrity seemed to Mrs Ramsay quite admirable. He never seemed for a moment to think, But how does this affect me? But then if you had the other temperament, which must have praise, which must have encouragement, naturally you began (and she knew that Mr Ramsay was beginning) to be uneasy; to want somebody to say, Oh, but your work will last, Mr Ramsay, or something like that. He showed his uneasiness quite clearly now by saying, with some irritation, that, anyhow, Scott (or was it Shakespeare?) would last him his lifetime. He said it irritably. Everybody, she thought, felt a little uncomfortable, without knowing why. Then Minta Doyle, whose instinct was fine, said bluffly, absurdly, that she did not believe that any one really enjoyed reading Shakespeare. Mr Ramsay said grimly (but his mind was turned away again) that very few people liked it as much as they said they did. But, he added, there is considerable merit in some of the plays nevertheless, and Mrs Ramsay saw that it would be all right for the moment anyhow; he would laugh at Minta, and she, Mrs Ramsay saw, realizing his extreme anxiety about himself, would, in her own

way, see that he was taken care of, and praise him, somehow or other.
But she wished it was not necessary: perhaps it was her fault that it
was necessary. Anyhow, she was free now to listen to what Paul
Rayley was trying to say about books one had read as a boy. They
lasted, he said. He had read some of Tolstoi at school. There was one
he always remembered, but he had forgotten the name. Russian
names were impossible, said Mrs Ramsay. 'Vronsky,' said Paul. He
remembered that because he always thought it such a good name for
a villain. 'Vronsky,' said Mrs Ramsay; 'O, *Anna Karenina*,'* but that
did not take them very far; books were not in their line. No, Charles
Tansley would put them both right in a second about books, but it
was all so mixed up with, Am I saying the right thing? Am I making a
good impression? that, after all, one knew more about him than
about Tolstoi, whereas what Paul said was about the thing simply,
not himself. Like all stupid people, he had a kind of modesty too, a
consideration for what you were feeling, which, once in a way at
least, she found attractive. Now he was thinking, not about himself
or about Tolstoi, but whether she was cold, whether she felt a
draught, whether she would like a pear.

No, she said, she did not want a pear. Indeed she had been keeping
guard over the dish of fruit (without realizing it) jealously, hoping
that nobody would touch it. Her eyes had been going in and out
among the curves and shadows of the fruit, among the rich purples
of the lowland grapes, then over the horny ridge of the shell, putting
a yellow against a purple, a curved shape against a round shape,
without knowing why she did it, or why, every time she did it, she
felt more and more serene; until, oh, what a pity that they should do
it—a hand reached out, took a pear, and spoilt the whole thing. In
sympathy she looked at Rose. She looked at Rose sitting between
Jasper and Prue. How odd that one's child should do that!

How odd to see them sitting there, in a row, her children, Jasper,
Rose, Prue, Andrew, almost silent, but with some joke of their own
going on, she guessed, from the twitching at their lips. It was
something quite apart from everything else, something they were
hoarding up to laugh over in their own room. It was not about their
father, she hoped. No, she thought not. What was it, she wondered,
sadly rather, for it seemed to her that they would laugh when she
was not there. There was all that hoarded behind those rather set,
still, mask-like faces, for they did not join in easily; they were like

watchers, surveyors, a little raised or set apart from the grown-up people. But when she looked at Prue tonight, she saw that this was not now quite true of her. She was just beginning, just moving, just descending. The faintest light was on her face, as if the glow of Minta opposite, some excitement, some anticipation of happiness was reflected in her, as if the sun of the love of men and women rose over the rim of the table-cloth, and without knowing what it was she bent towards it and greeted it. She kept looking at Minta, shyly, yet curiously, so that Mrs Ramsay looked from one to the other and said, speaking to Prue in her own mind. You will be as happy as she is one of these days. You will be much happier, she added, because you are my daughter, she meant; her own daughter must be happier than other people's daughters. But dinner was over. It was time to go. They were only playing with things on their plates. She would wait until they had done laughing at some story her husband was telling. He was having a joke with Minta about a bet. Then she would get up.

She liked Charles Tansley, she thought, suddenly; she liked his laugh. She liked him for being so angry with Paul and Minta. She liked his awkwardness. There was a lot in that young man after all. And Lily, she thought, putting her napkin beside her plate, she always has some joke of her own. One need never bother about Lily. She waited. She tucked her napkin under the edge of her plate. Well, were they done now? No. That story had led to another story. Her husband was in great spirits tonight, and wishing, she supposed, to make it all right with old Augustus after that scene about the soup, had drawn him in—they were telling stories about someone they had both known at college. She looked at the window in which the candle flames burnt brighter now that the panes were black, and looking at that outside the voices came to her very strangely, as if they were voices at a service in a cathedral, for she did not listen to the words. The sudden bursts of laughter and then one voice (Minta's) speaking alone, reminded her of men and boys crying out the Latin words of a service in some Roman Catholic cathedral. She waited. Her husband spoke. He was repeating something, and she knew it was poetry from the rhythm and the ring of exaltation and melancholy in his voice:

Come out and climb the garden path,*
    Luriana Lurilee.
The China rose is all abloom and buzzing with the yellow bee.

The words (she was looking at the window) sounded as if they were floating like flowers on water out there, cut off from them all, as if no one had said them, but they had come into existence of themselves.

> And all the lives we ever lived and all the lives to be
> Are full of trees and changing leaves.

She did not know what they meant, but like music, the words seemed to be spoken by her own voice, outside her self, saying quite easily and naturally what had been in her mind the whole evening while she said different things. She knew, without looking round, that everyone at the table was listening to the voice saying:

> I wonder if it seems to you
> Luriana, Lurilee

with the same sort of relief and pleasure that she had, as if this were, at last, the natural thing to say, this were their own voice speaking.

But the voice stopped. She looked round. She made herself get up. Augustus Carmichael had risen and, holding his table napkin so that it looked like a long white robe he stood chanting:

> To see the Kings go riding by
> Over lawn and daisy lea
> With their palm leaves and cedar sheaves,
> Luriana, Lurilee,

and as she passed him he turned slightly towards her repeating the last words:

> Luriana, Lurilee,

and bowed to her as if he did her homage. Without knowing why, she felt that he liked her better than he had ever done before; and with a feeling of relief and gratitude she returned his bow and passed through the door which he held open for her.

It was necessary now to carry everything a step further. With her foot on the threshold she waited a moment longer in a scene which was vanishing even as she looked, and then, as she moved and took Minta's arm and left the room, it changed, it shaped itself differently; it had become, she knew, giving one last look at it over her shoulder, already the past.

18

As usual, Lily thought. There was always something that had to be done at that precise moment, something that Mrs Ramsay had decided for reasons of her own to do instantly, it might be with everyone standing about making jokes, as now, not being able to decide whether they were going into the smoking-room, into the drawing-room, up to the attics. Then one saw Mrs Ramsay in the midst of this hubbub standing there with Minta's arm in hers, bethink her 'Yes, it is time for that now,' and so make off at once with an air of secrecy to do something alone. And directly she went a sort of disintegration set in; they wavered about, went different ways, Mr Bankes took Charles Tansley by the arm and went off to finish on the terrace the discussion they had begun at dinner about politics, thus giving a turn to the whole poise of the evening, making the weight fall in a different direction, as if, Lily thought, seeing them go, and hearing a word or two about the policy of the Labour Party,* they had gone up on the bridge of the ship and were taking their bearings; the change from poetry to politics struck her like that; so Mr Bankes and Charles Tansley went off, while the others stood looking at Mrs Ramsay going upstairs in the lamplight alone. Where, Lily wondered, was she going so quickly?

Not that she did in fact run or hurry; she went indeed rather slowly. She felt rather inclined just for a moment to stand still after all that chatter, and pick out one particular thing; the thing that mattered; to detach it; separate it off; clean it of all the emotions and odds and ends of things, and so hold it before her, and bring it to the tribunal where, ranged about in conclave, sat the judges she had set up to decide these things. Is it good, is it bad, is it right or wrong? Where are we going to? and so on. So she righted herself after the shock of the event, and quite unconsciously and incongruously, used the branches of the elm trees outside to help her to stabilize her position. Her world was changing: they were still. The event had given her a sense of movement. All must be in order. She must get that right and that right, she thought, insensibly, approving of the dignity of the trees' stillness, and now again of the superb upward rise (like the beak of a ship up a wave) of the elm branches as the

wind raised them. For it was windy (she stood a moment to look
out). It was windy, so that the leaves now and then brushed open a
star, and the stars themselves seemed to be shaking and darting light
and trying to flash out between the edges of the leaves. Yes, that was
done then, accomplished; and as with all things done, become solemn. Now one thought of it, cleared of chatter and emotion, it
seemed always to have been, only was shown now, and so being
shown struck everything into stability. They would, she thought,
going on again, however long they lived, come back to this night; this
moon; this wind; this house: and to her too. It flattered her, where
she was most susceptible of flattery, to think how, wound about
in their hearts, however long they lived she would be woven; and
this, and this, and this, she thought, going upstairs, laughing, but
affectionately, at the sofa on the landing (her mother's) at the rocking-
chair (her father's); at the map of the Hebrides. All that would be
revived again in the lives of Paul and Minta; 'the Rayleys'—she tried
the new name over; and she felt, with her hand on the nursery door,
that community of feeling with other people which emotion gives as
if the walls of partition had become so thin that practically (the
feeling was one of relief and happiness) it was all one stream, and
chairs, tables, maps, were hers, were theirs, it did not matter whose,
and Paul and Minta would carry it on when she was dead.

She turned the handle, firmly, lest it should squeak, and went in,
pursing her lips slightly, as if to remind herself that she must not
speak aloud. But directly she came in she saw, with annoyance, that
the precaution was not needed. The children were not asleep. It was
most annoying. Mildred should be more careful. There was James
wide awake and Cam sitting bolt upright, and Mildred out of bed in
her bare feet, and it was almost eleven and they were all talking. What
was the matter? It was that horrid skull again.* She had told Mildred
to move it, but Mildred, of course, had forgotten, and now there was
Cam wide awake and James wide awake quarrelling when they ought
to have been asleep hours ago. What had possessed Edward to send
them this horrid skull? She had been so foolish as to let them nail it
up there. It was nailed fast, Mildred said, and Cam couldn't go to
sleep with it in the room, and James screamed if she touched it.

Then Cam must go to sleep (it had great horns said Cam—) must
go to sleep and dream of lovely palaces, said Mrs Ramsay, sitting
down on the bed by her side. She could see the horns, Cam said,

all over the room. It was true. Wherever they put the light (and James could not sleep without a light) there was always a shadow somewhere.

'But think, Cam, it's only an old pig,' said Mrs Ramsay, 'a nice black pig like the pigs at the farm.' But Cam thought it was a horrid thing, branching at her all over the room.

'Well then,' said Mrs Ramsay, 'we will cover it up,' and they all watched her go to the chest of drawers, and open the little drawers quickly one after another, and not seeing anything that would do, she quickly took her own shawl off and wound it round the skull, round and round and round, and then she came back to Cam and laid her head almost flat on the pillow beside Cam's and said how lovely it looked now; how the fairies would love it; it was like a bird's nest; it was like a beautiful mountain such as she had seen abroad, with valleys and flowers and bells ringing and birds singing and little goats and antelopes . . . She could see the words echoing as she spoke them rhythmically in Cam's mind, and Cam was repeating after her how it was like a mountain, a bird's nest, a garden, and there were little antelopes, and her eyes were opening and shutting, and Mrs Ramsay went on saying still more monotonously, and more rhythmically and more nonsensically, how she must shut her eyes and go to sleep and dream of mountains and valleys and stars falling and parrots and antelopes and gardens, and everything lovely, she said, raising her head very slowly and speaking more and more mechanically, until she sat upright and saw that Cam was asleep.

Now, she whispered, crossing over to his bed, James must go to sleep too, for see, she said, the boar's skull was still there; they had not touched it; they had done just what he wanted; it was there quite unhurt. He made sure that the skull was still there under the shawl. But he wanted to ask her something more. Would they go to the Lighthouse tomorrow?

No, not tomorrow, she said, but soon, she promised him; the next fine day. He was very good. He lay down. She covered him up. But he would never forget, she knew, and she felt angry with Charles Tansley, with her husband, and with herself, for she had raised his hopes. Then feeling for her shawl and remembering that she had wrapped it round the boar's skull, she got up, and pulled the window down another inch or two, and heard the wind, and got a breath of the perfectly indifferent chill night air and murmured good-night to

Mildred and left the room and let the tongue of the door slowly lengthen in the lock and went out.

She hoped he would not bang his books on the floor above their heads, she thought, still thinking how annoying Charles Tansley was. For neither of them slept well; they were excitable children, and since he said things like that about the Lighthouse, it seemed to her likely that he would knock a pile of books over just as they were going to sleep, clumsily sweeping them off the table with his elbow. For she supposed that he had gone upstairs to work. Yet he looked so desolate; yet she would feel relieved when he went; yet she would see that he was better treated tomorrow; yet he was admirable with her husband; yet his manners certainly wanted improving; yet she liked his laugh—thinking this, as she came downstairs, she noticed that she could now see the moon itself through the staircase window— the yellow harvest moon—and turned, and they saw her, standing above them on the stairs.

'That's my mother,' thought Prue. Yes; Minta should look at her; Paul Rayley should look at her. That is the thing itself, she felt, as if there were only one person like that in the world; her mother. And, from having been quite grown up, a moment before, talking with the others, she became a child again, and what they had been doing was a game, and would her mother sanction their game, or condemn it, she wondered. And thinking what a chance it was for Minta and Paul and Lily to see her, and feeling what an extraordinary stroke of fortune it was for her to have her, and how she would never grow up and never leave home, she said, like a child, 'We thought of going down to the beach to watch the waves.'

Instantly, for no reason at all, Mrs Ramsay became like a girl of twenty, full of gaiety. A mood of revelry suddenly took possession of her. Of course they must go; of course they must go, she cried, laughing; and running down the last three or four steps quickly, she began turning from one to the other and laughing and drawing Minta's wrap round her and saying she only wished she could come too, and would they be very late, and had any of them got a watch?

'Yes, Paul has,' said Minta. Paul slipped a beautiful gold watch out of a little wash-leather case to show her. And as he held it in the palm of his hand before her, he felt, 'She knows all about it. I need not say anything.' He was saying to her as he showed her the watch, 'I've done it, Mrs Ramsay. I owe it all to you.' And seeing the gold watch lying in his hand, Mrs Ramsay felt, How extraordinarily lucky Minta is! She is marrying a man who has a gold watch in a wash-leather bag!

'How I wish I could come with you!' she cried. But she was withheld by something so strong that she never even thought of asking herself what it was. Of course it was impossible for her to go with them. But she would have liked to go, had it not been for the other thing, and tickled by the absurdity of her thought (how lucky to marry a man with a wash-leather bag for his watch) she went with a smile on her lips into the other room, where her husband sat reading.

19

OF course, she said to herself, coming into the room, she had to come here to get something she wanted. First she wanted to sit down in a particular chair under a particular lamp. But she wanted something more, though she did not know, could not think what it was that she wanted. She looked at her husband (taking up her stocking and beginning to knit), and saw that he did not want to be interrupted—that was clear. He was reading something that moved him very much. He was half smiling and then she knew he was controlling his emotion. He was tossing the pages over. He was acting it—perhaps he was thinking himself the person in the book. She wondered what book it was. Oh, it was one of old Sir Walter's,* she saw, adjusting the shade of her lamp so that the light fell on her knitting. For Charles Tansley had been saying (she looked up as if she expected to hear the crash of books on the floor above) had been saying that people don't read Scott any more. Then her husband thought, 'That's what they'll say of me;' so he went and got one of those books. And if he came to the conclusion 'That's true' what Charles Tansley said, he would accept it about Scott. (She could see that he was weighing, considering, putting this with that as he read.) But not about himself. He was always uneasy about himself. That troubled her. He would always be worrying about his own books—will they be read, are they good, why aren't they better, what do people think of me? Not liking to think of him so, and wondering if they had guessed at dinner why he suddenly became irritable when they talked about fame and books lasting, wondering if the children were laughing at that, she twitched the stocking out, and all the fine gravings came drawn with steel instruments about her lips and forehead, and she grew still like a tree which has been tossing and quivering and now, when the breeze falls, settles, leaf by leaf, into quiet.

It didn't matter, any of it, she thought. A great man, a great book, fame—who could tell? She knew nothing about it. But it was his way with him, his truthfulness—for instance at dinner she had been thinking quite instinctively, If only he would speak! She had complete trust in him. And dismissing all this, as one passes in diving now a weed, now a straw, now a bubble, she felt again, sinking deeper, as she had felt in the hall when the others were talking, There is something I want—something I have come to get, and she fell deeper and deeper without knowing quite what it was, with her eyes closed. And she waited a little, knitting, wondering, and slowly those words they had said at dinner, 'the China rose is all abloom and buzzing with the honey bee', began washing from side to side of her mind rhythmically, and as they washed, words, like little shaded lights, one red, one blue, one yellow, lit up in the dark of her mind, and seemed leaving their perches up there to fly across and across, or to cry out and to be echoed; so she turned and felt on the table beside her for a book.

> And all the lives we ever lived
> And all the lives to be,
> Are full of trees and changing leaves,

she murmured, sticking her needles into the stocking. And she opened the book and began reading here and there at random, and as she did so she felt that she was climbing backwards, upwards, shoving her way up under petals that curved over her, so that she only knew this is white, or this is red. She did not know at first what the words meant at all.

> Steer, hither steer your wingèd pines, all beaten Mariners*

she read and turned the page, swinging herself, zig-zagging this way and that, from one line to another as from one branch to another, from one red and white flower to another, until a little sound roused her—her husband slapping his thighs. Their eyes met for a second;

but they did not want to speak to each other. They had nothing to say, but something seemed, nevertheless, to go from him to her. It was the life, it was the power of it, it was the tremendous humour, she knew, that made him slap his thighs. Don't interrupt me, he seemed to be saying, don't say anything; just sit there. And he went on reading. His lips twitched. It filled him. It fortified him. He clean forgot all the little rubs and digs of the evening, and how it bored him unutterably to sit still while people ate and drank interminably, and his being so irritable with his wife and so touchy and minding when they passed his books over as if they didn't exist at all. But now, he felt, it didn't matter a damn who reached Z (if thought ran like an alphabet from A to Z). Somebody would reach it—if not he, then another. This man's strength and sanity, his feeling for straight-forward simple things, these fishermen, the poor old crazed creature in Mucklebackit's cottage* made him feel so vigorous, so relieved of something that he felt roused and triumphant and could not choke back his tears. Raising the book a little to hide his face he let them fall and shook his head from side to side and forgot himself completely (but not one or two reflections about morality and French novels and English novels and Scott's hands being tied but his view perhaps being as true as the other view) forgot his own bothers and failures completely in poor Steenie's drowning and Mucklebackit's sorrow (that was Scott at his best) and the astonishing delight and feeling of vigour that it gave him.

Well, let them improve upon that, he thought as he finished the chapter. He felt that he had been arguing with somebody, and had got the better of him. They could not improve upon that, whatever they might say; and his own position became more secure. The lovers were fiddlesticks, he thought, collecting it all in his mind again. That's fiddlesticks, that's first-rate, he thought, putting one thing beside another. But he must read it again. He could not remember the whole shape of the thing. He had to keep his judgement in suspense. So he returned to the other thought—if young men did not care for this, naturally they did not care for him either. One ought not to complain, thought Mr Ramsay, trying to stifle his desire to complain to his wife that young men did not admire him. But he was determined; he would not bother her again. Here he looked at her reading. She looked very peaceful, reading. He liked to think that everyone had taken themselves off and that he and she were alone. The whole of life did not consist in going to bed with a woman, he thought, returning to Scott and Balzac,* to the English novel and the French novel.

Mrs Ramsay raised her head and like a person in a light sleep seemed to say that if he wanted her to wake she would, she really would, but otherwise, might she go on sleeping, just a little longer, just a little longer? She was climbing up those branches, this way and that, laying hands on one flower and then another.

> Nor praise the deep vermilion in the rose,*

she read, and so reading she was ascending, she felt, on to the top, on to the summit. How satisfying! How restful! All the odds and ends of the day stuck to this magnet; her mind felt swept, felt clean. And then there it was, suddenly entire shaped in her hands, beautiful and reasonable, clear and complete, the essence sucked out of life and held rounded here—the sonnet.

But she was becoming conscious of her husband looking at her. He was smiling at her, quizzically, as if he were ridiculing her gently for being asleep in broad daylight, but at the same time he was thinking, Go on reading. You don't look sad now, he thought. And he wondered what she was reading, and exaggerated her ignorance, her simplicity, for he liked to think that she was not clever, not book-learned at all. He wondered if she understood what she was reading. Probably not, he thought. She was astonishingly beautiful. Her beauty seemed to him, if that were possible, to increase.

> Yet seem'd it winter still, and, you away,
> As with your shadow I with these did play,

she finished.

'Well?' she said, echoing his smile dreamily, looking up from her book.

> As with your shadow I with these did play,

she murmured putting the book on the table.

What had happened she wondered, as she took up her knitting, since she had last seen him alone? She remembered dressing, and seeing the moon; Andrew holding his plate too high at dinner; being depressed by something William had said; the birds in the trees; the sofa on the landing; the children being awake; Charles Tansley waking them with his books falling—oh no, that she had invented; and Paul having a wash-leather case for his watch. Which should she tell him about?

'They're engaged,' she said, beginning to knit, 'Paul and Minta.'

'So I guessed,' he said. There was nothing very much to be said about it. Her mind was still going up and down, up and down with the poetry; he was still feeling very vigorous, very forthright, after reading about Steenie's funeral. So they sat silent. Then she became aware that she wanted him to say something.

Anything, anything, she thought, going on with her knitting. Anything will do.

'How nice it would be to marry a man with a wash-leather bag for his watch,' she said, for that was the sort of joke they had together.

He snorted. He felt about this engagement as he always felt about any engagement; the girl is much too good for that young man. Slowly it came into her head, why is it then that one wants people to marry? What was the value, the meaning of things? (Every word they said now would be true.) Do say something, she thought, wishing only to hear his voice. For the shadow, the thing folding them in was beginning, she felt, to close round her again. Say anything, she begged, looking at him, as if for help.

He was silent, swinging the compass on his watch-chain to and fro, and thinking of Scott's novels and Balzac's novels. But through the crepuscular walls of their intimacy, for they were drawing together, involuntarily, coming side by side, quite close, she could feel his mind like a raised hand shadowing her mind; and he was beginning now that her thoughts took a turn he disliked—towards this 'pessimism' as he called it—to fidget, though he said nothing, raising his hand to his forehead, twisting a lock of hair, letting it fall again.

'You won't finish that stocking tonight,' he said, pointing to her stocking. That was what she wanted—the asperity in his voice reproving her. If he says it's wrong to be pessimistic probably it is wrong, she thought; the marriage will turn out all right.

'No,' she said, flattening the stocking out upon her knee, 'I shan't finish it.'

And what then? For she felt that he was still looking at her, but that his look had changed. He wanted something—wanted the thing she always found it so difficult to give him; wanted her to tell him that she loved him. And that, no, she could not do. He found talking so much easier than she did. He could say things—she never could. So naturally it was always he that said the things, and then for some reason he would mind this suddenly, and would reproach her. A heartless woman he called her; she never told him that she loved him. But it was not so—it was not so. It was only that she never could say what she felt. Was there no crumb on his coat? Nothing she could do for him? Getting up she stood at the window with the reddish-brown stocking in her hands, partly to turn away from him, partly because she did not mind looking now, with him watching, at the Lighthouse. For she knew that he had turned his head as she turned; he was watching her. She knew that he was thinking, You are more beautiful than ever. And she felt herself very beautiful. Will you not tell me just for once that you love me? He was thinking that, for he was roused, what with Minta and his book, and its being the end of the day and their having quarrelled about going to the Lighthouse. But she could not do it; she could not say it. Then, knowing that he was watching her, instead of saying anything she turned, holding her stocking, and looked at him. And as she looked at him she began to smile, for though she had not said a word, he knew, of course he knew, that she loved him. He could not deny it. And smiling she looked out of the window and said (thinking to herself, Nothing on earth can equal this happiness)—

'Yes, you were right. It's going to be wet tomorrow.' She had not said it, but he knew it. And she looked at him smiling. For she had triumphed again.

Beauty of opposition

II

TIME PASSES

1

'WELL, we must wait for the future to show,' said Mr Bankes, coming in from the terrace.*

'It's almost too dark to see,' said Andrew, coming up from the beach.

'One can hardly tell which is the sea and which is the land,' said Prue.

'Do we leave that light burning?' said Lily as they took their coats off indoors.

'No,' said Prue, 'not if everyone's in.'

'Andrew,' she called back, 'just put out the light in the hall.'

One by one the lamps were all extinguished,* except that Mr Carmichael, who liked to lie awake a little reading Virgil,* kept his candle burning rather longer than the rest.

2

SO with the lamps all put out, the moon sunk, and a thin rain drumming on the roof a downpouring of immense darkness began.* Nothing, it seemed, could survive the flood, the profusion of darkness which, creeping in at keyholes and crevices, stole round window blinds, came into bedrooms, swallowed up here a jug and basin, there a bowl of red and yellow dahlias, there the sharp edges and firm bulk of a chest of drawers. Not only was furniture confounded; there was scarcely anything left of body or mind by which one could say 'This is he' or 'This is she'. Sometimes a hand was raised as if to clutch something or ward off something, or somebody groaned, or somebody laughed aloud as if sharing a joke with nothingness.

Nothing stirred in the drawing-room or in the dining-room or on the staircase. Only through the rusty hinges and swollen sea-moistened woodwork certain airs, detached from the body of the wind (the house was ramshackle after all) crept round corners and ventured indoors. Almost one might imagine them, as they entered the drawing-room, questioning and wondering, toying with the flap of hanging wallpaper, asking, would it hang much longer, when would it fall? Then smoothly brushing the walls, they passed on musingly as if asking the red and yellow roses on the wallpaper whether they would fade, and questioning (gently, for there was time at their disposal) the torn letters in the wastepaper basket, the flowers, the books, all of which were now open to them and asking, Were they allies? Were they enemies? How long would they endure?

So some random light directing them from some uncovered star, or wandering ship, or the Lighthouse even, with its pale footfall upon stair and mat, the little airs mounted the staircase and nosed round bedroom doors. But here surely, they must cease. Whatever else may perish and disappear what lies here is steadfast. Here one might say to those sliding lights, those fumbling airs, that breathe and bend over the bed itself, here you can neither touch nor destroy. Upon which, wearily, ghostlily, as if they had feather-light fingers and the light persistency of feathers, they would look, once, on the shut eyes and the loosely clasping fingers, and fold their garments wearily and disappear. And so, nosing, rubbing, they went to the window on the staircase, to the servants' bedrooms, to the boxes in the attics; descending, blanched the apples on the dining-room table, fumbled the petals of roses, tried the picture on the easel, brushed the mat and blew a little sand along the floor. At length, desisting, all ceased together, gathered together, all sighed together; all together gave off an aimless gust of lamentation to which some door in the kitchen replied; swung wide; admitted nothing; and slammed to.

[Here Mr Carmichael, who was reading Virgil, blew out his candle. It was past midnight.]

3

BUT what after all is one night? A short space, especially when the darkness dims so soon, and so soon a bird sings, a cock crows, or a faint green quickens, like a turning leaf, in the hollow of the wave. Night, however, succeeds to night. The winter holds a pack of them in store and deals them equally, evenly, with indefatigable fingers. They lengthen; they darken. Some of them hold aloft clear planets, plates of brightness. The autumn trees, ravaged as they are, take on the flash of tattered flags kindling in the gloom of cool cathedral caves where gold letters on marble pages describe death in battle and how bones bleach and burn far away in Indian sands. The autumn trees gleam in the yellow moonlight, in the light of the harvest moons, the light which mellows the energy of labour, and smooths the stubble, and brings the wave lapping blue to the shore.

It seemed now as if, touched by human penitence and all its toil, divine goodness had parted the curtain and displayed behind it, single, distinct, the hare erect; the wave falling; the boat rocking, which, did we deserve them, should be ours always. But alas, divine goodness, twitching the cord, draws the curtain; it does not please him; he covers his treasures in a drench of hail, and so breaks them, so confuses them that it seems impossible that their calm should ever return or that we should ever compose from their fragments a perfect whole or read in the littered pieces the clear words of truth. For our penitence deserves a glimpse only; our toil respite only.

The nights now are full of wind and destruction; the trees plunge and bend and their leaves fly helter skelter until the lawn is plastered with them and they lie packed in gutters and choke rain pipes and scatter damp paths.* Also the sea tosses itself and breaks itself, and should any sleeper fancying that he might find on the beach an answer to his doubts, a sharer of his solitude, throw off his bed-clothes and go down by himself to walk on the sand, no image with semblance of serving and divine promptitude comes readily to hand bringing the night to order and making the world reflect the compass of the soul. The hand dwindles in his hand; the voice bellows in his ear. Almost it would appear that it is useless in such confusion to ask the night those questions as to what, and why, and wherefore, which tempt the sleeper from his bed to seek an answer.

[Mr Ramsay stumbling along a passage stretched his arms out one dark morning, but Mrs Ramsay having died rather suddenly the night before he stretched his arms out. They remained empty.]

4

So with the house empty and the doors locked and the mattresses rolled round, those stray airs, advance guards of great armies, blustered in, brushed bare boards, nibbled and fanned, met nothing in bedroom or drawing-room that wholly resisted them but only hangings that flapped, wood that creaked, the bare legs of tables, saucepans and china already furred, tarnished, cracked. What people had shed and left—a pair of shoes, a shooting cap, some faded skirts and coats in wardrobes—those alone kept the human shape and in the emptiness indicated how once they were filled and animated; how once hands were busy with hooks and buttons; how once the looking-glass had held a face; had held a world hollowed out in which a figure turned, a hand flashed, the door opened, in came children rushing and tumbling; and went out again. Now, day after day, light turned, like a flower reflected in water, its clear image on the wall opposite. Only the shadows of the trees, flourishing in the wind, made obeisance on the wall, and for a moment darkened the pool in which light reflected itself; or birds, flying, made a soft spot flutter slowly across the bedroom floor.

So loveliness reigned and stillness, and together made the shape of loveliness itself, a form from which life had parted; solitary like a pool at evening, far distant, seen from a train window, vanishing so quickly that the pool, pale in the evening, is scarcely robbed of its solitude, though once seen. Loveliness and stillness clasped hands in the bedroom, and among the shrouded jugs and sheeted chairs even the prying of the wind, and the soft nose of the clammy sea airs, rubbing, snuffling, iterating, and reiterating their questions—'Will you fade? Will you perish?'—scarcely disturbed the peace, the indifference, the air of pure integrity, as if the question they asked scarcely needed that they should answer: we remain.

Nothing it seemed could break that image, corrupt that innocence, or disturb the swaying mantle of silence which, week after week, in the empty room, wove into itself the falling cries of birds, ships hooting, the drone and hum of the fields, a dog's bark, a man's shout, and folded them round the house in silence. Once only a board sprang on the landing; once in the middle of the night with a roar, with a rupture, as after centuries of quiescence, a rock rends itself from the mountain and hurtles crashing into the valley, one fold of the shawl loosened and swung to and fro. Then again peace descended; and the shadow wavered; light bent to its own image in adoration on the bedroom wall; when Mrs McNab, tearing the veil of silence with hands that had stood in the wash-tub, grinding it with boots that had crunched the shingle, came as directed to open all windows, and dust the bedrooms.

5

As she lurched (for she rolled like a ship at sea) and leered (for her eyes fell on nothing directly, but with a sidelong glance that deprecated the scorn and anger of the world—she was witless, she knew it), as she clutched the banisters and hauled herself upstairs and rolled from room to room, she sang. Rubbing the glass of the long looking-glass and leering sideways at her swinging figure a sound issued from her lips—something that had been gay twenty years before on the stage perhaps, had been hummed and danced to, but now, coming from the toothless, bonneted, caretaking woman, was robbed of meaning, was like the voice of witlessness, humour, persistency itself, trodden down but springing up again, so that as she lurched, dusting, wiping, she seemed to say how it was one long sorrow and trouble, how it was getting up and going to bed again, and bringing things out and putting them away again. It was not easy or snug this world she had known for close on seventy years. Bowed down she was with weariness. How long, she asked, creaking and groaning on her knees under the bed, dusting the boards, how long shall it endure? but hobbled to her feet again, pulled herself up, and again with her sidelong leer which slipped and turned aside even from her own face, and her own sorrows, stood and gaped in the glass, aimlessly smiling, and began again the old amble and hobble, taking up mats, putting down china, looking sideways in the glass, as if, after all, she had her consolations, as if indeed there twined about her dirge some incorrigible hope. Visions of joy there must have been at the wash-tub, say with her children (yet two had been base-born and one had deserted her), at the public-house, drinking; turning over scraps in her drawers. Some cleavage of the dark there must have been, some channel in the depths of obscurity through which light enough issued to twist her face grinning in the glass and make her, turning to her job again, mumble out the old music hall song. Meanwhile the mystic, the visionary, walked the beach, stirred a puddle, looked at a stone, and asked themselves 'What am I?' 'What is this?' and suddenly an answer was vouchsafed them (what it was they could not say): so that they were warm in the frost and had comfort in the desert. But Mrs McNab continued to drink and gossip as before.

6

THE spring without a leaf to toss, bare and bright like a virgin fierce in her chastity, scornful in her purity, was laid out on fields wide-eyed and watchful and entirely careless of what was done or thought by the beholders.

[Prue Ramsay, leaning on her father's arm, was given in marriage that May. What, people said, could have been more fitting? And, they added, how beautiful she looked!]

As summer neared, as the evenings lengthened, there came to the wakeful, the hopeful, walking the beach, stirring the pool, imaginations of the strangest kind—of flesh turned to atoms which drove before the wind, of stars flashing in their hearts, of cliff, sea, cloud, and sky brought purposely together to assemble outwardly the scattered parts of the vision within. In those mirrors, the minds of men, in those pools of uneasy water, in which clouds for ever turn and shadows form, dreams persisted, and it was impossible to resist the strange intimation which every gull, flower, tree, man and woman, and the white earth itself seemed to declare (but if questioned at once to withdraw) that good triumphs, happiness prevails, order rules; or to resist the extraordinary stimulus to range hither and thither in search of some absolute good, some crystal of intensity, remote from the known pleasures and familiar virtues, something alien to the processes of domestic life, single, hard, bright, like a diamond in the sand, which would render the possessor secure. Moreover, softened and acquiescent, the spring with her bees humming and gnats dancing threw her cloak about her, veiled her eyes, averted her head, and among passing shadows and flights of small rain seemed to have taken upon her a knowledge of the sorrows of mankind.

[Prue Ramsay died that summer in some illness connected with childbirth,* which was indeed a tragedy, people said. They said nobody deserved happiness more.]

And now in the heat of summer the wind sent its spies about the house again. Flies wove a web in the sunny rooms; weeds that had grown close to the glass in the night tapped methodically at the window pane. When darkness fell, the stroke of the Lighthouse, which had laid itself with such authority upon the carpet in the darkness, tracing its pattern, came now in the softer light of spring mixed with moonlight gliding gently as if it laid its caress and lingered stealthily and looked and came lovingly again. But in the very lull of this loving caress, as the long stroke leant upon the bed, the rock was rent asunder; another fold of the shawl loosened; there it hung, and swayed. Through the short summer nights and the long summer days, when the empty rooms seemed to murmur with the echoes of the fields and the hum of flies, the long streamer waved gently, swayed aimlessly; while the sun so striped and barred the rooms and filled them with yellow haze that Mrs McNab, when she broke in and lurched about, dusting, sweeping, looked like a tropical fish oaring its way through sun-lanced waters.

But slumber and sleep though it might there came later in the summer ominous sounds like the measured blows of hammers dulled on felt, which, with their repeated shocks still further loosened the shawl and cracked the tea-cups. Now and again some glass tinkled in the cupboard as if a giant voice had shrieked so loud in its agony that tumblers stood inside a cupboard vibrated too. Then again silence fell; and then, night after night, and sometimes in plain mid-day when the roses were bright and light turned on the wall its shape clearly there seemed to drop into this silence this indifference, this integrity, the thud of something falling.

[A shell exploded. Twenty or thirty young men were blown up in France, among them Andrew Ramsay, whose death, mercifully, was instantaneous.]

At that season those who had gone down to pace the beach and ask of the sea and sky what message they reported or what vision they affirmed had to consider among the usual tokens of divine bounty — the sunset on the sea, the pallor of dawn, the moon rising, fishing-boats against the moon, and children pelting each other with handfuls of grass, something out of harmony with this jocundity, this serenity. There was the silent apparition of an ashen-coloured ship* for instance, come, gone; there was a purplish stain upon the bland surface of the sea as if something had boiled and bled, invisibly, beneath. This intrusion into a scene calculated to stir the most sublime reflections and lead to the most comfortable conclusions stayed their pacing. It was difficult blandly to overlook them, to abolish their significance in the landscape; to continue, as one walked by the sea, to marvel how beauty outside mirrored beauty within.

Did Nature supplement what man advanced? Did she complete what he began? With equal complacence she saw his misery, condoned his meanness, and acquiesced in his torture. That dream, then, of sharing, completing, finding in solitude on the beach an answer, was but a reflection in a mirror, and the mirror itself was but the surface glassiness which forms in quiescence when the nobler powers sleep beneath? Impatient, despairing yet loth to go (for beauty offers her lures, her consolations), to pace the beach was impossible; contemplation was unendurable; the mirror was broken.

[Mr Carmichael brought out a volume of poems that spring, which had an unexpected success. The war, people said, had revived their interest in poetry.]

7

Night after night, summer and winter, the torment of storms, the arrow-like stillness of fine weather, held their court without interference. Listening (had there been anyone to listen) from the upper rooms of the empty house only gigantic chaos streaked with lightning could have been heard tumbling and tossing, as the winds and waves disported themselves like the amorphous bulks of leviathans whose brows are pierced by no light of reason, and mounted one on top of another, and lunged and plunged in the darkness or the daylight (for night and day, month and year ran shapelessly together) in idiot games, until it seemed as if the universe were battling and tumbling, in brute confusion and wanton lust aimlessly by itself.

In spring the garden urns, casually filled with wind-blown plants, were gay as ever. Violets came and daffodils. But the stillness and the brightness of the day were as strange as the chaos and tumult of night, with the trees standing there, and the flowers standing there, looking before them, looking up, yet beholding nothing, eyeless, and thus terrible.

8

THINKING no harm, for the family would not come, never again, some said, and the house would be sold at Michaelmas* perhaps, Mrs McNab stooped and picked a bunch of flowers to take home with her. She laid them on the table while she dusted. She was fond of flowers. It was a pity to let them waste. Suppose the house were sold (she stood arms akimbo in front of the looking-glass) it would want seeing to—it would. There it had stood all these years without a soul in it. The books and things were mouldy, for, what with the war and help being hard to get, the house had not been cleaned as she could have wished. It was beyond one person's strength to get it straight now. She was too old. Her legs pained her. All those books needed to be laid out on the grass in the sun; there was plaster fallen in the hall; the rain-pipe had blocked over the study window and let the water in; the carpet was ruined quite. But people should come themselves; they should have sent somebody down to see. For there were clothes in the cupboards; they had left clothes in all the bedrooms. What was she to do with them? They had the moth in them—Mrs Ramsay's things. Poor lady! She would never want *them* again. She was dead, they said, years ago, in London. There was the old grey cloak she wore gardening (Mrs McNab fingered it). She could see her, as she came up the drive with the washing, stooping over her flowers (the garden was a pitiful sight now, all run to riot, and rabbits scuttling at you out of the beds)—she could see her with one of the children by her in that grey cloak. There were boots and shoes; and a brush and comb left on the dressing-table, for all the world as if she expected to come back tomorrow. (She had died very sudden at the end, they said.) And once they had been coming, but had put off coming, what with the war, and travel being so difficult these days;* they had never come all these years; just sent her money; but never wrote, never came, and expected to find things as they had left them, ah dear! Why the dressing-table drawers were full of things (she pulled them open), handkerchiefs, bits of ribbon. Yes, she could see Mrs Ramsay as she came up the drive with the washing.

'Good-evening, Mrs McNab,' she would say.

She had a pleasant way with her. The girls all liked her. But dear, many things had changed since then (she shut the drawer); many families had lost their dearest. So she was dead; and Mr Andrew killed; and Miss Prue dead too, they said, with her first baby; but everyone had lost someone these years. Prices had gone up shamefully, and didn't come down again neither. She could well remember her in her grey cloak.

'Good-evening, Mrs McNab,' she said, and told cook to keep a plate of milk soup for her*—quite thought she wanted it, carrying that heavy basket all the way up from town. She could see her now, stooping over her flowers; (and faint and flickering, like a yellow beam or the circle at the end of a telescope, a lady in a grey cloak, stooping over her flowers, went wandering over the bedroom wall, up the dressing-table, across the washstand, as Mrs McNab hobbled and ambled, dusting, straightening).

And cook's name now? Mildred? Marian?—some name like that. Ah, she had forgotten—she did forget things. Fiery, like all red-haired women. Many a laugh they had had. She was always welcome in the kitchen. She made them laugh, she did. Things were better then than now.

She sighed; there was too much work for one woman. She wagged her head this side and that. This had been the nursery. Why, it was all damp in here; the plaster was falling. Whatever did they want to hang a beast's skull there? gone mouldy too. And rats in all the attics. The rain came in. But they never sent; never came. Some of the locks had gone, so the doors banged. She didn't like to be up here at dusk alone neither. It was too much for one woman, too much, too much. She creaked, she moaned. She banged the door. She turned the key in the lock, and left the house shut up, locked, alone.

9

THE house was left; the house was deserted. It was left like a shell on a sand-hill to fill with dry salt grains now that life had left it. The long night seemed to have set in; the trifling airs, nibbling, the clammy breaths, fumbling, seemed to have triumphed. The saucepan had rusted and the mat decayed. Toads had nosed their way in. Idly, aimlessly, the swaying shawl swung to and fro. A thistle thrust itself between the tiles in the larder. The swallows nested in the drawing-room; the floor was strewn with straw; the plaster fell in shovelfuls; rafters were laid bare; rats carried off this and that to gnaw behind the wainscots. Tortoiseshell butterflies burst from the chrysalis and pattered their life out on the window-pane. Poppies sowed themselves among the dahlias;* the lawn waved with long grass; giant artichokes towered among roses; a fringed carnation flowered among the cabbages; while the gentle tapping of a weed at the window had become, on winters' nights, a drumming from sturdy trees and thorned briars which made the whole room green in summer.

What power could now prevent the fertility, the insensibility of nature? Mrs McNab's dream of a lady, of a child, of a plate of milk soup? It had wavered over the walls like a spot of sunlight and vanished. She had locked the door; she had gone. It was beyond the strength of one woman, she said. They never sent. They never wrote. There were things up there rotting in the drawers—it was a shame to leave them so, she said. The place was gone to rack and ruin. Only the Lighthouse beam entered the rooms for a moment, sent its sudden stare over bed and wall in the darkness of winter, looked with equanimity at the thistle and the swallow, the rat and the straw. Nothing now withstood them; nothing said no to them. Let the wind blow; let the poppy seed itself and the carnation mate with the cabbage. Let the swallow build in the drawing-room, and the thistle thrust aside the tiles, and the butterfly sun itself on the faded chintz of the armchairs. Let the broken glass and the china lie out on the lawn and be tangled over with grass and wild berries.

For now had come that moment, that hesitation when dawn trembles and night pauses, when if a feather alight in the scale it will be weighed down. One feather, and the house, sinking, falling, would have turned and pitched downwards to the depths of darkness. In the ruined room, picnickers would have lit their kettles; lovers sought shelter there, lying on the bare boards; and the shepherd stored his dinner on the bricks; and the tramp slept with his coat round him to ward off the cold. Then the roof would have fallen; briars and hemlocks would have blotted out path, step, and window; would have grown, unequally but lustily over the mound, until some trespasser, losing his way, could have told only by a red-hot poker among the nettles, or a scrap of china in the hemlock, that here once someone had lived; there had been a house.

If the feather had fallen, if it had tipped the scale downwards, the whole house would have plunged to the depths to lie upon the sands of oblivion. But there was a force working; something not highly conscious; something that leered, something that lurched; something not inspired to go about its work with dignified ritual or solemn chanting. Mrs McNab groaned; Mrs Bast creaked. They were old; they were stiff; their legs ached. They came with their brooms and pails at last; they got to work. All of a sudden, would Mrs McNab see that the house was ready, one of the young ladies wrote: would she get this done; would she get that done; all in a hurry. They might be coming for the summer; had left everything to the last; expected to find things as they had left them. Slowly and painfully, with broom and pail, mopping, scouring, Mrs McNab, Mrs Bast* stayed the corruption and the rot; rescued from the pool of Time that was fast closing over them now a basin, now a cupboard; fetched up from oblivion all the Waverley novels and a tea-set one morning; in the afternoon restored to sun and air a brass fender and a set of steel fire-irons. George, Mrs Bast's son, caught the rats, and cut the grass. They had the builders. Attended with the creaking of hinges and the screeching of bolts, the slamming and banging of damp-swollen woodwork, some rusty laborious birth seemed to be taking place, as the women, stooping, rising, groaning, singing, slapped and slammed, upstairs now, now down the cellars. Oh, they said, the work!

They drank their tea in the bedroom sometimes, or in the study; breaking off work at mid-day with the smudge on their faces, and their old hands clasped and cramped with the broom handles. Flopped on chairs they contemplated now the magnificent conquest over taps and bath; now the more arduous, more partial triumph over long rows of books, black as ravens once, now white-stained, breeding pale mushrooms and secreting furtive spiders. Once more, as she felt the tea warm in her, the telescope fitted itself to Mrs McNab's eyes, and in a ring of light she saw the old gentleman, lean as a rake, wagging his head, as she came up with the washing, talking to himself, she supposed, on the lawn. He never noticed her. Some said he was dead; some said she was dead. Which was it? Mrs Bast didn't know for certain either. The young gentleman was dead. That she was sure. She had read his name in the papers.

There was the cook now, Mildred, Marian, some such name as

that—a red-headed woman, quick-tempered like all her sort, but kind, too, if you knew the way with her. Many a laugh they had had together. She saved a plate of soup for Maggie; a bite of ham, sometimes; whatever was over. They lived well in those days. They had everything they wanted (glibly, jovially, with the tea hot in her, she unwound her ball of memories, sitting in the wicker armchair by the nursery fender). There was always plenty doing, people in the house, twenty staying sometimes, and washing up till long past midnight.

Mrs Bast (she had never known them; had lived in Glasgow at that time) wondered, putting her cup down, whatever they hung that beast's skull there for? Shot in foreign parts no doubt.

It might well be, said Mrs McNab, wantoning on with her memories; they had friends in eastern countries; gentlemen staying there, ladies in evening dress; she had seen them once through the dining-room door all sitting at dinner. Twenty she dared say in all their jewellery, and she asked to stay help wash up, might be till after midnight.

Ah, said Mrs Bast, they'd find it changed. She leant out of the window. She watched her son George scything the grass. They might well ask, what had been done to it? seeing how old Kennedy was supposed to have charge of it, and then his leg got so bad after he fell from the cart; and perhaps then no one for a year, or the better part of one; and then Davie Macdonald, and seeds might be sent, but who should say if they were ever planted? They'd find it changed.

She watched her son scything. He was a great one for work—one of those quiet ones. Well they must be getting along with the cupboards, she supposed. They hauled themselves up.

At last, after days of labour within, of cutting and digging without, dusters were flicked from the windows, the windows were shut to, keys were turned all over the house; the front door was banged; it was finished.

And now as if the cleaning and the scrubbing and the scything and the mowing had drowned it there rose that half-heard melody, that intermittent music which the ear half catches but lets fall; a bark, a bleat; irregular, intermittent, yet somehow related; the hum of an insect, the tremor of cut grass, disseevered yet somehow belonging; the jar of a dor beetle, the squeak of a wheel, loud, low, but mysteriously related; which the ear strains to bring together and is always on the verge of harmonizing but they are never quite heard, never fully harmonized, and at last, in the evening, one after another the sounds die out, and the harmony falters, and silence falls. With the sunset sharpness was lost, and like mist rising, quiet rose, quiet spread, the wind settled; loosely the world shook itself down to sleep, darkly here without a light to it, save what came green suffused through leaves, or pale on the white flowers by the window.

[Lily Briscoe had her bag carried up to the house late one evening in September. Mr Carmichael came by the same train.]

10

THEN indeed peace had come.* Messages of peace breathed from the sea to the shore. Never to break its sleep any more, to lull it rather more deeply to rest and whatever the dreamers dreamt holily, dreamt wisely, to confirm—what else was it murmuring—as Lily Briscoe laid her head on the pillow in the clean still room and heard the sea. Through the open window the voice of the beauty of the world came murmuring, too softly to hear exactly what it said—but what mattered if the meaning were plain?—entreating the sleepers (the house was full again; Mrs Beckwith was staying there, also Mr Carmichael), if they would not actually come down to the beach itself at least to lift the blind and look out. They would see then night flowing down in purple; his head crowned; his sceptre jewelled; and how in his eyes a child might look. And if they still faltered (Lily was tired out with travelling and slept almost at once; but Mr Carmichael read a book by candlelight), if they still said no, that it was vapour this splendour of his, and the dew had more power than he, and they preferred sleeping; gently then without complaint, or argument, the voice would sing its song. Gently the waves would break (Lily heard them in her sleep); tenderly the light fell (it seemed to come through her eyelids). And it all looked, Mr Carmichael thought, shutting his book, falling asleep, much as it used to look years ago.

Indeed the voice might resume, as the curtains of dark wrapped themselves over the house, over Mrs Beckwith, Mr Carmichael, and Lily Briscoe so that they lay with several folds of blackness on their eyes, why not accept this, be content with this, acquiesce and resign? The sigh of all the seas breaking in measure round the isles soothed them; the night wrapped them; nothing broke their sleep, until, the birds beginning and the dawn weaving their thin voices into its whiteness, a cart grinding, a dog somewhere barking, the sun lifted the curtains, broke the veil on their eyes, and Lily Briscoe stirring in her sleep clutched at her blankets as a faller clutches at the turf on the edge of a cliff. Her eyes opened wide. Here she was again, she thought, sitting bolt upright in bed. Awake.

III

THE LIGHTHOUSE

1

WHAT does it mean then, what can it all mean? Lily Briscoe asked herself, wondering whether, since she had been left alone, it behoved her to go to the kitchen to fetch another cup of coffee or wait here. What does it mean?—a catchword that was, caught up from some book, fitting her thought loosely, for she could not, this first morning with the Ramsays, contract her feelings, could only make a phrase resound to cover the blankness of her mind until these vapours had shrunk. For really, what did she feel, come back after all these years and Mrs Ramsay dead? Nothing, nothing—nothing that she could express at all.

She had come late last night when it was all mysterious, dark. Now she was awake, at her old place at the breakfast table, but alone. It was very early too, not yet eight. There was this expedition—they were going to the Lighthouse, Mr Ramsay, Cam, and James. They should have gone already—they had to catch the tide or something. And Cam was not ready and James was not ready and Nancy had forgotten to order the sandwiches and Mr Ramsay had lost his temper and banged out of the room.

'What's the use of going now?' he had stormed.

Nancy had vanished. There he was, marching up and down the terrace in a rage. One seemed to hear doors slamming and voices calling all over the house. Now Nancy burst in, and asked, looking round the room, in a queer half dazed, half desperate way, 'What does one send to the Lighthouse?' as if she were forcing herself to do what she despaired of ever being able to do.

What does one send to the Lighthouse indeed! At any other time Lily could have suggested reasonably tea, tobacco, newspapers. But this morning everything seemed so extraordinarily queer that a question like Nancy's—What does one send to the Lighthouse?—opened doors in one's mind that went banging and swinging to and fro and made one keep asking, in a stupefied gape, What does one send? What does one do? Why is one sitting here after all?

Sitting alone (for Nancy went out again) among the clean cups at the long table she felt cut off from other people, able only to go on watching, asking, wondering. The house, the place, the morning, all seemed strangers to her. She had no attachment here, she felt, no relations with it, anything might happen, and whatever did happen, a step outside, a voice calling ('It's not in the cupboard; it's on the landing,' someone cried), was a question, as if the link that usually bound things together had been cut, and they floated up here, down there, off, anyhow. How aimless it was, how chaotic, how unreal it was, she thought, looking at her empty coffee cup. Mrs Ramsay dead; Andrew killed; Prue dead too—repeat it as she might, it roused no feeling in her. And we all get together in a house like this on a morning like this, she said, looking out of the window—it was a beautiful still day.

Suddenly Mr Ramsay raised his head as he passed and looked straight at her, with his distraught wild gaze which was yet so pene-trating, as if he saw you, for one second, for the first time, for ever; and she pretended to drink out of her empty coffee cup so as to escape him—to escape his demand on her, to put aside a moment longer that imperious need. And he shook his head at her, and strode on ('Alone' she heard him say, 'Perished'* she heard him say) and like everything else this strange morning the words became symbols, wrote themselves all over the grey-green walls. If only she could put them together, she felt, write them out in some sentence, then she would have got at the truth of things. Old Mr Carmichael came padding softly in, fetched his coffee, took his cup and made off to sit in the sun. The extraordinary unreality was frightening; but it was also exciting. Going to the Lighthouse. But what does one send to the Lighthouse? Perished. Alone. The grey-green light on the wall opposite. The empty places. Such were some of the parts, but how bring them together? she asked. As if any interruption would break the frail shape she was building on the table she turned her back to the window lest Mr Ramsay should see her. She must escape some-how, be alone somewhere. Suddenly she remembered. When she had sat there last ten years ago there had been a little sprig or leaf pattern on the table-cloth, which she had looked at in a moment of revela-tion.* There had been a problem about a foreground of a picture. Move the tree to the middle, she had said. She had never finished that picture. It had been knocking about in her mind all these years. She would paint that picture now. Where were her paints, she won-dered? Her paints, yes. She had left them in the hall last night. She would start at once. She got up quickly, before Mr Ramsay turned.

She fetched herself a chair. She pitched her easel with her precise old maidish movements on the edge of the lawn, not too close to Mr Carmichael, but close enough for his protection. Yes, it must have been precisely here that she had stood ten years ago. There was the wall; the hedge; the tree. The question was of some relation between those masses. She had borne it in her mind all these years. It seemed as if the solution had come to her: she knew now what she wanted to do.

But with Mr Ramsay bearing down on her, she could do nothing. Every time he approached—he was walking up and down the terrace—ruin approached, chaos approached. She could not paint. She stooped, she turned; she took up this rag; she squeezed that tube. But all she did was to ward him off a moment. He made it impossible for her to do anything. For if she gave him the least chance, if he saw her disengaged a moment, looking his way a moment, he would be on her, saying, as he had said last night, 'You find us much changed.' Last night he had got up and stopped before her, and said that. Dumb and staring though they had all sat, the six children whom they used to call after the Kings and Queens of England—the Red, the Fair, the Wicked, the Ruthless,—she felt how they raged under it. Kind old Mrs Beckwith said something sensible. But it was a house full of unrelated passions—she had felt that all the evening. And on top of this chaos Mr Ramsay got up, pressed her hand, and said: 'You will find us much changed' and none of them had moved or had spoken; but had sat there as if they were forced to let him say it. Only James (certainly the Sullen) scowled at the lamp; and Cam screwed her handkerchief round her finger. Then he reminded them that they were going to the Lighthouse tomorrow. They must be ready, in the hall, on the stroke of half-past seven. Then, with his hand on the door, he stopped; he turned upon them. Did they not want to go? he demanded. Had they dared say No (he had some reason for wanting it) he would have flung himself tragically backwards into the bitter waters of despair. Such a gift he had for gesture. He looked like a king in exile. Doggedly James said yes. Cam stumbled more wretchedly. Yes, oh yes, they'd both be ready, they said. And it struck her, this was tragedy—not palls, dust, and the shroud; but children coerced, their spirits subdued. James was sixteen, Cam seventeen, perhaps. She had looked round for someone who was not there, for Mrs Ramsay, presumably. But there was only kind Mrs

Beckwith turning over her sketches under the lamp. Then, being tired, her mind still rising and falling with the sea, the taste and smell that places have after long absence possessing her, the candles wavering in her eyes, she had lost herself and gone under. It was a wonderful night, starlit; the waves sounded as they went upstairs; the moon surprised them, enormous, pale, as they passed the staircase window. She had slept at once.

She set her clean canvas firmly upon the easel, as a barrier, frail, but she hoped sufficiently substantial to ward off Mr Ramsay and his exactingness. She did her best to look, when his back was turned, at her picture; that line there, that mass there. But it was out of the question. Let him be fifty feet away, let him not even speak to you, let him not even see you, he permeated, he prevailed, he imposed himself. He changed everything. She could not see the colour; she could not see the lines; even with his back turned to her, she could only think, But he'll be down on me in a moment, demanding— something she felt she could not give him. She rejected one brush; she chose another. When would those children come? When would they all be off? she fidgeted. That man, she thought, her anger rising in her, never gave; that man took. She, on the other hand, would be forced to give. Mrs Ramsay had given. Giving, giving, giving, she had died—and had left all this. Really, she was angry with Mrs Ramsay. With the brush slightly trembling in her fingers she looked at the hedge, the step, the wall. It was all Mrs Ramsay's doing. She was dead. Here was Lily, at forty-four,* wasting her time, unable to do a thing, standing there, playing at painting, playing at the one thing one did not play at, and it was all Mrs Ramsay's fault. She was dead. The step where she used to sit was empty. She was dead.

But why repeat this over and over again? Why be always trying to bring up some feeling she had not got? There was a kind of blasphemy in it. It was all dry: all withered: all spent. They ought not to have asked her; she ought not to have come. One can't waste one's time at forty-four, she thought. She hated playing at painting. A brush, the one dependable thing in a world of strife, ruin, chaos— that one should not play with, knowingly even: she detested it. But he made her. You shan't touch your canvas, he seemed to say, bearing down on her, till you've given me what I want of you. Here he was, close upon her again, greedy, distraught. Well, thought Lily in despair, letting her right hand fall at her side, it would be simpler then to have it over. Surely she could imitate from recollection the glow, the rhapsody, the self-surrender she had seen on so many women's faces (on Mrs Ramsay's, for instance) when on some occasion like this they blazed up—she could remember the look on Mrs Ramsay's face—into a rapture of sympathy, of delight in the reward they had, which, though the reason of it escaped her, evidently conferred on them the most supreme bliss of which human nature was capable. Here he was, stopped by her side. She would give him what she could.

2

SHE seemed to have shrivelled slightly, he thought. She looked a little skimpy, wispy; but not unattractive. He liked her. There had been some talk of her marrying William Bankes once, but nothing had come of it. His wife had been fond of her. He had been a little out of temper too at breakfast. And then, and then—this was one of those moments when an enormous need urged him, without being conscious what it was, to approach any woman, to force them, he did not care how, his need was so great, to give him what he wanted: sympathy.

Was anybody looking after her? he said. Had she everything she wanted?

'Oh, thanks, everything,' said Lily Briscoe nervously. No; she could not do it. She ought to have floated off instantly upon some wave of sympathetic expansion: the pressure on her was tremendous. But she remained stuck. There was an awful pause. They both looked at the sea. Why, thought Mr Ramsay, should she look at the sea when I am here? She hoped it would be calm enough for them to land at the Lighthouse, she said. The Lighthouse! The Lighthouse! What's that got to do with it? he thought impatiently. Instantly, with the force of some primeval gust (for really he could not restrain himself any longer), there issued from him such a groan that any other woman in the whole world would have done something, said something—all except myself, thought Lily, girding at herself bitterly, who am not a woman, but a peevish, ill-tempered, dried-up old maid presumably.

Mr Ramsay sighed to the full. He waited. Was she not going to say

anything? Did she not see what he wanted from her? Then he said he
had a particular reason for wanting to go to the Lighthouse. His wife
used to send the men things. There was a poor boy with a tuberculous hip, the lightkeeper's son. He sighed profoundly. He sighed
significantly. All Lily wished was that this enormous flood of grief,
this insatiable hunger for sympathy, this demand that she should
surrender herself up to him entirely, and even so he had sorrows
enough to keep her supplied for ever, should leave her, should be
diverted (she kept looking at the house, hoping for an interruption)
before it swept her down in its flow.

'Such expeditions', said Mr Ramsay, scraping the ground with his
toe, 'are very painful.' Still Lily said nothing. (She is a stock, she is a
stone, he said to himself.) 'They are very exhausting,' he said, looking, with a sickly look that nauseated her (he was acting, she felt, this
great man was dramatizing himself), at his beautiful hands. It was
horrible, it was indecent. Would they never come, she asked, for she
could not sustain this enormous weight of sorrow, support these
heavy draperies of grief (he had assumed a pose of extreme decrepitude; he even tottered a little as he stood there) a moment longer.

Still she could say nothing; the whole horizon seemed swept bare
of objects to talk about; could only feel, amazedly, as Mr Ramsay
stood there, how his gaze seemed to fall dolefully over the sunny
grass and discolour it, and cast over the rubicund, drowsy, entirely
contented figure of Mr Carmichael, reading a French novel on a
deck-chair, a veil of crape, as if such an existence, flaunting its pros-
perity in a world of woe were enough to provoke the most dismal
thoughts of all. Look at him, he seemed to be saying, look at me; and
indeed, all the time he was feeling, Think of me, think of me. Ah,
could that bulk only be wafted alongside of them, Lily wished; had
she only pitched her easel a yard or two closer to him; a man, any
man, would staunch this effusion, would stop these lamentations. A
woman, she had provoked this horror; a woman, she should have
known how to deal with it. It was immensely to her discredit, sexu-
ally, to stand there dumb. One said—what did one say?—Oh, Mr
Ramsay! Dear Mr Ramsay! That was what that kind old lady who
sketched, Mrs Beckwith, would have said instantly, and rightly. But
no. They stood there, isolated from the rest of the world. His
immense self-pity, his demand for sympathy poured and spread
itself in pools at her feet, and all she did, miserable sinner that she

was, was to draw her skirts a little closer round her ankles, lest she should get wet. In complete silence she stood there, grasping her paint brush.

Heaven could never be sufficiently praised! She heard sounds in the house. James and Cam must be coming. But Mr Ramsay, as if he knew that his time ran short, exerted upon her solitary figure the immense pressure of his concentrated woe; his age; his frailty; his desolation; when suddenly, tossing his head impatiently, in his annoyance—for, after all, what woman could resist him?—he noticed that his boot-laces were untied. Remarkable boots they were too, Lily thought, looking down at them: sculptured; colossal; like everything that Mr Ramsay wore, from his frayed tie to his half-buttoned waistcoat, his own indisputably. She could see them walking to his room of their own accord, expressive in his absence of pathos, surliness, ill-temper, charm.

'What beautiful boots!' she exclaimed. She was ashamed of herself. To praise his boots when he asked her to solace his soul; when he had shown her his bleeding hands, his lacerated heart, and asked her to pity them, then to say, cheerfully, 'Ah, but what beautiful boots you wear!' deserved, she knew, and she looked up expecting to get it, in one of his sudden roars of ill-temper, complete annihilation.

Instead, Mr Ramsay smiled. His pall, his draperies, his infirmities fell from him. Ah yes, he said, holding his foot up for her to look at, they were first-rate boots. There was only one man in England who could make boots like that. Boots are among the chief curses of mankind, he said. 'Bootmakers make it their business', he exclaimed, 'to cripple and torture the human foot.' They are also the most obstinate and perverse of mankind. It had taken him the best part of his youth to get boots made as they should be made. He would have her observe (he lifted his right foot and then his left) that she had never seen boots made quite that shape before. They were made of the finest leather in the world, also. Most leather was mere brown paper and cardboard. He looked complacently at his foot, still held in the air. They had reached, she felt, a sunny island where peace dwelt, sanity reigned and the sun for ever shone, the blessed island of good boots. Her heart warmed to him. 'Now let me see if you can tie a knot,' he said. He poohpoohed her feeble system. He showed her his own invention. Once you tied it, it never came undone. Three times he knotted her shoe; three times he unknotted it.

Why, at this completely inappropriate moment, when he was
stooping over her shoe, should she be so tormented with sympathy
for him that, as she stooped too, the blood rushed to her face, and,
thinking of her callousness (she had called him a play-actor) she felt
her eyes swell and tingle with tears? Thus occupied he seemed to her
a figure of infinite pathos. He tied knots. He bought boots. There
was no helping Mr Ramsay on the journey he was going. But now
just as she wished to say something, could have said something,
perhaps, here they were—Cam and James. They appeared on the
terrace. They came, lagging, side by side, a serious, melancholy
couple.

But why was it like *that* that they came? She could not help feeling
annoyed with them; they might have come more cheerfully; they
might have given him what, now that they were off, she would not
have the chance of giving him. For she felt a sudden emptiness; a
frustration. Her feeling had come too late; there it was ready; but he
no longer needed it. He had become a very distinguished, elderly
man, who had no need of her whatsoever. She felt snubbed. He slung
a knapsack round his shoulders. He shared out the parcels—there
were a number of them, ill tied, in brown paper. He sent Cam for a
cloak. He had all the appearance of a leader making ready for an
expedition. Then, wheeling about, he led the way with his firm
military tread, in those wonderful boots, carrying brown paper parcels, down the path, his children following him. They looked, she
thought, as if fate had devoted them to some stern enterprise, and
they went to it, still young enough to be drawn acquiescent in their
father's wake, obediently, but with a pallor in their eyes which made
her feel that they suffered something beyond their years in silence.
So they passed the edge of the lawn, and it seemed to Lily that she
watched a procession go, drawn on by some stress of common feeling
which made it, faltering and flagging as it was, a little company
bound together and strangely impressive to her. Politely, but very
distantly, Mr Ramsay raised his hand and saluted her as they passed.

But what a face, she thought, immediately finding the sympathy
which she had not been asked to give troubling her for expression.
What had made it like that? Thinking, night after night, she supposed—about the reality of kitchen tables, she added, remembering
the symbol which in her vagueness as to what Mr Ramsay did think
about Andrew had given her. (He had been killed by the splinter of a

shell instantly, she bethought her.) The kitchen table was something visionary, austere; something bare, hard, not ornamental. There was no colour to it; it was all edges and angles; it was uncompromisingly plain. But Mr Ramsay kept always his eyes fixed upon it, never allowed himself to be distracted or deluded, until his face became worn too and ascetic and partook of this unornamented beauty which so deeply impressed her. Then, she recalled (standing where he had left her, holding her brush), worries had fretted it—not so nobly. He must have had his doubts about that table, she supposed; whether the table was a real table; whether it was worth the time he gave to it; whether he was able after all to find it. He had had doubts, she felt, or he would have asked less of people. That was what they talked about late at night sometimes, she suspected; and then next day Mrs Ramsay looked tired, and Lily flew into a rage with him over some absurd little thing. But now he had nobody to talk to about that table, or his boots, or his knots; and he was like a lion seeking whom he could devour, and his face had that touch of desperation, of exaggeration in it which alarmed her, and made her pull her skirts about her. And then, she recalled, there was that sudden revivification, that sudden flare (when she praised his boots), that sudden recovery of vitality and interest in ordinary human things, which too passed and changed (for he was always changing, and hid nothing) into that other final phase which was new to her and had, she owned, made herself ashamed of her own irritability, when it seemed as if he had shed worries and ambitions, and the hope of sympathy and the desire for praise, had entered some other region, was drawn on, as if by curiosity, in dumb colloquy, whether with himself or another, at the head of that little procession out of one's range. An extraordinary face! The gate banged.

3

So they're gone, she thought, sighing with relief and disappointment. Her sympathy seemed to fly back in her face, like a bramble sprung. She felt curiously divided, as if one part of her were drawn out there—it was a still day, hazy; the Lighthouse looked this morning at an immense distance; the other had fixed itself doggedly, solidly, here on the lawn. She saw her canvas as if it had floated up and placed itself white and uncompromising directly before her. It seemed to rebuke her with its cold stare for all this hurry and agitation; this folly and waste of emotion; it drastically recalled her and spread through her mind first a peace, as her disorderly sensations (he had gone and she had been so sorry for him and she had said nothing) trooped off the field; and then, emptiness. She looked blankly at the canvas, with its uncompromising white stare; from the canvas to the garden. There was something (she stood screwing up her little Chinese eyes in her small puckered face) something she remembered in the relations of those lines cutting across, slicing down, and in the mass of the hedge with its green cave of blues and browns, which had stayed in her mind; which had tied a knot in her mind so that at odds and ends of time, involuntarily, as she walked along the Brompton Road, as she brushed her hair, she found herself painting that picture, passing her eye over it, and untying the knot in imagination. But there was all the difference in the world between this planning airily away from the canvas, and actually taking her brush and making the first mark.

She had taken the wrong brush in her agitation at Mr Ramsay's presence, and her easel, rammed into the earth so nervously, was at the wrong angle. And now that she had put that right, and in so doing had subdued the impertinences and irrelevances that plucked her attention and made her remember how she was such and such a person, had such and such relations to people, she took her hand and raised her brush. For a moment it stayed trembling in a painful but exciting ecstasy in the air. Where to begin?—that was the question; at what point to make the first mark? One line placed on the canvas committed her to innumerable risks, to frequent and irrevocable decisions. All that in idea seemed simple became in practice immediately complex; as the waves shape themselves symmetrically from the cliff top, but to the swimmer among them are divided by steep gulfs, and foaming crests. Still the risk must be run; the mark made.

With a curious physical sensation, as if she were urged forward and at the same time must hold herself back, she made her first quick decisive stroke. The brush descended. It flickered brown over the white canvas; it left a running mark. A second time she did it—a third time. And so pausing and so flickering, she attained a dancing rhythmical movement, as if the pauses were one part of the rhythm and the strokes another, and all were related; and so, lightly and swiftly pausing, striking, she scored her canvas with brown running nervous lines which had no sooner settled there than they enclosed (she felt it looming out at her) a space. Down in the hollow of one wave she saw the next wave towering higher and higher above her. For what could be more formidable than that space? Here she was again, she thought, stepping back to look at it, drawn out of gossip, out of living, out of community with people into the presence of this formidable ancient enemy of hers—this other thing, this truth, this reality, which suddenly laid hands on her, emerged stark at the back of appearances and commanded her attention. She was half unwilling, half reluctant. Why always be drawn out and haled away? Why not left in peace, to talk to Mr Carmichael on the lawn? It was an exacting form of intercourse anyhow. Other worshipful objects were content with worship; men, women, God, all let one kneel prostrate; but this form, were it only the shape of a white lamp-shade looming on a wicker table, roused one to perpetual combat, challenged one to a fight in which one was bound to be worsted. Always (it was in her nature, or in her sex, she did not know which) before she exchanged the fluidity of life for the concentration of painting she had a few moments of nakedness when she seemed like an unborn soul, a soul reft of body, hesitating on some windy pinnacle and exposed without protection to all the blasts of doubt. Why then did she do it? She looked at the canvas, lightly scored with running lines. It would be hung in the servants' bedrooms. It would be rolled up and stuffed under a sofa. What was the good of doing it then, and she heard some voice saying she couldn't paint, saying she couldn't create, as if she were caught up in one of those habitual currents which after a certain time forms experience in the mind, so that one repeats words without being aware any longer who originally spoke them.

Can't paint, can't write, she murmured monotonously, anxiously considering what her plan of attack should be. For the mass loomed before her; it protruded; she felt it pressing on her eyeballs. Then, as if some juice necessary for the lubrication of her faculties were spontaneously squirted, she began precariously dipping among the blues and umbers, moving her brush hither and thither, but it was now heavier and went slower, as if it had fallen in with some rhythm which was dictated to her (she kept looking at the hedge, at the canvas) by what she saw, so that while her hand quivered with life, this rhythm was strong enough to bear her along with it on its current. Certainly she was losing consciousness of outer things. And as she lost consciousness of outer things, and her name and her personality and her appearance, and whether Mr Carmichael was there or not, her mind kept throwing up from its depths, scenes, and names, and sayings, and memories and ideas, like a fountain spurting over that glaring, hideously difficult white space, while she modelled it with greens and blues.

Charles Tansley used to say that, she remembered, women can't paint, can't write. Coming up behind her he had stood close beside her, a thing she hated, as she painted here on this very spot. 'Shag tobacco,' he said, 'fivepence an ounce,' parading his poverty, his principles. (But the war had drawn the sting of her femininity. Poor devils one thought, poor devils of both sexes, getting into such messes.) He was always carrying a book about under his arm—a purple book. He 'worked'. He sat, she remembered, working in a blaze of sun. At dinner he would sit right in the middle of the view. And then, she reflected, there was that scene on the beach. One must remember that. It was a windy morning. They had all gone to the beach. Mrs Ramsay sat and wrote letters by a rock.* She wrote and wrote. 'Oh,' she said, looking up at last at something floating in the sea, 'is it a lobster pot? Is it an upturned boat?' She was so short-sighted that she could not see, and then Charles Tansley became as nice as he could possibly be. He began playing ducks and drakes. They chose little flat black stones and sent them skipping over the waves. Every now and then Mrs Ramsay looked up over her spectacles and laughed at them. What they said she could not remember, but only she and Charles throwing stones and getting on very well all of a sudden and Mrs Ramsay watching them. She was highly conscious of that. Mrs Ramsay, she thought, stepping back and screwing up her eyes. (It must have altered the design a good deal when she was sitting on the step with James. There must have been a shadow.) Mrs Ramsay. When she thought of herself and Charles throwing ducks and drakes and of the whole scene on the beach, it seemed to depend somehow upon Mrs Ramsay sitting under the rock, with a pad on her knee, writing letters. (She wrote innumerable letters, and sometimes the wind took them and she and Charles just saved a page from the sea.) But what a power was in the human soul! she thought. That woman sitting there, writing under the rock resolved everything into simplicity; made these angers, irritations fall off like old rags; she brought together this and that and then this, and so made out of that miserable silliness and spite (she and Charles squabbling, sparring, had been silly and spiteful) something—this scene on the beach for example, this moment of friendship and liking—which survived, after all these years, complete, so that she dipped into it to re-fashion her memory of him, and it stayed in the mind almost like a work of art.

'Like a work of art,' she repeated, looking from her canvas to the drawing-room steps and back again. She must rest for a moment. And, resting, looking from one to the other vaguely, the old question which traversed the sky of the soul perpetually, the vast, the general question which was apt to particularize itself at such moments as these, when she released faculties that had been on the strain, stood over her, paused over her, darkened over her. What is the meaning of life? That was all—a simple question; one that tended to close in on one with years. The great revelation had never come. The great revelation perhaps never did come. Instead there were little daily miracles, illuminations, matches struck unexpectedly in the dark; here was one. This, that, and the other; herself and Charles Tansley and the breaking wave; Mrs Ramsay bringing them together; Mrs Ramsay saying 'Life stand still here'; Mrs Ramsay making of the moment something permanent (as in another sphere Lily herself tried to make of the moment something permanent)—this was of the nature of a revelation. In the midst of chaos there was shape; this external passing and flowing (she looked at the clouds going and the leaves shaking) was stuck into stability. Life stand still here, Mrs Ramsay said. 'Mrs Ramsay! Mrs Ramsay!' she repeated. She owed this revelation to her.

All was silence. Nobody seemed yet to be stirring in the house. She looked at it there sleeping in the early sunlight with its windows green and blue with the reflected leaves. The faint thought she was thinking of Mrs Ramsay seemed in consonance with this quiet house; this smoke; this fine early morning air. Faint and unreal, it was amazingly pure and exciting. She hoped nobody would open the window or come out of the house, but that she might be left alone to go on thinking, to go on painting. She turned to her canvas. But impelled by some curiosity, driven by the discomfort of the sympathy which she held undischarged, she walked a pace or so to the end of the lawn to see whether, down there on the beach, she could

This is what Woolf is trying to do with her art.

see that little company setting sail. Down there among the little boats
which floated, some with their sails furled, some slowly, for it was
very calm, moving away, there was one rather apart from the others.
The sail was even now being hoisted. She decided that there in that
very distant and entirely silent little boat Mr Ramsay was sitting with
Cam and James. Now they had got the sail up; now after a little
flagging and hesitation the sails filled and, shrouded in profound
silence, she watched the boat take its way with deliberation past the
other boats out to sea.

4

THE sails flapped over their heads. The water chuckled and slapped
the sides of the boat, which drowsed motionless in the sun. Now and
then the sails rippled with a little breeze in them, but the ripple ran
over them and ceased. The boat made no motion at all. Mr Ramsay
sat in the middle of the boat. He would be impatient in a moment,
James thought, and Cam thought, looking at their father, who sat in
the middle of the boat between them (James steered; Cam sat alone
in the bow) with his legs tightly curled. He hated hanging about.
Sure enough, after fidgeting a second or two, he said something
sharp to Macalister's boy, who got out his oars and began to row. But
their father, they knew, would never be content until they were flying
along. He would keep looking for a breeze, fidgeting, saying things
under his breath, which Macalister and Macalister's boy would over-
hear, and they would both be made horribly uncomfortable. He had
made them come. He had forced them to come. In their anger they
hoped that the breeze would never rise, that he might be thwarted in
every possible way, since he had forced them to come against their
wills.

All the way down to the beach they had lagged behind together,
though he bade them 'Walk up, walk up', without speaking. Their
heads were bent down, their heads were pressed down by some
remorseless gale. Speak to him they could not. They must come;
they must follow. They must walk behind him carrying brown paper
parcels. But they vowed, in silence, as they walked, to stand by each
other and carry out the great compact—to resist tyranny to the
death. So there they would sit, one at one end of the boat, one at the

other, in silence. They would say nothing, only look at him now and then where he sat with his legs twisted, frowning and fidgeting, and pishing and pshawing and muttering things to himself, and waiting impatiently for a breeze. And they hoped it would be calm. They hoped he would be thwarted. They hoped the whole expedition would fail, and they would have to put back, with their parcels, to the beach.

But now, when Macalister's boy had rowed a little way out, the sails slowly swung round, the boat quickened itself, flattened itself, and shot off. Instantly, as if some great strain had been relieved, Mr Ramsay uncurled his legs, took out his tobacco pouch, handed it with a little grunt to Macalister, and felt, they knew, for all they suffered, perfectly content. Now they would sail on for hours like this, and Mr Ramsay would ask old Macalister a question—about the great storm last winter probably—and old Macalister would answer it, and they would puff their pipes together, and Macalister would take a tarry rope in his fingers, tying or untying some knot, and the boy would fish, and never say a word to anyone. James would be forced to keep his eye all the time on the sail. For if he forgot, then the sail puckered, and shivered, and the boat slackened, and Mr Ramsay would say sharply, 'Look out! Look out!' and old Macalister would turn slowly on his seat. So they heard Mr Ramsay asking some question about the great storm at Christmas. 'She comes driving round the point,' old Macalister said, describing the great storm last Christmas, when ten ships had been driven into the bay for shelter;* and he had seen 'one there, one there, one there' (he pointed slowly round the bay. Mr Ramsay followed him, turning his head.) He had seen three men clinging to the mast. Then she was gone. 'And at last we shoved her off,' he went on (but in their anger and their silence they only caught a word here and there, sitting at opposite ends of the boat, united by their compact to fight tyranny to the death). At last they had shoved her off, they had launched the lifeboat, and they had got her out past the point—Macalister told the story; and though they only caught a word here and there, they were conscious all the time of their father—how he leant forward, how he brought his voice into tune with Macalister's voice; how, puffing at his pipe, and looking there and there where Macalister pointed, he relished the thought of the storm and the dark night and the fishermen striving there. He liked that men should labour and sweat on the windy beach at night, pitting muscle and brain against the waves and the wind; he liked men to work like that, and women to keep house, and sit beside sleeping children indoors, while men were drowned, out there in a storm. So James could tell, so Cam could tell (they looked at him, they looked at each other), from his toss and his vigilance and the ring in his voice, and the little tinge of Scottish accent which came into his voice, making him seem like a peasant himself, as he questioned Macalister about the eleven ships that had been driven into the bay in a storm. Three had sunk.

He looked proudly where Macalister pointed; and Cam thought, feeling proud of him without knowing quite why, had he been there he would have launched the lifeboat, he would have reached the wreck, Cam thought. He was so brave, he was so adventurous, Cam thought. But she remembered. There was the compact; to resist tyranny to the death. Their grievance weighed them down. They had been forced; they had been bidden. He had borne them down once more with his gloom and his authority, making them do his bidding, on this fine morning, come, because he wished it, carrying these parcels to the Lighthouse; take part in those rites he went through for his own pleasure in memory of dead people, which they hated, so that they lagged after him, and all the pleasure of the day was spoilt.

Yes, the breeze was freshening. The boat was leaning, the water was sliced sharply and fell away in green cascades, in bubbles, in cataracts. Cam looked down into the foam, into the sea with all its treasure in it, and its speed hypnotized her, and the tie between her and James sagged a little. It slackened a little. She began to think, How fast it goes. Where are we going? and the movement hypnotized her, while James, with his eye fixed on the sail and on the horizon, steered grimly. But he began to think as he steered that he might escape; he might be quit of it all. They might land somewhere; and be free then. Both of them, looking at each other for a moment, had a sense of escape and exaltation, what with the speed and the change. But the breeze bred in Mr Ramsay too the same excitement, and, as old Macalister turned to fling his line overboard, he cried aloud, 'We perished,' and then again, 'each alone'.* And then with his usual spasm of repentance or shyness, pulled himself up, and waved his hand towards the shore.

'See the little house,' he said pointing, wishing Cam to look. She raised herself reluctantly and looked. But which was it? She could no longer make out, there on the hillside, which was their house. All looked distant and peaceful and strange. The shore seemed refined, far away, unreal. Already the little distance they had sailed had put them far from it and given it the changed look, the composed look, of something receding in which one has no longer any part. Which was their house? She could not see it.

'But I beneath a rougher sea,' Mr Ramsay murmured. He had found the house and so seeing it, he had also seen himself there; he had seen himself walking on the terrace, alone. He was walking up and down between the urns; and he seemed to himself very old, and bowed. Sitting in the boat he bowed, he crouched himself, acting instantly his part—the part of a desolate man, widowed, bereft; and so called up before him in hosts people sympathizing with him; staged for himself as he sat in the boat, a little drama; which required of him decrepitude and exhaustion and sorrow (he raised his hands and looked at the thinness of them, to confirm his dream) and then there was given him in abundance women's sympathy, and he imagined how they would soothe him and sympathize with him, and so getting in his dream some reflection of the exquisite pleasure women's sympathy was to him, he sighed and said gently and mournfully,

> But I beneath a rougher sea
> Was whelmed in deeper gulfs than he,*

so that the mournful words were heard quite clearly by them all. Cam half started on her seat. It shocked her—it outraged her. The movement roused her father; and he shuddered, and broke off, exclaiming: 'Look! Look!' so urgently that James also turned his head to look over his shoulder at the island. They all looked. They looked at the island.

But Cam could see nothing. She was thinking how all those paths and the lawn, thick and knotted with the lives they had lived there, were gone: were rubbed out; were past; were unreal, and now this was real; the boat and the sail with its patch; Macalister with his earrings; the noise of the waves—all this was real. Thinking this, she was murmuring to herself 'We perished, each alone,' for her father's words broke and broke again in her mind, when her father, seeing her gazing so vaguely, began to tease her. Didn't she know the points of the compass? he asked. Didn't she know the North from the South? Did she really think they lived right out there? And he pointed again, and showed her where their house was, there, by those trees. He wished she would try to be more accurate, he said: 'Tell me—which is East, which is West?' he said, half laughing at her, half scolding her, for he could not understand the state of mind of any-one, not absolutely imbecile, who did not know the points of the compass. Yet she did not know. And seeing her gazing, with her vague, now rather frightened, eyes fixed where no house was Mr Ramsay forgot his dream; how he walked up and down between the urns on the terrace; how the arms were stretched out to him. He thought, women are always like that; the vagueness of their minds is hopeless; it was a thing he had never been able to understand; but so it was. It had been so with her—his wife. They could not keep anything clearly fixed in their minds. But he had been wrong to be angry with her; moreover, did he not rather like this vagueness in women? It was part of their extraordinary charm. I will make her smile at me, he thought. She looks frightened. She was so silent. He clutched his fingers, and determined that his voice and his face and all the quick expressive gestures which had been at his command making people pity him and praise him all these years should subdue themselves. He would make her smile at him. He would find some simple easy thing to say to her. But what? For, wrapped up in his work as he was, he forgot the sort of thing one said. There was a puppy. They had a puppy. Who was looking after the puppy today? he asked. Yes, thought James pitilessly, seeing his sister's head against the sail, now she will give way. I shall be left to fight the tyrant alone. The compact would be left to him to carry out. Cam would never resist tyranny to the death, he thought grimly, watching her face, sad, sulky, yielding. And as sometimes happens when a cloud falls on a green hillside and gravity descends and there among all the surrounding hills is gloom and sorrow, and it seems as if the hills themselves must ponder the fate of the clouded, the darkened, either in pity, or maliciously rejoicing in her dismay: so Cam now felt herself overcast, as she sat there among calm, resolute people and wondered how to answer her father about the puppy; how to resist his entreaty—forgive me, care for me; while James the lawgiver, with the tablets of eternal wisdom laid open on his knee (his hand on the tiller had become symbolical to her), said, Resist him. Fight him. He said so rightly; justly. For they must fight tyranny to the death, she thought. Of all human qualities she reverenced justice most. Her brother was most god-like, her father most suppliant. And to which did she yield, she thought, sitting between them, gazing at the shore whose points were all unknown to her, and thinking how the lawn and the terrace and the house were smoothed away now and peace dwelt there.

'Jasper,' she said sullenly. He'd look after the puppy.

And what was she going to call him? her father persisted. He had had a dog when he was a little boy, called Frisk. She'll give way, James thought, as he watched a look come upon her face, a look he remembered. They look down, he thought, at their knitting or something. Then suddenly they look up. There was a flash of blue, he remembered, and then somebody sitting with him laughed, surrendered, and he was very angry. It must have been his mother, he thought, sitting on a low chair, with his father standing over her. He began to search among the infinite series of impressions which time had laid down, leaf upon leaf, fold upon fold softly, incessantly upon his brain; among scents, sounds; voices, harsh, hollow, sweet; and lights passing, and brooms tapping; and the wash and hush of the sea, how a man had marched up and down and stopped dead, upright, over them. Meanwhile, he noticed, Cam dabbled her fingers in the water, and stared at the shore and said nothing. No, she won't give way, he thought; she's different, he thought. Well, if Cam would not answer him, he would not bother her, Mr Ramsay decided, feeling in his pocket for a book. But she would answer him; she wished, passionately, to move some obstacle that lay upon her tongue and to say, Oh yes, Frisk. I'll call him Frisk. She wanted even to say, Was that the dog that found its way over the moor alone? But try as she might, she could think of nothing to say like that, fierce and loyal to the compact, yet passing on to her father, unsuspected by James, a private token of the love she felt for him. For she thought, dabbling her hand (and now Macalister's boy had caught a mackerel, and it lay kicking on the floor, with blood on its gills) for she thought, looking at James who kept his eyes dispassionately on the sail, or glanced now and then for a second at the horizon, you're not exposed to it, to this pressure and division of feeling, this extraordinary temptation. Her father was feeling in his pockets; in another second, he would have found his book. For no one attracted her more; his hands were beautiful to her and his feet, and his voice, and his words, and his haste, and his temper, and his oddity, and his passion, and his saying straight out before everyone, we perish, each alone, and his remoteness. (He had opened his book.) But what remained intolerable, she thought, sitting upright, and watching Macalister's boy tug the hook out of the gills of another fish, was that crass blindness and tyranny of his which had poisoned her childhood and raised bitter storms, so that even now she woke in the night trembling with rage and remembered some command of his; some insolence: 'Do this,' 'Do that,' his dominance: his 'Submit to me.'

So she said nothing, but looked doggedly and sadly at the shore, wrapped in its mantle of peace; as if the people there had fallen asleep, she thought; were free like smoke, were free to come and go like ghosts. They have no suffering there, she thought.

5

YES, that is their boat, Lily Briscoe decided, standing on the edge of the lawn. It was the boat with greyish-brown sails, which she saw now flatten itself upon the water and shoot off across the bay. There he sits, she thought, and the children are quite silent still. And she could not reach him either. The sympathy she had not given him weighed her down. It made it difficult for her to paint.

She had always found him difficult. She had never been able to praise him to his face, she remembered. And that reduced their relationship to something neutral, without that element of sex in it which made his manner to Minta so gallant, almost gay. He would pick a flower for her, lend her his books. But could he believe that Minta read them? She dragged them about the garden, sticking in leaves to mark the place.

'D'you remember, Mr Carmichael?' she was inclined to ask, looking at the old man. But he had pulled his hat half over his forehead; he was asleep, or he was dreaming, or he was lying there catching words, she supposed.

'D'you remember?' she felt inclined to ask him as she passed him, thinking again of Mrs Ramsay on the beach; the cask bobbing up and down; and the pages flying. Why, after all these years had that survived, ringed round, lit up, visible to the last detail, with all before it blank and all after it blank, for miles and miles?

'Is it a boat? Is it a cork?' she would say, Lily repeated, turning back, reluctantly again, to her canvas. Heaven be praised for it, the problem of space remained, she thought, taking up her brush again. It glared at her. The whole mass of the picture was poised upon that weight. Beautiful and bright it should be on the surface, feathery and evanescent, one colour melting into another like the colours on a butterfly's wing; but beneath the fabric must be clamped together with bolts of iron. It was to be a thing you could ruffle with your breath; and a thing you could not dislodge with a team of horses. And she began to lay on a red, a grey, and she began to model her way into the hollow there. At the same time, she seemed to be sitting beside Mrs Ramsay on the beach.

'Is it a boat? Is it a cask?' Mrs Ramsay said. And she began hunting round for her spectacles. And she sat, having found them, silent, looking out to sea. And Lily, painting steadily, felt as if a door had opened, and one went in and stood gazing silently about in a high cathedral-like place, very dark, very solemn. Shouts came from a world far away. Steamers vanished in stalks of smoke on the horizon. Charles threw stones and sent them skipping.

Mrs Ramsay sat silent. She was glad, Lily thought, to rest in silence, uncommunicative; to rest in the extreme obscurity of human relationships. Who knows what we are, what we feel? Who knows even at the moment of intimacy. This is knowledge? Aren't things spoilt then, Mrs Ramsay may have asked (it seemed to have happened so often, this silence by her side) by saying them? Aren't we more expressive thus? The moment at least seemed extraordinarily fertile. She rammed a little hole in the sand and covered it up, by way of burying in it the perfection of the moment. It was like a drop of silver in which one dipped and illumined the darkness of the past.

Lily stepped back to get her canvas—so—into perspective. It was an odd road to be walking, this of painting. Out and out one went, further and further, until at last one seemed to be on a narrow plank, perfectly alone, over the sea. And as she dipped into the blue paint, she dipped too into the past there. Now Mrs Ramsay got up, she remembered. It was time to go back to the house—time for luncheon. And they all walked up from the beach together, she walking behind with William Bankes, and there was Minta in front of them with a hole in her stocking. How that little round hole of pink heel seemed to flaunt itself before them! How William Bankes deplored it, without, so far as she could remember, saying anything about it! It meant to him the annihilation of womanhood, and dirt and disorder, and servants leaving and beds not made at mid-day—all the things he most abhorred. He had a way of shuddering and spreading his fingers out as if to cover an unsightly object, which he did now— holding his hand in front of him. And Minta walked on ahead, and presumably Paul met her and she went off with Paul in the garden.

The Rayleys, thought Lily Briscoe, squeezing her tube of green paint. She collected her impressions of the Rayleys. Their lives appeared to her in a series of scenes; one, on the staircase at dawn. Paul had come in and gone to bed early; Minta was late. There was Minta, wreathed, tinted, garish on the stairs about three o'clock in the morning. Paul came out in his pyjamas carrying a poker in case of burglars. Minta was eating a sandwich, standing half-way up by a window, in the cadaverous early morning light, and the carpet had a hole in it. But what did they say? Lily asked herself, as if by looking she could hear them. Something violent. Minta went on eating her sandwich, annoyingly, while he spoke. He spoke indignant, jealous words, abusing her, in a mutter so as not to wake the children, the two little boys. He was withered, drawn; she flamboyant, careless. For things had worked loose after the first year or so; the marriage had turned out rather badly.

And this, Lily thought, taking the green paint on her brush, this making up scenes about them, is what we call 'knowing' people, 'thinking' of them, 'being fond' of them! Not a word of it was true; she had made it up; but it was what she knew them by all the same. She went on tunnelling her way into her picture, into the past.

Another time, Paul said he 'played chess in coffee-houses'. She had built up a whole structure of imagination on that saying too. She remembered how, as he said it, she thought how he rang up the servant, and she said 'Mrs Rayley's out, sir', and he decided that he would not come home either. She saw him sitting in the corner of some lugubrious place where the smoke attached itself to the red plush seats, and the waitresses got to know you, playing chess with a little man who was in the tea trade and lived at Surbiton,* but that was all Paul knew about him. And then Minta was out when he came home and then there was that scene on the stairs, when he got the poker in case of burglars (no doubt to frighten her too) and spoke so bitterly, saying she had ruined his life. At any rate when she went down to see them at a cottage near Rickmansworth,* things were horribly strained. Paul took her down the garden to look at the Belgian hares which he bred, and Minta followed them, singing, and put her bare arm on his shoulder, lest he should tell her anything.

Minta was bored by hares, Lily thought. But Minta never gave herself away. She never said things like that about playing chess in coffee-houses. She was far too conscious, far too wary. But to go on with their story—they had got through the dangerous stage by now. She had been staying with them last summer some time and the car broke down and Minta had to hand him his tools. He sat on the road mending the car, and it was the way she gave him the tools—business-like, straightforward, friendly—that proved it was all right now. They were 'in love' no longer; no, he had taken up with another woman, a serious woman, with her hair in a plait and a case in her hand (Minta had described her gratefully, almost admiringly), who went to meetings and shared Paul's views (they had got more and more pronounced) about the taxation of land values and a capital levy.* Far from breaking up the marriage, that alliance had righted it. They were excellent friends, obviously, as he sat on the road and she handed him his tools.

So that was the story of the Rayleys, Lily smiled. She imagined herself telling it to Mrs Ramsay, who would be full of curiosity to know what had become of the Rayleys. She would feel a little triumphant, telling Mrs Ramsay that the marriage had not been a success.

But the dead, thought Lily, encountering some obstacle in her design which made her pause and ponder, stepping back a foot or so, Oh the dead! she murmured, one pitied them, one brushed them aside, one had even a little contempt for them. They are at our mercy. Mrs Ramsay has faded and gone, she thought. We can override her wishes, improve away her limited, old-fashioned ideas. She recedes further and further from us. Mockingly she seemed to see her there at the end of the corridor of years saying, of all incongruous things, 'Marry, marry!' (sitting very upright early in the morning with the birds beginning to cheep in the garden outside). And one would have to say to her, It has all gone against your wishes. They're happy like that; I'm happy like this. Life has changed completely. At

that all her being, even her beauty, became for a moment, dusty and
out of date. For a moment Lily, standing there, with the sun hot on
her back, summing up the Rayleys, triumphed over Mrs Ramsay,
who would never know how Paul went to coffee-houses and had a
mistress; how he sat on the ground and Minta handed him his tools;
how she stood here painting, had never married, not even William
Bankes.

Mrs Ramsay had planned it. Perhaps, had she lived, she would
have compelled it. Already that summer he was 'the kindest of men'.
He was 'the first scientist of his age, my husband says'. He was also
'poor William—it makes me so unhappy, when I go to see him, to
find nothing nice in his house—no one to arrange the flowers'. So
they were sent for walks together, and she was told, with that faint
touch of irony that made Mrs Ramsay slip through one's fingers,
that she had a scientific mind; she liked flowers; she was so exact.
What was this mania of hers for marriage? Lily wondered, stepping
to and fro from her easel.

(Suddenly, as suddenly as a star slides in the sky, a reddish light
seemed to burn in her mind, covering Paul Rayley, issuing from him.
It rose like a fire sent up in token of some celebration by savages on a
distant beach. She heard the roar and the crackle. The whole sea for
miles round ran red and gold. Some winy smell mixed with it and
intoxicated her, for she felt again her own headlong desire to throw
herself off the cliff and be drowned looking for a pearl brooch on a
beach. And the roar and the crackle repelled her with fear and dis-
gust, as if while she saw its splendour and power she saw too how
it fed on the treasure of the house, greedily, disgustingly, and she
loathed it. But for a sight, for a glory it surpassed everything in her
experience, and burnt year after year like a signal fire on a desert
island at the edge of the sea, and one had only to say 'in love' and
instantly, as happened now, up rose Paul's fire again. And it sank
and she said to herself, laughing, 'The Rayleys'; how Paul went to
coffee-houses and played chess.)

She had only escaped by the skin of her teeth though, she
thought. She had been looking at the table-cloth, and it had flashed
upon her that she would move the tree to the middle, and need never
marry anybody, and she had felt an enormous exultation. She had
felt now she could stand up to Mrs Ramsay—a tribute to the astonishing power that Mrs Ramsay had over one. Do this, she said, and

one did it. Even her shadow at the window with James was full of authority. She remembered how William Bankes had been shocked by her neglect of the significance of mother and son. Did she not admire their beauty? he said. But William, she remembered, had listened to her with his wise child's eyes when she explained how it was not irreverence: how a light there needed a shadow there and so on. She did not intend to disparage a subject which, they agreed, Raphael had treated divinely.* She was not cynical. Quite the contrary. Thanks to his scientific mind he understood—a proof of disinterested intelligence which had pleased her and comforted her enormously. One could talk of painting then seriously to a man. Indeed, his friendship had been one of the pleasures of her life. She loved William Bankes.

They went to Hampton Court* and he always left her, like the perfect gentleman he was, plenty of time to wash her hands, while he strolled by the river. That was typical of their relationship. Many things were left unsaid. Then they strolled through the courtyards, and admired, summer after summer, the proportions and the flowers, and he would tell her things, about perspective, about architecture, as they walked, and he would stop to look at a tree, or the view over the lake, and admire a child (it was his great grief—he had no daughter) in the vague aloof way that was natural to a man who spent so much time in laboratories that the world when he came out seemed to dazzle him, so that he walked slowly, lifted his hand to screen his eyes and paused, with his head thrown back, merely to breathe the air. Then he would tell her how his housekeeper was on her holiday; he must buy a new carpet for the staircase. Perhaps she would go with him to buy a new carpet for the staircase. And once something led him to talk about the Ramsays and he had said how when he first saw her she had been wearing a grey hat; she was not more than nineteen or twenty. She was astonishingly beautiful. There he stood looking down the avenue at Hampton Court, as if he could see her there among the fountains.

She looked now at the drawing-room step. She saw, through William's eyes, the shape of a woman, peaceful and silent, with downcast eyes. She sat musing, pondering (she was in grey that day, Lily thought). Her eyes were bent. She would never lift them. Yes, thought Lily, looking intently, I must have seen her look like that, but not in grey; nor so still, nor so young, nor so peaceful. The figure came readily enough. She was astonishingly beautiful, William said. But beauty was not everything. Beauty had this penalty—it came too readily, came too completely. It stilled life—froze it. One forgot the little agitations; the flush, the pallor, some queer distortion, some light or shadow, which made the face unrecognizable for a moment and yet added a quality one saw for ever after. It was simpler to smooth that all out under the cover of beauty. But what was the look she had, Lily wondered, when she clapped her deer-stalker's hat on her head, or ran across the grass, or scolded Kennedy, the gardener? Who could tell her? Who could help her?

Against her will she had come to the surface, and found herself half out of the picture, looking, a little dazedly, as if at unreal things, at Mr Carmichael. He lay on his chair with his hands clasped above his paunch not reading, or sleeping, but basking like a creature gorged with existence. His book had fallen on to the grass.

She wanted to go straight up to him and say, 'Mr Carmichael!' Then he would look up benevolently as always, from his smoky vague green eyes. But one only woke people if one knew what one wanted to say to them. And she wanted to say not one thing, but everything. Little words that broke up the thought and dismembered it said nothing. 'About life, about death; about Mrs Ramsay'—no, she thought, one could say nothing to nobody. The urgency of the moment always missed its mark. Words fluttered sideways and struck the object inches too low. Then one gave it up; then the idea sunk back again; then one became like most middle-aged people, cautious, furtive, with wrinkles between the eyes and a look of perpetual apprehension. For how could one express in words these emotions of the body? express that emptiness there? (She was looking at the drawing-room steps; they looked extraordinarily empty.) It was one's body feeling, not one's mind. The physical sensations that went with the bare look of the steps had become suddenly extremely unpleasant. To want and not to have, sent all up her body a hardness, a hollowness, a strain. And then to want and not to have—to want and want—how that wrung the heart, and wrung it again and again! Oh Mrs Ramsay! she called out silently, to that essence which sat by the boat, that abstract one made of her, that woman in grey, as if to abuse her for having gone, and then having gone, come back again. It had seemed so safe, thinking of her. Ghost, air, nothingness, a thing you could play with easily and safely at any time of day or night, she had been that, and then suddenly she put her hand out and wrung the heart thus. Suddenly, the empty drawing-room steps, the frill of the chair inside, the puppy tumbling on the terrace, the whole wave and whisper of the garden became like curves and arabesques flourishing round a centre of complete emptiness.

'What does it mean? How do you explain it all?' she wanted to say, turning to Mr Carmichael again. For the whole world seemed to have dissolved in this early morning hour into a pool of thought, a deep basin of reality, and one could almost fancy that had Mr Carmichael spoken, a little tear would have rent the surface of the pool. And then? Something would emerge. A hand would be shoved up, a blade would be flashed.* It was nonsense of course.

A curious notion came to her that he did after all hear the things she could not say. He was an inscrutable old man, with the yellow stain on his beard, and his poetry, and his puzzles, sailing serenely through a world which satisfied all his wants, so that she thought he had only to put down his hand where he lay on the lawn to fish up anything he wanted. She looked at her picture. That would have been his answer, presumably—how 'you' and 'I' and 'she' pass and vanish; nothing stays; all changes; but not words, not paint. Yet it would be hung in the attics, she thought; it would be rolled up and flung under a sofa; yet even so, even of a picture like that, it was true. One might say, even of this scrawl, not of that actual picture, perhaps, but of what it attempted, that it 'remained for ever', she was going to say, or, for the word spoken sounded even to herself, too boastful, to hint, wordlessly; when, looking at the picture, she was surprised to find that she could not see it. Her eyes were full of a hot liquid (she did not think of tears at first) which, without disturbing the firmness of her lips, made the air thick, rolled down her cheeks. She had perfect control of herself—Oh yes!— in every other way. Was she crying then for Mrs Ramsay, without being aware of any unhappiness? She addressed old Mr Carmichael again. What was it then? What did it mean? Could things thrust their hands up and grip one; could the blade cut; the fist grasp? Was there no safety? No learning by heart of the ways of the world? No guide, no shelter, but all was miracle, and leaping from the pinnacle of a tower into the air? Could it be, even for elderly people, that this was life?—startling, unexpected, unknown? For one moment she felt that if they both got up, here, now on the lawn, and demanded an explanation, why was it

so short, why was it so inexplicable, said it with violence, as two fully
equipped human beings from whom nothing should be hid might
speak, then, beauty would roll itself up; the space would fill; those
empty flourishes would form into shape; if they shouted loud
enough Mrs Ramsay would return. 'Mrs Ramsay!' she said aloud,
'Mrs Ramsay!' The tears ran down her face.

6

[Macalister´s boy took one of the fish and cut a square out of its
side to bait his hook with. The mutilated body (it was alive still) was
thrown back into the sea.]

7

'Mrs Ramsay!' Lily cried, 'Mrs Ramsay!' But nothing happened.
The pain increased. That anguish could reduce one to such a pitch
of imbecility, she thought! Anyhow the old man had not heard her.
He remained benignant, calm—if one chose to think it, sublime.
Heaven be praised, no one had heard her cry that ignominious cry,
stop pain, stop! She had not obviously taken leave of her senses. No
one had seen her step off her strip of board into the waters of
annihilation. She remained a skimpy old maid, holding a paint-brush
on the lawn.

And now slowly the pain of the want, and the bitter anger (to be
called back, just as she thought she would never feel sorrow for Mrs
Ramsay again. Had she missed her among the coffee cups at breakfast? not in the least) lessened; and of their anguish left, as antidote, a
relief that was balm in itself, and also, but more mysteriously, a sense
of someone there, of Mrs Ramsay, relieved for a moment of the
weight that the world had put on her, staying lightly by her side and
then (for this was Mrs Ramsay in all her beauty) raising to her
forehead a wreath of white flowers* with which she went. Lily
squeezed her tubes again. She attacked that problem of the hedge. It
was strange how clearly she saw her, stepping with her usual quick-
ness across the fields among whose folds, purplish and soft, among
whose flowers, hyacinths or lilies, she vanished. It was some trick of

the painter's eye. For days after she had heard of her death she had seen her thus, putting her wreath to her forehead and going unquestioningly with her companion, a shadow, across the fields. The sight, the phrase, had its power to console. Wherever she happened to be, painting, here, in the country or in London, the vision would come to her, and her eyes, half closing, sought something to base her vision on. She looked down the railway carriage, the omnibus; took a line from shoulder or cheek; looked at the windows opposite; at Piccadilly,* lamp-strung in the evening. All had been part of the fields of death. But always something—it might be a face, a voice, a paper boy crying *Standard, News**—thrust through, snubbed her, waked her, required and got in the end an effort of attention, so that the vision must be perpetually remade. Now again, moved as she was by some instinctive need of distance and blue, she looked at the bay beneath her, making hillocks of the blue bars of the waves, and stony fields of the purpler spaces. Again she was roused as usual by something incongruous. There was a brown spot in the middle of the bay. It was a boat. Yes, she realized that after a second. But whose boat? Mr Ramsay's boat, she replied. Mr Ramsay; the man who had marched past her, with his hand raised, aloof, at the head of a procession, in his beautiful boots, asking her for sympathy, which she had refused. The boat was now half-way across the bay.

So fine was the morning except for a streak of wind here and there that the sea and sky looked all one fabric, as if sails were stuck high up in the sky, or the clouds had dropped down into the sea. A steamer far out at sea had drawn in the air a great scroll of smoke which stayed there curving and circling decoratively, as if the air were a fine gauze which held things and kept them softly in its mesh, only gently swaying them this way and that. And as happens sometimes when the weather is very fine, the cliffs looked as if they were conscious of the ships, and the ships looked as if they were conscious of the cliffs, as if they signalled to each other some secret message of their own. For sometimes quite close to the shore, the Lighthouse looked this morning in the haze an enormous distance away.

'Where are they now?' Lily thought, looking out to sea. Where was he, that very old man who had gone past her silently, holding a brown paper parcel under his arm? The boat was in the middle of the bay.

8

THEY don't feel a thing there, Cam thought, looking at the shore, which, rising and falling, became steadily more distant and more peaceful. Her hand cut a trail in the sea, as her mind made the green swirls and streaks into patterns and, numbed and shrouded, wandered in imagination in that underworld of waters where the pearls stuck in clusters to white sprays, where in the green light a change came over one's entire mind and one's body shone half transparent enveloped in a green cloak.

Then the eddy slackened round her hand. The rush of the water ceased; the world became full of little creaking and squeaking sounds. One heard the waves breaking and flapping against the side of the boat as if they were anchored in harbour. Everything became very close to one. For the sail, upon which James had his eyes fixed until it had become to him like a person whom he knew, sagged entirely; there they came to a stop, flapping about waiting for a breeze, in the hot sun, miles from shore, miles from the Lighthouse. Everything in the whole world seemed to stand still. The Lighthouse became immovable, and the line of the distant shore became fixed. The sun grew hotter and everybody seemed to come very close together and to feel each other's presence, which they had almost forgotten. Macalister's fishing-line went plumb down into the sea. But Mr Ramsay went on reading with his legs curled under him.

He was reading a little shiny book with covers mottled like a plover's egg. Now and again, as they hung about in that horrid calm, he turned a page. And James felt that each page was turned with a peculiar gesture aimed at him: now assertively, now commandingly; now with the intention of making people pity him; and all the time, as his father read and turned one after another of those little pages, James kept dreading the moment when he would look up and speak sharply to him about something or other. Why were they lagging about here? he would demand, or something quite unreasonable like that. And if he does, James thought, then I shall take a knife and strike him to the heart.

He had always kept this old symbol of taking a knife and striking his father to the heart. Only now, as he grew older, and sat staring at his father in an impotent rage, it was not him, that old man reading, whom he wanted to kill, but it was the thing that descended on him—without his knowing it perhaps: that fierce sudden black-winged harpy, with its talons and its beak all cold and hard, that struck and struck at you (he could feel the beak on his bare legs, where it had struck when he was a child) and then made off, and there he was again, an old man, very sad, reading his book. That he would kill, that he would strike to the heart. Whatever he did—(and he might do anything, he felt, looking at the Lighthouse and the distant shore) whether he was in a business, in a bank, a barrister, a man at the head of some enterprise, that he would fight, that he would track down and stamp out—tyranny, despotism, he called it—making people do what they did not want to do, cutting off their right to speak. How could any of them say, But I won't, when he said, Come to the Lighthouse. Do this. Fetch me that. The black wings spread, and the hard beak tore. And then next moment, there he sat reading his book; and he might look up—one never knew—quite reasonably. He might talk to the Macalisters. He might be pressing a sovereign into some frozen old woman's hand in the street, James thought; he might be shouting out at some fisherman's sports; he might be waving his arms in the air with excitement. Or he might sit at the head of the table dead silent from one end of dinner to the other. Yes, thought James, while the boat slapped and dawdled there in the hot sun; there was a waste of snow and rock very lonely and austere; and there he had come to feel, quite often lately, when his father said something which surprised the others, were two pairs of footprints only; his own and his father's. They alone knew each other. What then was this terror, this hatred? Turning back among the many leaves which the past had folded in him, peering into the heart of that forest where light and shade so chequer each other that all shape is distorted, and one blunders, now with the sun in one's eyes, now with a dark shadow, he sought an image to cool and detach and round off his feeling in a concrete shape. Suppose then that as a child sitting helpless in a perambulator, or on someone's knee, he had seen a waggon crush ignorantly and innocently, someone's foot? Suppose he had seen the foot first, in the grass, smooth, and whole; then the wheel; and the same foot, purple, crushed. But the wheel was innocent. So now, when his father came striding down the passage knocking them up early in the morning to go to the Lighthouse down it came over his foot, over Cam's foot, over anybody's foot. One sat and watched it.

But whose foot was he thinking of, and in what garden did all this happen? For one had settings for these scenes; trees that grew there; flowers; a certain light; a few figures. Everything tended to set itself in a garden where there was none of this gloom and none of this throwing of hands about; people spoke in an ordinary tone of voice. They went in and out all day long. There was an old woman gossiping in the kitchen; and the blinds were sucked in and out by the breeze; all was blowing, all was growing; and over all those plates and bowls and tall brandishing red and yellow flowers a very thin yellow veil would be drawn, like a vine leaf, at night. Things became stiller and darker at night. But the leaf-like veil was so fine that lights lifted it, voices crinkled it; he could see through it a figure stooping, hear, coming close, going away, some dress rustling, some chain tinkling.

It was in this world that the wheel went over the person's foot. Something, he remembered, stayed and darkened over him; would not move; something flourished up in the air, something arid and sharp descended even there, like a blade, a scimitar, smiting through the leaves and flowers even of that happy world and making them shrivel and fall.

'It will rain,' he remembered his father saying. 'You won't be able to go to the Lighthouse.'

The Lighthouse was then a silvery, misty-looking tower with a yellow eye that opened suddenly and softly in the evening. Now—

James looked at the Lighthouse. He could see the white-washed rocks; the tower, stark and straight; he could see that it was barred with black and white; he could see windows in it; he could even see washing spread on the rocks to dry. So that was the Lighthouse, was it?

No, the other was also the Lighthouse. For nothing was simply one thing. The other was the Lighthouse too. It was sometimes hardly to be seen across the bay. In the evening one looked up and saw the eye opening and shutting and the light seemed to reach them in that airy sunny garden where they sat.

But he pulled himself up. Whenever he said 'they' or 'a person', and then began hearing the rustle of someone coming, the tinkle of someone going, he became extremely sensitive to the presence of whoever might be in the room. It was his father now. The strain

Oedipal here

became acute. For in one moment if there was no breeze, his father would slap the covers of his book together, and say: 'What's happening now? What are we dawdling about here for, eh?' as, once before he had brought his blade down among them on the terrace and she had gone stiff all over, and if there had been an axe handy, a knife, or anything with a sharp point he would have seized it and struck his father through the heart. His mother had gone stiff all over, and then, her arm slackening, so that he felt she listened to him no longer, she had risen somehow and gone away and left him there, impotent, ridiculous, sitting on the floor grasping a pair of scissors.

Not a breath of wind blew. The water chuckled and gurgled in the bottom of the boat where three or four mackerel beat their tails up and down in a pool of water not deep enough to cover them. At any moment Mr Ramsay (James scarcely dared look at him) might rouse himself, shut his book, and say something sharp; but for the moment he was reading, so that James stealthily, as if he were stealing downstairs on bare feet, afraid of waking a watch-dog by a creaking board, went on thinking what was she like, where did she go that day? He began following her from room to room and at last they came to a room where in a blue light, as if the reflection came from many china dishes, she talked to somebody; he listened to her talking. She talked to a servant, saying simply whatever came into her head. 'We shall need a big dish tonight. Where is it—the blue dish?' She alone spoke the truth; to her alone could he speak it. That was the source of her everlasting attraction for him, perhaps; she was a person to whom one could say what came into one's head. But all the time he thought of her, he was conscious of his father following his thought, shadowing it, making it shiver and falter.

At last he ceased to think; there he sat with his hand on the tiller in the sun, staring at the Lighthouse, powerless to move, powerless to flick off these grains of misery which settled on his mind one after another. A rope seemed to bind him there, and his father had knotted it and he could only escape by taking a knife and plunging it . . . But at that moment the sail swung slowly round, filled slowly out, the boat seemed to shake herself, and then to move off half conscious in her sleep, and then she woke and shot through the waves. The relief was extraordinary. They all seemed to fall away from each other again and to be at their ease and the fishing-lines slanted taut across the side of the boat. But his father did not rouse himself. He only raised his right hand mysteriously high in the air, and let it fall upon his knee again as if he were conducting some secret symphony.

9

[THE sea without a stain on it, thought Lily Briscoe, still standing and looking out over the bay. The sea is stretched like silk across the bay. Distance had an extraordinary power; they had been swallowed up in it, she felt, they were gone for ever, they had become part of the nature of things. It was so calm; it was so quiet. The steamer itself had vanished, but the great scroll of smoke still hung in the air and drooped like a flag mournfully in valediction.]

10

IT was like that then, the island, thought Cam, once more drawing her fingers through the waves. She had never seen it from out at sea before. It lay like that on the sea, did it, with a dent in the middle and two sharp crags, and the sea swept in there, and spread away for miles and miles on either side of the island. It was very small; shaped something like a leaf stood on end. So we took a little boat, she thought, beginning to tell herself a story of adventure about escaping from a sinking ship. But with the sea streaming through her fingers, a spray of seaweed vanishing behind them, she did not want to tell herself seriously a story; it was the sense of adventure and escape that she wanted, for she was thinking, as the boat sailed on, how her father's anger about the points of the compass, James's obstinacy about the compact, and her own anguish, all had slipped, all had passed, all had streamed away. What then came next? Where were they going? From her hand, ice cold, held deep in the sea, there spurted up a fountain of joy at the change, at the escape, at the adventure (that she should be alive, that she should be there). And the drops falling from this sudden and unthinking fountain of joy fell here and there on the dark, the slumbrous shapes in her mind; shapes of a world not realized* but turning in their darkness, catching here and there, a spark of light; Greece, Rome, Constantinople. Small as it was, and shaped something like a leaf stood on end with the gold sprinkled waters flowing in and about it, it had, she supposed, a place in the universe—even that little island? The old gentlemen in the study she thought could have told her. Sometimes she strayed in from the garden purposely to catch them at it. There they were (it might be Mr Carmichael or Mr Bankes, very old, very stiff) sitting opposite each other in their low armchairs. They were crackling in front of them the pages of *The Times*, when she came in from the garden, all in a muddle, about something someone had said about Christ; a mammoth had been dug up in a London street; what was the great Napoleon like? Then they took all this with their clean hands (they wore grey-coloured clothes; they smelt of heather) and they brushed the scraps together, turning the paper, crossing their knees, and said something now and then very brief. In a kind of trance she would take a book from the shelf and stand there, watching her father write, so equally, so neatly from one side of the page to another, with a little cough now and then, or something said briefly to the other old gentleman opposite. And she thought, standing there with her book open, here one could let whatever one thought expand like a leaf in water; and if it did well here, among the old gentlemen smoking and *The Times* crackling, then it was right. And watching her father as he wrote in his study, she thought (now sitting in the boat) he was most lovable, he was most wise; he was not vain nor a tyrant. Indeed, if he saw she was there, reading a book, he would ask her, as gently as any one could, Was there nothing he could give her?

Lest this should be wrong, she looked at him reading the little book with the shiny cover mottled like a plover's egg. No; it was right. Look at him now, she wanted to say aloud to James. (But James had his eye on the sail.) He is a sarcastic brute, James would say. He brings the talk round to himself and his books, James would say. He is intolerably egotistical. Worst of all, he is a tyrant. But look! she said, looking at him. Look at him now. She looked at him reading the little book with his legs curled; the little book whose yellowish pages she knew, without knowing what was written on them. It was small; it was closely printed; on the fly-leaf, she knew, he had written that he had spent fifteen francs on dinner; the wine had been so much; he had given so much to the waiter; all was added up neatly at the bottom of the page. But what might be written in the book which had rounded its edges off in his pocket, she did not know. What he thought they none of them knew. But he was absorbed in it, so that when he looked up, as he did now for an instant, it was not to see anything; it was to pin down some thought more exactly. That done, his mind flew back again and he plunged into his reading. He read, she thought, as if he were guiding something, or wheedling a large flock of sheep, or pushing his way up and up a single narrow path; and sometimes he went fast and straight, and broke his way through the thicket, and sometimes it seemed a branch struck at him, a bramble blinded him, but he was not going to let himself be beaten by that; on he went, tossing over page after page. And she went on telling herself a story about escaping from a sinking ship, for she was safe, while he sat there; safe, as she felt herself when she crept in from the garden, and took a book down, and the old gentleman, lowering the paper suddenly, said something very brief over the top of it about the character of Napoleon.*

She gazed back over the sea, at the island. But the leaf was losing its sharpness. It was very small; it was very distant. The sea was more important now than the shore. Waves were all round them, tossing and sinking, with a log wallowing down one wave; a gull riding on another. About here, she thought, dabbling her fingers in the water, a ship had sunk, and she murmured, dreamily, half asleep, how we perished, each alone.

11

So much depends then, thought Lily Briscoe, looking at the sea which had scarcely a stain on it, which was so soft that the sails and the clouds seemed set in its blue, so much depends, she thought, upon distance: whether people are near us or far from us; for her feeling for Mr Ramsay changed as he sailed further and further across the bay. It seemed to be elongated, stretched out; he seemed to become more and more remote. He and his children seemed to be swallowed up in that blue, that distance; but here, on the lawn, close at hand, Mr Carmichael suddenly grunted. She laughed. He clawed his book up from the grass. He settled into his chair again puffing and blowing like some sea monster. That was different altogether, because he was so near. And now again all was quiet. They must be out of bed by this time, she supposed, looking at the house, but nothing appeared there. But then, she remembered, they had always made off directly a meal was over, on business of their own. It was all in keeping with this silence, this emptiness, and the unreality of the early morning hour. It was a way things had sometimes, she thought, lingering for a moment and looking at the long glittering windows and the plume of blue smoke: they became unreal. So coming back from a journey, or after an illness, before habits had spun themselves across the surface, one felt that same unreality, which was so start-ling; felt something emerge. Life was most vivid then. One could be at one's ease. Mercifully one need not say, very briskly, crossing the lawn to greet old Mrs Beckwith, who would be coming out to find a corner to sit in, 'Oh good-morning, Mrs Beckwith! What a lovely day! Are you going to be so bold as to sit in the sun? Jasper's hidden the chairs. Do let me find you one!' and all the rest of the usual chatter. One need not speak at all. One glided, one shook one's sails (there was a good deal of movement in the bay, boats were starting off) between things, beyond things. Empty it was not, but full to the brim. She seemed to be standing up to the lips in some substance, to move and float and sink in it, yes, for these waters were unfathom-ably deep. Into them had spilled so many lives. The Ramsays'; the children's; and all sorts of waifs and strays of things besides. A washerwoman with her basket; a rook; a red-hot poker; the purples and grey-greens of flowers; some common feeling which held the whole together.

It was some such feeling of completeness perhaps which, ten years ago, standing almost where she stood now, had made her say that she must be in love with the place. Love had a thousand shapes. There might be lovers whose gift it was to choose out the elements of things and place them together and so, giving them a wholeness not theirs in life, make of some scene, or meeting of people (all now gone and separate), one of those globed compacted things over which thought lingers, and love plays.

Her eyes rested on the brown speck of Mr Ramsay's sailing boat. They would be at the Lighthouse by lunch-time she supposed. But the wind had freshened, and, as the sky changed slightly and the sea changed slightly and the boats altered their positions, the view, which a moment before had seemed miraculously fixed, was now unsatisfactory. The wind had blown the trail of smoke about; there was something displeasing about the placing of the ships.

The disproportion there seemed to upset some harmony in her own mind. She felt an obscure distress. It was confirmed when she turned to her picture. She had been wasting her morning. For whatever reason she could not achieve that razor edge of balance between two opposite forces; Mr Ramsay and the picture; which was necessary. There was something perhaps wrong with the design? Was it, she wondered, that the line of the wall wanted breaking, was it that the mass of the trees was too heavy? She smiled ironically; for had she not thought, when she began, that she had solved her problem?

What was the problem then? She must try to get hold of something that evaded her. It evaded her when she thought of Mrs Ramsay; it evaded her now when she thought of her picture. Phrases came. Visions came. Beautiful phrases. But what she wished to get hold of was that very jar on the nerves, the thing itself before it has been made anything. Get that and start afresh; get that and start afresh; she said desperately, pitching herself firmly again before her easel. It was a miserable machine, an inefficient machine, she thought, the human apparatus for painting or for feeling; it always broke down at the critical moment; heroically, one must force it on. She stared, frowning. There was the hedge, sure enough. But one got nothing by soliciting urgently. One got only a glare in the eye from looking at the line of the wall, or from thinking—she wore a grey hat. She was astonishingly beautiful. Let it come, she thought, if it will come. For there are moments when one can neither think nor feel. And if one can neither think nor feel, she thought, where is one?

Here on the grass, on the ground, she thought, sitting down, and examining with her brush a little colony of plantains.* For the lawn was very rough. Here sitting on the world, she thought, for she could not shake herself free from the sense that everything this morning was happening for the first time, perhaps for the last time, as a traveller, even though he is half asleep, knows, looking out of the train window, that he must look now, for he will never see that town, or that mule-cart, or that woman at work in the fields, again. The lawn was the world; they were up here together, on this exalted station, she thought, looking at old Mr Carmichael, who seemed (though they had not said a word all this time) to share her thoughts. And she would never see him again perhaps. He was growing old. Also, she remembered, smiling at the slipper that dangled from his foot, he was growing famous.* People said that his poetry was 'so beautiful'. They went and published things he had written forty years ago. There was a famous man now called Carmichael, she smiled, thinking how many shapes one person might wear, how he was that in the newspapers, but here the same as he had always been. He looked the same—greyer, rather. Yes, he looked the same, but somebody had said, she recalled, that when he had heard of Andrew Ramsay's death (he was killed in a second by a shell; he should have been a great mathematician) Mr Carmichael had 'lost all interest in life'. What did it mean—that? she wondered. Had he marched through Trafalgar Square grasping a big stick?* Had he turned pages over and over, without reading them, sitting in his room in St John's Wood alone? She did not know what he had done, when he heard that Andrew was killed, but she felt it in him all the same. They only mumbled at each other on staircases; they looked up at the sky and said it will be fine or it won't be fine. But this was one way of knowing people, she thought: to know the outline, not the detail, to sit in one's garden and look at the slopes of a hill running purple down into the distant heather. She knew him in that way. She knew that he had changed somehow. She had never read a line of his poetry. She thought that she knew how it went though, slowly and sonorously. It was seasoned and mellow. It was about the desert and the camel. It was about the palm tree and the sunset. It was extremely impersonal; it said something about death; it said very little about love. There was an aloofness about him. He wanted very little of other people. Had he not always lurched rather awkwardly past the drawing-room window with some newspaper under his arm, trying to avoid Mrs Ramsay whom for some reason he did not much like? On that account, of course, she would always try to make him stop. He would bow to her. He would halt unwillingly and bow profoundly. Annoyed that he did not want anything of her, Mrs Ramsay would ask him (Lily could hear her) wouldn't he like a coat, a rug, a newspaper? No, he wanted nothing. (Here he bowed.) There was some quality in her which he did not much like. It was perhaps her masterfulness, her positiveness, something matter-of-fact in her. She was so direct.

(A noise drew her attention to the drawing-room window—the squeak of a hinge. The light breeze was toying with the window.)

There must have been people who disliked her very much, Lily thought (Yes; she realized that the drawing-room step was empty, but it had no effect on her whatever. She did not want Mrs Ramsay now.)—People who thought her too sure, too drastic. Also her beauty offended people probably. How monotonous, they would say, and the same always! They preferred another type—the dark, the vivacious. Then she was weak with her husband. She let him make those scenes. Then she was reserved. Nobody knew exactly what had happened to her. And (to go back to Mr Carmichael and his dislike) one could not imagine Mrs Ramsay standing painting, lying reading, a whole morning on the lawn. It was unthinkable. Without saying a word, the only token of her errand a basket on her arm, she went off to the town, to the poor, to sit in some stuffy little bedroom. Often and often Lily had seen her go silently in the midst of some game, some discussion, with her basket on her arm, very upright. She had noted her return. She had thought, half laughing (she was so methodical with the tea cups) half moved (her beauty took one's breath away), eyes that are closing in pain have looked on you. You have been with them there.

And then Mrs Ramsay would be annoyed because somebody was late, or the butter not fresh, or the teapot chipped. And all the time she was saying that the butter was not fresh one would be thinking of Greek temples, and how beauty had been with them there. She never talked of it—she went, punctually, directly. It was her instinct to go, an instinct like the swallows for the south, the artichokes for the sun, turning her infallibly to the human race, making her nest in its heart. And this, like all instincts, was a little distressing to people who did not share it; to Mr Carmichael perhaps, to herself certainly. Some notion was in both of them about the ineffectiveness of action, the supremacy of thought. Her going was a reproach to them, gave a different twist to the world, so that they were led to protest, seeing their own prepossessions disappear, and clutch at them vanishing. Charles Tansley did that too: it was part of the reason why one disliked him. He upset the proportions of one's world. And what had happened to him, she wondered, idly stirring the plantains with her brush. He had got his fellowship. He had married; he lived at Golders Green.*

She had gone one day into a Hall and heard him speaking during the war. He was denouncing something: he was condemning somebody. He was preaching brotherly love. And all she felt was how could he love his kind who did not know one picture from another, who had stood behind her smoking shag ('fivepence an ounce, Miss Briscoe') and making it his business to tell her women can't write, women can't paint, not so much that he believed it, as that for some odd reason he wished it? There he was, lean and red and raucous, preaching love from a platform (there were ants crawling about among the plantains which she disturbed with her brush—red, energetic ants, rather like Charles Tansley). She had looked at him ironically from her seat in the half-empty hall, pumping love into that chilly space, and suddenly, there was the old cask or whatever it was bobbing up and down among the waves and Mrs Ramsay looking for her spectacle case among the pebbles. 'Oh dear! What a nuisance! Lost again. Don't bother, Mr Tansley. I lose thousands every summer,' at which he pressed his chin back against his collar, as if afraid to sanction such exaggeration, but could stand it in her whom he liked, and smiled very charmingly. He must have confided in her on one of those long expeditions when people got separated and walked back alone. He was educating his little sister, Mrs Ramsay had told her. It was immensely to his credit. Her own idea of him was grotesque, Lily knew well, stirring the plantains with her brush. Half one's notions of other people were, after all, grotesque. They served private purposes of one's own. He did for her instead of a whipping-boy. She found herself flagellating his lean flanks when she was out of temper. If she wanted to be serious about him she had to help herself to Mrs Ramsay's sayings, to look at him through her eyes.

She raised a little mountain for the ants to climb over. She reduced them to a frenzy of indecision by this interference in their cosmogony. Some ran this way, others that.

One wanted fifty pairs of eyes to see with, she reflected. Fifty pairs of eyes were not enough to get round that one woman with, she thought. Among them, must be one that was stone blind to her beauty. One wanted most some secret sense, fine as air, with which to steal through keyholes and surround her where she sat knitting, talking, sitting silent in the window alone; which took to itself and treasured up like the air which held the smoke of the steamer, her thoughts, her imaginations, her desires. What did the hedge mean to her, what did the garden mean to her, what did it mean to her when a wave broke? (Lily looked up, as she had seen Mrs Ramsay look up; she too heard a wave falling on the beach.) And then what stirred and trembled in her mind when the children cried, 'How's that? How's that?' cricketing? She would stop knitting for a second. She would look intent. Then she would lapse again, and suddenly Mr Ramsay stopped dead in his pacing in front of her, and some curious shock passed through her and seemed to rock her in profound agitation on its breast when stopping there he stood over her, and looked down at her. Lily could see him.

He stretched out his hand and raised her from her chair. It seemed somehow as if he had done it before; as if he had once bent in the same way and raised her from a boat which, lying a few inches off some island, had required that the ladies should thus be helped on shore by the gentlemen. An old-fashioned scene that was, which required, very nearly, crinolines and peg-top trousers.* Letting herself be helped by him, Mrs Ramsay had thought (Lily supposed) the time has come now; Yes, she would say it now. Yes, she would marry him. And she stepped slowly, quietly on shore. Probably she said one word only, letting her hand rest still in his. I will marry you, she might have said, with her hand in his; but no more. Time after time the same thrill had passed between them—obviously it had, Lily thought, smoothing a way for her ants. She was not inventing; she was only trying to smooth out something she had been given years ago folded up; something she had seen. For in the rough and tumble of daily life, with all those children about, all those visitors, one had constantly a sense of repetition—of one thing falling where another had fallen, and so setting up an echo which chimed in the air and made it full of vibrations.

But it would be a mistake, she thought, thinking how they walked off together, she in her green shawl, he with his tie flying, arm in arm, past the greenhouse, to simplify their relationship. It was no monotony of bliss—she with her impulses and quicknesses; he with his shudders and glooms. Oh no. The bedroom door would slam violently early in the morning. He would start from the table in a temper. He would whizz his plate through the window. Then all through the house there would be a sense of doors slamming and blinds fluttering as if a gusty wind were blowing and people scudded about trying in a hasty way to fasten hatches and make things ship-shape. She had met Paul Rayley like that one day on the stairs. They had laughed and laughed, like a couple of children, all because Mr Ramsay, finding an earwig in his milk at breakfast had sent the whole thing flying through the air on to the terrace outside. 'An earwig,' Prue murmured, awestruck, 'in his milk.' Other people might find centipedes. But he had built round him such a fence of sanctity, and occupied the space with such a demeanour of majesty that an earwig in his milk was a monster.

But it tired Mrs Ramsay, it cowed her a little—the plates whizzing and the doors slamming. And there would fall between them some-times long rigid silences, when, in a state of mind which annoyed Lily in her, half plaintive, half resentful, she seemed unable to sur-mount the tempest calmly, or to laugh as they laughed, but in her weariness perhaps concealed something. She brooded and sat silent. After a time he would hang stealthily about the places where she was—roaming under the window where she sat writing letters or talking, for she would take care to be busy when he passed, and evade him, and pretend not to see him. Then he would turn smooth as silk, affable, urbane, and try to win her so. Still she would hold off, and now she would assert for a brief season some of those prides and airs the due of her beauty which she was generally utterly without; would turn her head; would look so, over her shoulder, always with some Minta, Paul, or William Bankes at her side. At length, standing outside the group the very figure of a famished wolfhound (Lily got up off the grass and stood looking at the steps, at the window, where she had seen him), he would say her name* once only, for all the world like a wolf barking in the snow, but still she held back; and he would say it once more, and this time something in the tone would rouse her, and she would go to him, leaving them all of a sudden, and they would walk off together among the pear trees, the cabbages, and the raspberry beds. They would have it out together. But with what attitudes and with what words? Such a dignity was theirs in this relationship that, turning away, she and Paul and Minta would hide their curiosity and their discomfort, and begin picking flowers, throwing balls, chattering, until it was time for dinner, and there they were, he at one end of the table, she at the other, as usual.

'Why don't some of you take up botany? . . . With all those legs and arms why doesn't one of you . . .?' So they would talk as usual, laughing, among the children. All would be as usual, save only for some quiver, as of a blade in the air, which came and went between them as if the usual sight of the children sitting round their soup plates had freshened itself in their eyes after that hour among the pears and the cabbages. Especially, Lily thought, Mrs Ramsay would glance at Prue. She sat in the middle between brothers and sisters, always so occupied, it seemed, seeing that nothing went wrong that she scarcely spoke herself. How Prue must have blamed herself for that earwig in the milk! How white she had gone when Mr Ramsay threw his plate through the window! How she drooped under those long silences between them! Anyhow, her mother now would seem to be making it up to her; assuring her that everything was well; promising her that one of these days that same happiness would be hers. She had enjoyed it for less than a year, however.

She had let the flowers fall from her basket, Lily thought, screwing up her eyes and standing back as if to look at her picture, which she was not touching, however, with all her faculties in a trance, frozen over superficially but moving underneath with extreme speed.

She let her flowers fall from her basket, scattered and tumbled them on to the grass and, reluctantly and hesitatingly, but without question or complaint—had she not the faculty of obedience to perfection?—went too. Down fields, across valleys, white, flower-strewn—that was how she would have painted it. The hills were austere. It was rocky; it was steep. The waves sounded hoarse on the stones beneath. They went, the three of them together, Mrs Ramsay walking rather fast in front, as if she expected to meet someone round the corner.

Suddenly the window at which she was looking was whitened by some light stuff behind it. At last then somebody had come into the drawing-room; somebody was sitting in the chair. For Heaven's sake, she prayed, let them sit still there and not come floundering out to talk to her. Mercifully, whoever it was stayed still inside; had settled by some stroke of luck so as to throw an odd-shaped triangular shadow over the step. It altered the composition of the picture a little. It was interesting. It might be useful. Her mood was coming back to her. One must keep on looking without for a second relaxing the intensity of emotion, the determination not to be put off, not to be bamboozled. One must hold the scene—so—in a vice and let nothing come in and spoil it. One wanted, she thought, dipping her brush deliberately, to be on a level with ordinary experience, to feel simply that's a chair, that's a table, and yet at the same time, It's a miracle, it's an ecstasy. The problem might be solved after all. Ah, but what had happened? Some wave of white went over the window pane. The air must have stirred some flounce in the room. Her heart leapt at her and seized her and tortured her.

'Mrs Ramsay! Mrs Ramsay!' she cried, feeling the old horror come back—to want and want and not to have. Could she inflict that still? And then, quietly, as if she refrained, that too became part of ordinary experience, was on a level with the chair, with the table. Mrs Ramsay—it was part of her perfect goodness to Lily—sat there quite simply, in the chair, flicked her needles to and fro, knitted her reddish-brown stocking, cast her shadow on the step. There she sat.

And as if she had something she must share, yet could hardly leave her easel, so full her mind was of what she was thinking, of what she was seeing, Lily went past Mr Carmichael holding her brush to the edge of the lawn. Where was that boat now? Mr Ramsay? She wanted him.

12

MR Ramsay had almost done reading. One hand hovered over the page as if to be in readiness to turn it the very instant he had finished it. He sat there bareheaded with the wind blowing his hair about, extraordinarily exposed to everything. He looked very old. He looked, James thought, getting his head now against the Lighthouse, now against the waste of waters running away into the open, like some old stone lying on the sand; he looked as if he had become physically what was always at the back of both of their minds that loneliness which was for both of them the truth about things.

He was reading very quickly, as if he were eager to get to the end. Indeed they were very close to the Lighthouse now. There it loomed up, stark and straight, glaring white and black, and one could see the waves breaking in white splinters like smashed glass upon the rocks. One could see lines and creases in the rocks. One could see the windows clearly; a dab of white on one of them, and a little tuft of green on the rock. A man had come out and looked at them through a glass and gone in again. So it was like that, James thought, the Lighthouse one had seen across the bay all these years; it was a stark tower on a bare rock. It satisfied him. It confirmed some obscure feeling of his about his own character. The old ladies, he thought, thinking of the garden at home, went dragging their chairs about on the lawn. Old Mrs Beckwith, for example, was always saying how nice it was and how sweet it was and how they ought to be so proud and they ought to be so happy, but as a matter of fact James thought, looking at the Lighthouse stood there on its rock, it's like that. He looked at his father reading fiercely with his legs curled tight. They shared that knowledge. 'We are driving before a gale—we must sink,' he began saying to himself, half aloud exactly as his father said it.

Nobody seemed to have spoken for an age. Cam was tired of looking at the sea. Little bits of black cork had floated past,* the fish were dead in the bottom of the boat. Still her father read, and James looked at him and she looked at him, and they vowed that they would fight tyranny to the death, and he went on reading quite unconscious of what they thought. It was thus that he escaped, she thought. Yes, with his great forehead and his great nose, holding his little mottled book firmly in front of him, he escaped. You might try to lay hands on him, but then like a bird, he spread his wings, he floated off to settle out of your reach somewhere far away on some desolate stump. She gazed at the immense expanse of the sea. The island had grown so small that it scarcely looked like a leaf any longer. It looked like the top of a rock which some big wave would cover. Yet in its frailty were all those paths, those terraces, those bedrooms—all those innumerable things. But as, just before sleep, things simplify themselves so that only one of all the myriad details has power to assert itself, so, she felt, looking drowsily at the island, all those paths and terraces and bedrooms were fading and disappearing, and nothing was left but a pale blue censer swinging rhythmically this way and that across her mind. It was a hanging garden; it was a valley, full of birds, and flowers, and antelopes . . . She was falling asleep.

'Come now,' said Mr Ramsay, suddenly shutting his book.

Come where? To what extraordinary adventure? She woke with a start. To land somewhere, to climb somewhere? Where was he leading them? For after his immense silence the words startled them. But it was absurd. He was hungry, he said. It was time for lunch. Besides, look, he said. There's the Lighthouse. 'We're almost there.'

'He's doing very well,' said Macalister, praising James. 'He's keeping her very steady.'

But his father never praised him, James thought grimly.

Mr Ramsay opened the parcel and shared out the sandwiches among them. Now he was happy, eating bread and cheese with these fishermen. He would have liked to live in a cottage and lounge about in the harbour spitting with the other old men, James thought, watching him slice his cheese into thin yellow sheets with his penknife.

This is right, this is it, Cam kept feeling, as she peeled her hard-boiled egg. Now she felt as she did in the study when the old men were reading *The Times*. Now I can go on thinking whatever I like, and I shan't fall over a precipice or be drowned, for there he is, keeping his eye on me, she thought.

At the same time they were sailing so fast along by the rocks that it was very exciting—it seemed as if they were doing two things at once; they were eating their lunch here in the sun and they were also making for safety in a great storm after a shipwreck. Would the water last? Would the provisions last? she asked herself, telling herself a story but knowing at the same time what was the truth.

They would soon be out of it, Mr Ramsay was saying to old Macalister; but their children would see some strange things. Macalister said he was seventy-five last March; Mr Ramsay was seventy-one. Macalister said he had never seen a doctor; he had never lost a tooth. And that's the way I'd like my children to live—Cam was sure that her father was thinking that, for he stopped her throwing a sandwich into the sea and told her, as if he were thinking of the fishermen and how they live, that if she did not want it she should put it back in the parcel. She should not waste it. He said it so wisely, as if he knew so well the things that happened in the world, that she put it back at once, and then he gave her, from his own parcel, a gingerbread nut, as if he were a great Spanish gentleman, she thought, handing a flower to a lady at a window (so courteous his manner was). But he was shabby, and simple, eating bread and cheese; and yet he was leading them on a great expedition where, for all she knew, they would be drowned.

'That was where she sunk,' said Macalister's boy suddenly.

'Three men were drowned where we are now,' said the old man. He had seen them clinging to the mast himself. And Mr Ramsay taking a look at the spot was about, James and Cam were afraid, to burst out:

> But I beneath a rougher sea,

and if he did, they could not bear it; they would shriek aloud; they could not endure another explosion of the passion that boiled in him; but to their surprise all he said was 'Ah' as if he thought to himself, But why make a fuss about that? Naturally men are drowned in a storm, but it is a perfectly straightforward affair, and the depths of the sea (he sprinkled the crumbs from his sandwich paper over them) are only water after all. Then having lighted his pipe he took out his watch. He looked at it attentively; he made, perhaps, some mathematical calculation. At last he said, triumphantly:

'Well done!' James had steered them like a born sailor.

There! Cam thought, addressing herself silently to James. You've got it at last. For she knew that this was what James had been wanting, and she knew that now he had got it he was so pleased that he would not look at her or at his father or at anyone. There he sat with his hand on the tiller sitting bolt upright, looking rather sulky and frowning slightly. He was so pleased that he was not going to let anybody take away a grain of his pleasure. His father had praised him. They must think that he was perfectly indifferent. But you've got it now, Cam thought.

They had tacked, and they were sailing swiftly, buoyantly on long rocking waves which handed them on from one to another with an extraordinary lilt and exhilaration beside the reef. On the left a row of rocks showed brown through the water which thinned and became greener and on one, a higher rock, a wave incessantly broke and spurted a little column of drops which fell down in a shower. One could hear the slap of the water and the patter of falling drops and a kind of hushing and hissing sound from the waves rolling and gambolling and slapping the rocks as if they were wild creatures who were perfectly free and tossed and tumbled and sported like this for ever.

Now they could see two men on the Lighthouse, watching them and making ready to meet them.

Mr Ramsay buttoned his coat, and turned up his trousers. He took the large, badly packed, brown paper parcel which Nancy had got ready and sat with it on his knee. Thus in complete readiness to land he sat looking back at the island. With his long-sighted eyes perhaps he could see the dwindled leaf-like shape standing on end on a plate of gold quite clearly. What could he see? Cam wondered. It was all a blur to her. What was he thinking now? she wondered. What was it he sought, so fixedly, so intently, so silently? They watched him, both of them, sitting bareheaded with his parcel on his knee staring and staring at the frail blue shape which seemed like the vapour of something that had burnt itself away. What do you want? they both wanted to ask. They both wanted to say, Ask us anything and we will give it you. But he did not ask them anything. He sat and looked at the island and he might be thinking, We perished, each alone, or he might be thinking, I have reached it. I have found it, but he said nothing.

Then he put on his hat.

'Bring those parcels,' he said, nodding his head at the things Nancy had done up for them to take to the Lighthouse. 'The parcels for the Lighthouse men,' he said. He rose and stood in the bow of the boat, very straight and tall, for all the world, James thought, as if he were saying, 'There is no God,' and Cam thought, as if he were leaping into space, and they both rose to follow him as he sprang, lightly like a young man, holding his parcel, on to the rock.

13

'He must have reached it,' said Lily Briscoe aloud, feeling suddenly completely tired out. For the Lighthouse had become almost invisible, had melted away into a blue haze, and the effort of looking at it and the effort of thinking of him landing there, which both seemed to be one and the same effort, had stretched her body and mind to the utmost. Ah, but she was relieved. Whatever she had wanted to give him, when he left her that morning, she had given him at last.

'He has landed,' she said aloud. 'It is finished.' Then, surging up, puffing slightly, old Mr Carmichael stood beside her, looking like an old pagan god, shaggy, with weeds in his hair and the trident (it was only a French novel) in his hand.* He stood by her on the edge of the lawn, swaying a little in his bulk, and said, shading his eyes with his hand: 'They will have landed,' and she felt that she had been right. They had not needed to speak. They had been thinking the same things and he had answered her without her asking him anything. He stood there spreading his hands over all the weakness and suffering of mankind; she thought he was surveying, tolerantly, compassionately, their final destiny. Now he has crowned the occasion, she thought, when his hand slowly fell, as if she had seen him let fall from his great height a wreath of violets and asphodels* which, fluttering slowly, lay at length upon the earth.

Quickly, as if she were recalled by something over there, she turned to her canvas. There it was—her picture. Yes, with all its green and blues, its lines running up and across, its attempt at something. It would be hung in the attics, she thought; it would be destroyed. But what did that matter? she asked herself, taking up her brush again. She looked at the steps; they were empty; she looked at her canvas; it was blurred. With a sudden intensity, as if she saw it clear for a second, she drew a line there, in the centre. It was done; it was finished. Yes, she thought, laying down her brush in extreme fatigue, I have had my vision.

EXPLANATORY NOTES

In preparing the following Notes and in every other aspect of this edition, I have benefited from the sage and generous advice of Stephen Barkway and Stuart N. Clarke. To both I am very grateful.

ABBREVIATIONS

MausB   *Sir Leslie Stephen's Mausoleum Book*, ed. Alan Bell (Oxford: Clarendon Press, 1977).

MB   Virginia Woolf, *Moments of Being: Autobiographical Writings*, ed. Jeanne Schulkind, rev. Hermione Lee (London: Pimlico, 2002).

OHD   Virginia Woolf, *To the Lighthouse: The Original Holograph Draft*, transcribed and ed. Susan Dick (London: Hogarth Press, 1983).

PA   Virginia Woolf, *A Passionate Apprentice: The Early Journals and 'Carlyle's House and Other Sketches'*, ed. Mitchell A. Leaska (London: Pimlico, 2004).

THE WINDOW

7 *Ramsay*: in view of the novel's strong political currents, it would be satisfying to speculate that Woolf plumped for the name Ramsay having come across a copy of Alasdair Alpin MacGregor's *Over the Sea to Skye* (1926), published with a foreword by the Scottish socialist (James) Ramsay Macdonald (1866–1937), the first Labour prime minister, who held office for nine months in 1924. But the accession stamp in the Bodleian Library's copy is 'Jul[y] 29 1926' and other sources confirm that MacGregor's book was published that month, which means that Woolf had already chosen her principal family's surname by the time *Over the Sea to Skye* came out. But given that James Ramsay, the youngest of the eight Ramsay siblings, is the ex-premier's namesake, and the fact that Ramsay Macdonald was by far the most famous Scotsman of his day (let alone the most prominent socialist), he remains the most likely source for the fictional family's name. Alternatively, it may simply have been the geographical proximity of Raasay to Skye (it lies a short distance off Skye's east coast) that prompted Woolf to opt for the similar sounding Ramsay. It is also possible that the distinguished Scottish portrait painter Allan Ramsay (1713–84), appointed court painter to George III in 1767 and celebrated for his portraits of women in particular (including Flora Macdonald: see Introduction, pp. xxix, xxx), may also have had some bearing on Woolf's choice of surname. Or she could have had in mind the Scottish chemist and 1904 Nobel Prize winner Sir William Ramsay (1852–1916), discoverer of

argon, neon, helium, and other inert gases. But Ramsay Macdonald and Raasay are the leading contenders.

7 *Army and Navy Stores*: the 'Army and Navy Co-operative Society Ltd, or the "Stores" as it was more commonly known . . . was incorporated in 1871 with a capital of £15,000. Its object was to act as general dealers for the purpose of supplying its shareholders and subscribers, and their friends, with food, drink, clothes and articles of general use at the lowest prices made possible by bulk buying and small profits . . . All members were subject to approval of the Board of Directors, made up almost entirely of senior officers. The patrons listed on the first prospectus of the Society included Officers in the Militia and Yeomanry; Irish, Indian and Colonial Constabulary were also eligible, as were peers, Privy Councillors, English and foreign ambassadors and officials of the Foreign Office, cabinet ministers and the more senior civil servants and substantial professional men, all of whom were entitled to nominate friends and relatives as life or annual members on payment of the appropriate fee' (R. H. Langbridge (comp.), *Edwardian Shopping: A Selection from the Army & Navy Stores Catalogues 1898–1913* (Newton Abbot and London: David & Charles, 1975), [p.1]). 'When far from England, the great cloth-bound catalogue kept you in touch with "home"—was, indeed, a very tangible part of "home". In 1901 branches were opened in Bombay, Delhi, Calcutta and Karachi, the price lists issued in Indian currency. The Indian princes became loyal customers' (Alison Adburgham (introd.), *Yesterday's Shopping: The Army & Navy Stores Catalogue 1907. A Facsimile of the Army & Navy Co-operative Society's 1907 Issue of Rules of the Society and Price List of Articles Sold at the Stores* (Newton Abbot: David & Charles, 1969), n.p.).

refrigerator: for illustrations of the Army and Navy's range of refrigerators, see *Yesterday's Shopping: The Army & Navy Stores Catalogue 1907*, 211–12. 'By the 1880s refrigerating machines were being used in ships, transporting meat successfully on long sea journeys. The first mechanically operated domestic refrigerator was developed c.1880 from the cooling apparatus used by the brewing industry, powered by a small steam pump; electric refrigerators appeared in the 1920s' (*The Oxford English Reference Dictionary*, ed. Judy Pearsall and Bill Trumble (Oxford: Oxford University Press, 1995), 1213).

his high forehead and his fierce blue eyes: James is a miniature Leslie Stephen. As Woolf recalled, her father's 'forehead rose and swelled; his skull was magnificent . . . and though his eyes were very small . . . they were pure bright forget-me-not blue' (*MB*, p. 120).

all red and ermine on the Bench: short for the King's or Queen's Bench, a division of the High Court of Justice, at which the monarch formerly presided.

8 *Lighthouse*: based on the Godrevy Lighthouse, located on Godrevy Island, three and a half miles across St Ives Bay from St Ives itself. In the 'Hyde Park Gate News' (the Stephen family newspaper) of 12 September

1892, we read: 'On Saturday morning Master Hilary Hunt and Master Basil Smith came up to Talland House and asked Master Thoby and Miss Virginia Stephen to accompany them to the light-house as Freeman the boatman said that there was a perfect tide and wind for going there. Master Adrian Stephen was much disappointed at not being allowed to go' (Virginia Woolf and Vanessa Bell, with Thoby Stephen, *Hyde Park Gate News: The Stephen Family Newspaper*, ed. Gill Lowe (London: Hesperus Press, 2005), 108–9).

the terrace: photographs of the terrace and many other scenes from the Stephen family's tenancy of Talland House are illustrated in Marion Dell and Marion Whybrow, *Virginia Woolf and Vanessa Bell: Remembering St Ives* (Padstow: Tabb House, 2004). For the terrace in particular, see pp. 30, 38, and 108.

9 *Hebrides*: a group of islands off the west coast of Scotland, subdivided into the Inner and Outer Hebrides and separated by the North Minch and the South Minch sea channels.

ruled India: Woolf's mother was born in Calcutta in 1846 and before he married Virginia Stephen in 1912, Leonard Woolf had been a colonial administrator (1904–11) in Ceylon (Sri Lanka), then part of the Indian Empire. The British presence in India grew steadily and purposefully after the Indian Mutiny of 1857. See also note to p. 67 about Woolf's uncle James Fitzjames Stephen and his time in and attitude to India.

her hair grey, her cheek sunk, at fifty: Woolf's mother died of influenza in May 1895, aged 49 and similarly exhausted from her 'laborious' life of charitable good works and demanding household management.

10 *Isle of Skye*: the largest and most northerly of the Inner Hebrides group. The main town in the Edwardian period was (and remains) Portree.

'ablest fellow in Balliol': one of the oldest of the colleges of Oxford University, Balliol was founded in 1263 by John of Balliol, King of Scots (1292–6), and his wife Dervorguilla of Galloway. Leslie Stephen was educated at Trinity Hall, Cambridge.

buried his light temporarily at Bristol or Bedford: University College, Bristol, was founded in 1876, but Bedford has never had a university. Woolf probably had in mind Bedford College, London, founded for women in 1849 by Elisabeth Jesser Reid. The college was incorporated into the University of London in 1900 and in 1985 it merged with Royal Holloway College to form Royal Holloway and Bedford New College, more commonly known as Royal Holloway.

Prolegomena: introductions or prefaces to books, especially of a philosophical or mathematical kind.

11 *the passing of the Reform Bill*: probably a reference to the Reform Act of 1832. Others followed in 1867 and 1884 with the cumulative effect of extending the male suffrage. This part of the novel is set in September 1909 and so the issue remained topical in the lead up to the Parliament

Act of 1911 which emphatically took away the remnants of political power from the aristocracy.

11 *the Grisons*: the largest and most easterly canton of Switzerland, known in German as Graubünden. It is almost entirely mountainous. The Stephen family had a Swiss servant for a time at their 22 Hyde Park Gate home in London.

12 *a dull errand in the town*: this description of the town is far more redolent of St Ives than Portree (see note to p. 10). In his *Mausoleum Book*, Leslie Stephen describes Julia Stephen's dedication to the poor and sick of St Ives and how she 'got up a subscription to set up a nurse for the town' (*MausB*, p. 63).

Carmichael: based on a man named Wolstenholme, 'a man whom [Leslie Stephen] had first known as a brilliant mathematician at Cambridge, whose Bohemian tastes and heterodox opinions had made a Cambridge career unadvisable, who had tried to become a hermit in Wastdale [in the Lake District]. He had emerged [and] married an uncongenial and rather vulgar Swiss girl . . . he was despondent and dissatisfied and consoled himself with mathematics and opium . . . Julia . . . took him under her protection, encouraged him and petted him, and had him to stay every summer with us in the country. There he could at least be without his wife' (*MausB*, p. 79). See also *MB*, p. 86.

a few drops of something: perhaps laudanum, a tincture of opium. See the previous note.

Hindustanee: or Hindustani is an Indo-Aryan language that originated in the dialect of the Delhi district. Like the Moguls, the British promoted the use of Hindustani as a lingua franca throughout India.

13 *gowned and hooded, walking in a procession*: Tansley is currently 'at college' (p. 13), almost certainly an undergraduate at either Oxford or Cambridge. At both of these (and, indeed, at other British universities) formal academic processions would occur and still occur on Congregation days and Degree days, etc., where all the participants are appropriately 'gowned and hooded'.

14 *readership*: in a university, 'a lecturer of the highest grade below professor' (*OED*).

Ibsen . . . He was an awful prig: the point is that the Norwegian dramatist Henrik Ibsen (1828–1906) was not only the most influential dramatist of his age but also a radical artist who had been explicated and lionized by George Bernard Shaw in *The Quintessence of Ibsenism* (1891). Shaw, one of the most prominent Fabian socialists of his day, would have been a political hero of Tansley's.

settlements . . . helping our own class: from around the late nineteenth century, a settlement came to mean 'An establishment in a poor part of a large city lived in by people engaged or interested in social work or reform' (*OED*). The first such settlement was Toynbee Hall, founded in

1884 by the friends of the social reformer Arnold Toynbee (1852–83) in the Whitechapel area of London's East End. It quickly became established as a place where undergraduates from Oxford and Cambridge could spend their vacations living among and helping to improve the lives of the urban poor.

artists had come here: St Ives became a well-known artists' colony at about the time the Stephen family began spending its summers there. See Dell and Whybrow, *Virginia Woolf and Vanessa Bell: Remembering St Ives*, 12–16, 58–61.

pink women on the beach: the unnamed artist is merely a slavish imitator of the imaginary Paunceforte, but given that his pictures comprise seascapes and beach scenes and his palette is 'pale, elegant, semi-transparent' (p. 19) and 'etherealized' (p. 42), Paunceforte may well have been based on the English Impressionist Philip Wilson Steer (1860–1942), who had painted at St Ives, but who more famously brought the same kind of artistic fashionableness to Southwold and Walberswick on the Suffolk coast as Paunceforte has brought to Skye.

15 *must keep the windows open and the doors shut*: probably to defend the house against both dampness and the threat of tuberculosis. See Introduction, p. xxiii.

Queen Victoria wearing the blue ribbon of the Garter: Queen Victoria (reigned 1837–1901) was made Empress of India in 1876 and in *Moments of Being* Woolf recalled that Julia Stephen 'with her natural impetuosity' sometimes 'despatch[ed] difficulties with a high hand, like some commanding Empress' (*MB*, p. 7). The sovereign is always a member of the Order of the Garter, the oldest and highest order of knighthood, founded in 1348 by Edward III. The Order is limited to the sovereign, the Prince of Wales, and no more than twenty-four knights companions. A member of the Order wears a Star, a garter below the left knee, and a diagonal blue ribbon.

16 *the tap of balls . . . cricket*: in her preliminary notes for the novel, Woolf wrote: 'Topics that may come in' and one of these was 'The waves breaking. Tapping of cricket balls. The bark "How's that?" ' (*OHD*, p. 49).

17 *something between a croak and a song*: in her 'Leslie Stephen, The Philosopher at Home: A Daughter's Memories' (*The Times*, 28 November 1932, pp. 15–16), Woolf recalled that her father would often burst 'into a strange rhythmical chant, for verse of all kinds, both "utter trash" as he called it, and the most sublime words of Milton and Wordsworth, stuck in his memory, and the act of walking or climbing seemed to inspire him to recite whichever it was that came uppermost or suited his mood' (repr. in Virginia Woolf, *Collected Essays*, iv (London: Hogarth Press, 1967), 76–80).

a pocket knife with six blades: there are no fewer than nine pages of pocket knives illustrated in *Yesterday's Shopping* (pp. 985–93) and a number of them have six blades.

17 *Stormed at with shot and shell*: the first of a number of quotations from
    'The Charge of the Light Brigade' (1854), by Alfred, Lord Tennyson
    (1809–92). The poem commemorates the notorious cavalry charge dur-
    ing the Battle of Balaclava (25 October 1854), a key engagement of the
    Crimean War (1853–6), when 247 men out of the 673-strong Light
    Brigade were either killed or wounded after senior officers misunderstood
    a command. Stanzas 2 and 3 read:

> 'Forward, the Light Brigade!'
> Was there a man dismayed?
> Not though the soldiers knew
> Some one had blundered:
> Their's not to make reply,
> Their's not to reason why,
> Their's but to do and die:
> Into the valley of Death
> Rode the six hundred.
>
> Cannon to the right of them,
> Cannon to left of them,
> Cannon in front of them
> Volleyed and thundered;
> Stormed at with shot and shell,
> Boldly they rode and well,
> Into the jaws of Death,
> Into the mouth of Hell
> Rode the six hundred.

    It was largely due to the impact of this poem that the Charge became
    synonymous both with military incompetence and disciplined, military
    valour.

    Chinese eyes: see also pp. 24, 74, 85, and 130, and the similar stress on
    Elizabeth Dalloway's 'Chinese eyes' in Virginia Woolf, *Mrs Dalloway*, ed.
    David Bradshaw (Oxford: Oxford University Press, 2000), 104, 114.

18 *the heights of Balaclava*: see also note to p. 17. On 25 October 1854, in one
    of the principal engagements of the Crimean War, the Russians
    attempted to lift the siege of Sebastopol by moving against the British
    base at Balaclava. In view of the novel's setting on the Isle of Skye, it is
    worth noting that the Russian cavalrymen were repulsed by the cele-
    brated 'thin red line' of the 93rd Highlanders, many of whom would have
    been Skyemen. This incident was followed by an attack on the main body
    of the Russian cavalry by the Heavy Brigade (of British cavalry) and then
    the infamous Charge of the Light Brigade. In the event, Balaclava was a
    victory for the allies (Britain, France, Sardinia, and Turkey), though
    the Russians kept control of the Causeway Heights, the 'heights' in
    question here.

jacmanna: this is the hybrid cultivar *Clematis × jackmanii*, a widespread ornamental plant which flowers in summer and autumn and which was first produced at Jackman's nurseries at Woking, Surrey, in 1860. More commonly known as purple clematis, it is a hybrid between *Clematis lanuginosa* (China) and *Clematis viticella* (S. Europe).

Her shoes were excellent . . . expansion: William Bankes is at least partly based on Sir George Darwin, second son of Charles Darwin and from 1883 Plumian Professor of Astronomy and Experimental Philosophy at Cambridge, who, Woolf wrote in 1909, 'likes punctuality, good manners and tidiness; lectured us, for instance, upon the importance (often overlooked by young ladies) of good shoes' (*PA*, p. 417).

19 *off the Brompton Road*: the Brompton Road extends from Knightsbridge to the Fulham Road in south-west central London.

20 *pampas grass . . . red-hot pokers*: pampas grass was brought to Europe from South America and New Zealand and was a feature of the garden at Talland House (*MB*, p. 134). The red-hot poker, or torch lily, was brought to Europe from South Africa.

a road in Westmorland: until the local government reorganization of 1974, Westmorland was a county in north-west England. It now forms part of Cumbria.

21 *Cam*: presumably a contraction of Camilla. It is likely that the Ramsays' youngest daughter has been named after Mrs Ramsay's beautiful Aunt Camilla (see p. 56). But Cam's name probably carries with it more than a mere family nicety because 'known only from Virgil's *Aeneid* . . . [Camilla was] a maiden-warrior of the Volsci, and ally of Turnus. When she was a baby her father, Metabus, king of the Volscians, was driven out for his cruelty, and arrived with his baby daughter at the flooded river Amasenus. He tied Camilla to a spear, dedicated her to the goddess Diana (Lat. *camilla*, "religious attendant"), and threw her across the river to safety. He then swam across himself. In the *Aeneid* she is killed by the Etruscan Arruns' (*The Concise Oxford Companion to Classical Literature*, ed. M. C. Howatson and Ian Chilvers (Oxford and New York: Oxford University Press, 1993), 105–6). This possibly helps to explain why Cam is 'wild and fierce' (p. 21) and why she flies about like a 'projectile' (p. 46).

22 *the Kings and Queens of England . . . Prue the Fair*: there have been no Kings or Queens of England with the same names as the eight Ramsay children, except James. Nor have there been monarchs called 'the Red' (apart from William Rufus), the Fair, the Wicked, the Ruthless. See also p. 123.

a picture of Vesuvius in eruption: there were seven paroxysmal eruptions of the famous volcano between the beginning of the photographic age and 1927: 1839, 1850, 1855, 1861, 1868, 1872, and 1906 (probably the one in question).

a large kitchen table . . . 'Subject and object and the nature of reality':

Mr Ramsay is an exponent of philosophical idealism. Similarly, in an essay called 'What is Materialism', Leslie Stephen writes: 'we cannot get outside our own consciousness. We know nothing directly except the modifications of our consciousness, thoughts, sensations, emotions, volitions and so forth; and all statements of knowledge carry with them a reference, explicit or implicit, to the knower. An object without a subject is a meaningless phrase' (*An Agnostic's Apology and Other Essays* (London: Smith, Elder, 1893), 127–67; quote from p. 135). A little further on Stephen writes: ' "This is a table" is a phrase which in the first place asserts that I have a certain set of organised sense-impressions' (p. 137).

23 *sections of potatoes*: to examine under a microscope.

salt in vegetables: the over-boiling or over-cooking of vegetables will ensure that 'the vegetable salts are lost' (p. 43). See also pp. 61, 82.

25 *one old woman*: the first of a number of references to Mrs McNab. See also pp. 47, 112, 152, 157.

the rent was precisely twopence halfpenny: even if we take inflation into account, and no matter whether this figure of two and a half old pennies refers to the daily, weekly, or monthly rent, it is a remarkably cheap rent for the scale of house involved (see Introduction, p. xxxiii). Notwithstanding 'precisely', this expression may simply mean that the rent was extremely low. See also note to p. 35 below.

three hundred miles: the distance between London and Skye is actually well over six hundred miles.

'For her whose wishes . . . Helen of our days': in *She* (1887) by H. Rider Haggard, Queen Ayesha of the Amahaggar is otherwise known as 'She-who-must-be-obeyed'. The Helen in question is Helen of Troy, who, in eloping with the Trojan Paris while her husband Menelaus of Sparta was at a funeral, precipitated the Trojan War and the eventual sack of Troy by the Greeks. If this is taken to imply that Mrs Ramsay's name was Helen, then it is interesting that in the holograph her name is Sara (see note to p. 163). But this is also a somewhat ambiguous compliment in that throughout history Helen has been portrayed as a woman of easy virtue: see Bettany Hughes, *Helen of Troy: Goddess, Princess, Whore* (London: Jonathan Cape, 2005).

Croom on the Mind and Bates . . . Customs of Polynesia: George Croom Robertson (1842–92) was from 1866 Grote Professor of Logic at University College, London, and first editor of the leading philosophical journal *Mind* (started 1876). 'If you look in his *Remains* [1894]', Leslie Stephen told his children, 'you will find in the biographical preface a letter in which I have recorded my affection for him. He was one of my very best friends' (*MausB*, p. 79). Polynesia, the large collection of island-groups in the central and western Pacific, including New Zealand, Hawaii, and Samoa, had already received a great deal of attention by 1910 and would receive much more with the development of the academic disciplines of anthropology and ethnography, but no one called 'Bates' had written about Polynesia's 'Savage Customs' prior to or during the Edwardian period.

26 *Cashmere shawl*: see Introduction, p. xxxiv.

Never did anybody look so sad: in *Moments of Being* Woolf remarked that her mother had 'a background of knowledge that made her sad. She had her own sorrow waiting behind her to dip into privately . . . she looked very sad when she was not talking' (*MB*, p. 94).

27 *Graces . . . meadows of asphodel*: in Greek mythology, the three Graces that enhance the enjoyment of life—grace, charm, and beauty—are personified by Thalia, Euphrosyne, and Aglaia, three minor goddesses who were daughters of Zeus and Hera. The Plain of Asphodel, in Homer's *Odyssey*, is 'the place in the Underworld . . . where the dead dwell, leading a shadowy continuance of their former life in the world. The asphodel (whence "daffodil") is a flowering plant of the lily family' (*Concise Oxford Companion to Classical Literature*, 66).

Euston: opened in 1837, this once elegant London railway terminus, whence trains ran to Birmingham, Manchester, Liverpool, Glasgow, and beyond, was controversially demolished in 1963 and replaced by the distinctly less inspiring structure we have today.

Knitting . . . stocking: in *Moments of Being*, Woolf can still 'see her [mother] knitting on the hall step while we play cricket' (*MB*, p. 95).

28 *authenticated masterpiece by Michael Angelo*: this is a mystery as it is inconceivable that Woolf means that the Ramsays actually own a *picture* by the great Renaissance artist Michelangelo Buonarroti (1475–1564), as such a work, even in the Edwardian period, would have been almost priceless. So this must be some kind of print after or reproduction of one of Michelangelo's works. Conceivably, Woolf has in mind a print or reproduction of a work by Michelangelo that had only recently been authenticated. But whatever it is precisely, why leave a 'masterpiece' in such a damp house where it will be ruined?

30 *the great sea lion at the Zoo*: the first sea lion arrived at the London Zoological Gardens in Regent's Park in 1856 and a new sea-lion pool was completed in 1905 and opened to public acclaim. But whether any of the sea lions it held grew to a 'great' size must remain a matter of conjecture. See John Edwards (comp.), *London Zoo from Old Photographs 1852–1914* (London: John Edwards, 1996), 55, 57, 59. 'In this pool', however, 'the Zoo for some time showed an occasional walrus—a beast that, after the Great War, was automatically christened "Old Bill"' (L. R. Brightwell, *The Zoo You Knew* (Oxford: Basil Blackwell, 1936), 182) and it is possible that Woolf has Old Bill in mind at this point.

'in June he gets out of tune': this is probably a variation on a traditional rhyme about the cuckoo:

> The cuckoo comes in April,
> He sings his song in May;

In the middle of June
He changes his tune,
And then he flies away

(*The Oxford Nursery Rhyme Book*, assembled by Iona and Peter Opie (Oxford: Oxford University Press, 1955; 16th impression, 1997), 118.)

30 *the letter Q*: this passage is ironic (in more ways than one) in that Mr Ramsay, as a self-respecting Victorian paterfamilias, might be expected to 'mind his Ps and Qs', that is, be circumspect in his behaviour, as opposed to making a great exhibition of himself.

the stone urn: another feature borrowed from Talland House. See Introduction, p. xii.

31 *a failure*: Leslie Stephen gave in to a profound sense of underachievement towards the end of his life, writing in his *Mausoleum Book*: 'The sense in which I do take myself to be a failure is this: I have scattered myself too much. I think that I had it in me to make something like a real contribution to philosophical or ethical thought. Unluckily, what with journalism and dictionary making, I have been a jack of all trades; and instead of striking home have only done enough to persuade friendly judges that I could have struck . . . [I]f . . . the history of English thought in the nineteenth century should ever be written, my name will only be mentioned in small type and footnotes whereas, had my energies been wisely directed, I might have had the honour of a paragraph in full sized type or even a section in a chapter all to myself' (*MausB*, p. 93). As a literary critic, however, 'Stephen need not have feared. After Matthew Arnold's death in 1888 he was regarded as the first man of English letters and an eminent Victorian' (Noel Annan, *Leslie Stephen: The Godless Victorian* (London: Weidenfeld and Nicolson, 1984), 112).

expedition across the icy solitudes of the Polar region: in her 1932 essay on her father Woolf wrote: 'to the end of his days he would speak of great climbers and explorers with a peculiar mixture of admiration and envy' ('Leslie Stephen, The Philosopher at Home', in Woolf, *Collected Essays*, iv. 76–80). Mr Ramsay most obviously identifies with Robert Falcon Scott (1868–1912) at this point. Scott led a successful Antarctic expedition in 1902–4 and a far more famous one which began in 1910 and ended in failure in 1912. His account of his first expedition, *The Voyage of the 'Discovery'*, was a 1905 best-seller.

32 *forlorn hope*: 'The phrase has its origin in Dutch *verloren hoop*, "lost troop". The French equivalent is *enfants perdus*, "lost children". The forlorn hope was a picked body of men sent in front to begin an attack, particularly the body of volunteers who first entered a breach when storming a defensive fortification' (*Brewer's Dictionary of Phrase and Fable*).

34 *Grimm's fairy story*: this is 'The Fisherman and his Wife'. It is the story of a poor fisherman who catches an enchanted prince in the guise of an enormous flounder. The prince asks to be returned to the sea and the fisherman obliges, only to be berated by his wife on returning home for

having returned the prince without asking him to grant their wish for better accommodation. The fisherman returns to the shore, summons the prince, and their wish is granted in the form of a splendid cottage and garden. The fisherman's domineering wife proceeds to make her husband ask the prince to grant her increasingly outrageous wishes—for a castle; to be made king; to be made emperor; to be made pope—and they are all granted, but when she demands to be given the powers of God and sends her husband off to the shore to ask the flounder to grant this wish, the fisherman finds a storm raging and the prince returns him and his wife to their hovel, where they remain for the rest of their days. The quotations on pp. 37, 47, 48, 49, 51, and 52 are all from the two-volume *Grimm's Household Tales*, trans. Margaret Hunt (London: George Bell and Sons, 1884), i. 78–85.

35 *fifty pounds, perhaps, to mend it*: it could be that one of the reasons why the rent on the house is so extraordinarily low is that the Ramsays are solely responsible for its upkeep. See note to p. 25.

36 *St John's Wood*: a residential area of inner north-west London. In the Victorian period, 'the variety and charm of the comparatively inexpensive houses . . . and the convenience of its proximity to [central] London, combined with the purity of the air, made this an area chosen and inhabited by artists, authors, philosophers and scientists as well by more prosaic members of the middle classes' (*The London Encyclopaedia*, ed. Ben Weinreb and Christopher Hibbert (London and Basingstoke: Macmillan, 1993), 747). Among other nineteenth-century residents of distinction were George Eliot and T. H. Huxley.

37 *the existence of a slave class. The liftman in the Tube*: Clive Bell would argue that a slave class is necessary for the creation of culture in his *Civilization* (1928): see Introduction, pp. xxxv–xxxvi. The reference to the Tube or London Underground is one of three such allusions in the novel (the other two are on pp. 60 and 75).

38 *the young men at Cardiff*: University College, Cardiff, was founded in 1883.

39 *Locke, Hume, Berkeley, and the causes of the French Revolution*: John Locke (1632–1704) was the founder of the British empiricist school of philosophy and author of *An Essay Concerning Human Understanding* (1690); the Scottish philosopher David Hume (1711–76) developed Locke's ideas in his *Enquiry Concerning Human Understanding* (1748); Bishop George Berkeley (1685–1753) argued that things could not exist independently of perception: *esse est percipii* (Lat. 'to be is to perceive'). Naturally, Leslie Stephen discusses the work of all three philosophers in his *History of English Thought in the Eighteenth Century* (1876; 3rd edn. 1902), but does not link their work to the French Revolution of 1789.

Swansea . . . Exeter, Southampton, Kidderminster: university colleges had been established at Swansea in 1920, at Exeter in 1922, and at Southampton in 1902; for Cardiff, see note to p. 38. Kidderminster, a market town on the River Stour in Worcestershire, was until fairly recently synonymous with the manufacture of carpets, but that would not have precluded an appreciation of philosophy among its inhabitants.

40 *Carlyle*: Woolf closely associated the Scottish historian and man of letters Thomas Carlyle (1795–1881) with her father. She visited Carlyle's House in Chelsea with her father in January 1897 (*PA*, p. 24) and she returned the following year and in 1909 (*PA*, pp. 415–16). Leslie Stephen wrote the entry on Carlyle for his *Dictionary of National Biography* and after the death of Julia in 1895 he brooded anxiously in the *Mausoleum Book* on similarities between his own conduct towards his wife and Carlyle's notorious and deeply regretted treatment of his own spouse: 'If I felt that I had a burthen on my conscience like that which tortured poor Carlyle, I think that I should be almost tempted to commit suicide. I cannot, I am thankful to say, feel that. Yet neither can I feel myself to be so absolutely free from blame as I should wish to feel. I am like my father "skinless": over-sensitive and nervously irritable . . . I am, I think, one of the most easily bored of mankind; I cannot bear long sittings with dull people and even when alone in my family I am sometimes as restless as a hyena. I remember—and certainly not without compunction—how bored I was with certain guests of ours—at St. Ives, for example . . . and how I used to plunge away into my back den and leave them, I fear, to bore Julia. All this comes back to me . . . and prevents me from saying, as I would so gladly have said, that I never gave her anxiety or caused her needless annoyance' (*MausB*, p. 89). Stephen once asked Woolf: 'I was not as bad as Carlyle, was I?' (*MB*, p. 13).

44 *treasures in the tombs of kings, tablets bearing sacred inscriptions*: these words anticipate the discovery of the tomb of the boy-pharaoh Tutankhamun (d.1323 BC) in 1922 and the 'Tutmania' which ensued, but they also allude to the many other less spectacular discoveries by Egyptologists which had occurred over the previous 150 years.

the dome-shaped hive: here and a few lines further on when Lily tells Mr Bankes that she sees Mrs Ramsay as 'an august shape; the shape of a dome', it helps to know that in her 'Sketch of the Past' Woolf placed her mother 'in the very centre of that great Cathedral space which was childhood' (*MB*, p. 93). Later on, when Lily feels she has got to grips with Mrs Ramsay and the past and her paint is beginning to flow, she feels 'as if a door had opened, and one went in and stood gazing silently about in a high cathedral-like place, very dark, very solemn' (p. 141).

45 *she had made no attempt at likeness*: Lily's approach to her art is indebted to the post-Impressionists, of whom Woolf's friend Roger Fry wrote in 1912: 'it is not the object of these artists to exhibit their skill or proclaim their knowledge, but only to attempt to express by pictorial and plastic form certain spiritual experiences . . . They do not seek to imitate form, but to create form, not to imitate life, but to find an equivalent for life' (quoted in Virginia Woolf, *Roger Fry: A Biography* (London: Hogarth Press, 1940), 177–8).

the banks of the Kennet: a river flowing through Wiltshire and into Berkshire before joining the River Thames.

47 *an old woman in the kitchen . . . soup out of a basin*: Mrs McNab again. See p. 112, where Mrs McNab remembers the cook giving her 'a plate of milk soup'.

49 *Finlay*: the name of the house or, less likely, an invented Skye place name.

hospitals and drains and the dairy: in Julia Stephen's short book of advice for nurses, there are precise instructions about milk: 'The nurse must see the milkman herself and impress on him the importance of sweet fresh milk from one cow being always brought. When brought she must empty the milk into a flat pan, such as is used for rising cream in a dairy; this pan must be placed in a cool place, and must be well scalded each time it is emptied' (Mrs Leslie Stephen, *Notes from Sick Rooms* (London: Smith, Elder, 1883), 39).

53 *the Indian plains*: central India consists of a plateau called the Deccan flanked by the mountains of the Western and Eastern Ghats. North of the Deccan lies the Indo-Gangetic plain.

the thick leather curtain of a church in Rome: such a curtain would hang before the main door of a church. Woolf visited Rome in April 1927, just before *To the Lighthouse* was published, and wrote: 'I like the Roman Catholic religion . . . I am sure Rome is the city where I shall come to die' (*The Letters of Virginia Woolf*, ed. Nigel Nicolson and Joanne Trautmann (6 vols.; London: Hogarth Press, 1975–80), iii. 360–1). Given that she thought of her childhood as a 'great Cathedral space' (see note to p. 44), it is interesting that she writes of 'the leathern curtain of the heart' in that part of the fifth chapter of *Jacob's Room* which is set in St Paul's Cathedral (Virginia Woolf, *Jacob's Room*, ed. Kate Flint (Oxford: Oxford University Press, 1992), 87).

We are in the hands of the Lord: Mrs Ramsay has in mind either Ecclesiastes 2: 18: 'We will fall into the hands of the Lord, and not into the hands of men; for as His majesty is, so is His mercy' or 2 Samuel 24: 14: 'And David said unto God, I am in a great strait: let us fall now into the hand of the Lord; for his mercies *are* great: and let me not fall into the hand of man.'

54 *Hume . . . had stuck in a bog*: the story of the philosopher getting stuck in a bog was recalled by Leslie Stephen in his *Dictionary of National Biography* (1891) entry on the philosopher: 'He had grown very fat, and was once rescued by an old woman from a bog into which he had fallen on condition of repeating the Creed and the Lord's Prayer.'

56 *scholarship*: to either Oxford or Cambridge.

57 *Hume was stuck in a bog*: see note to p. 54.

off for a day's walk if the weather held: before the onset of old age, Leslie Stephen was a stupendous walker. See Noel Annan, *Leslie Stephen: The Godless Victorian*, 97–8.

59 *Best and brightest, come away!*: the first line of P. B. Shelley's poem, 'To Jane: The Invitation' (first published 1824).

They must marry!: in the *Mausoleum Book*, Leslie Stephen describes Julia as 'a bit of a matchmaker' with 'exalted views of love and marriage' (*MausB*, pp. 75, 77).

60 *Amsterdam . . . the Prado*: the Rijksmuseum in Amsterdam contains many works by the great Dutch master Rembrandt van Rijn (1606–69). The Prado gallery in Madrid was founded by Ferdinand VII in 1818. It houses some of the most acclaimed works by many of the world's great artists, including Velázquez, Goya, El Greco, and Titian (see third note for this page).

Sistine Chapel . . . Giottos: with a painted ceiling by Michelangelo, the Sistine Chapel is part of the Vatican palace. Giotto di Bondone (?1267–1337) was the artist responsible for the frescos on the walls of the Arena Chapel in Padua.

Titians and we can't all be Darwins: given that Woolf has drawn on her memories of Sir George Darwin for William Bankes (see second note for p. 18), this is ironic. Leslie Stephen greatly admired and was immensely influenced by Charles Darwin (1809–82). Titian, or Tiziano Vecellio (1488–1576), was one of the great painters of the high Renaissance.

61 *Constantinople seen through a mist . . . 'Is that the Golden Horn?'*: ancient Byzantium was renamed Constantinople in 330, when Emperor Constantine I declared it the capital of the Eastern Roman Empire. It was the capital of the Byzantine Empire until captured by the Ottoman Turks in 1453. The Ottomans renamed the city Istanbul and made it the capital of their empire in 1457. Built as a Christian cathedral by Emperor Justinian the Great in 532–7, Santa Sofia became a mosque when Constantinople was absorbed into the Ottoman empire and is now a museum. The dome collapsed in 558 and was rebuilt in 563. The Golden Horn is an inlet of the Bosporus (the narrow, 19-mile strait which separates Europe from Asia, connecting the Sea of Marmara with the Black Sea) which serves as Istanbul's harbour. Woolf visited Constantinople in 1906 with her sister Vanessa and her brother Thoby. Both caught typhoid and, while Vanessa recovered, Thoby died of the disease soon after the siblings returned to London. In her 1906 journal Woolf wrote: 'But on the whole the most splendid thing in Constantinople . . . is the prospect of the roofs of the town, seen from the high ground of Pera. For in the morning a mist lies like a veil that muffles treasures across all the houses & all the mosques' (*PA*, p. 351). Earlier in the same journal she describes Santa Sofia, as seen from a boat, as being 'like a treble globe of bubbles frozen solid, floating out to meet us. For it is fashioned in the shape of some fine substance, thin as glass, blown in plump curves; save that it is also as substantial as a pyramid' (*PA*, p. 347).

62 *Damn your eyes, damn your eyes*: the refrain from the once popular ballad, 'Samuel Hall' or 'Sam Hall'.

the Pope's Nose: probably a rock formation, but the term more generally means the rump of a fowl (also called the Parson's Nose).

63 *lost her grandmother's brooch*: a visitor to Talland House once lost her brooch (*MB*, p. 137).

65 *People were getting ready for dinner*: note how the Ramsays put on formal 'dress clothes' for dinner (p. 70) even during their summer holiday.

Lights, lights, lights: Paul is thinking of Polonius' words following the Mouse-trap scene in *Hamlet*, III. ii. 270: 'Lights, lights, lights!'.

66 *Empress of Mexico*: a year after the French invasion of Mexico in 1863, Maximilian I, Archduke of Austria, was installed as emperor. He was married to Princess Charlotte of Belgium, who became known as Empress Carlota of Mexico. In 1867, Maximilian was shot dead during the successful anti-French revolution led by Benito Juárez. The Empress of Mexico escaped to Europe and died after many years of seclusion and emotional turmoil in the same year *To the Lighthouse* was published.

might choose which jewels she was to wear: as a child, Woolf sometimes 'chose the jewels [her mother] was to wear' (*MB*, p. 105) for dinner.

fifteen people sitting down to dinner: in fact, fourteen—Andrew, Jasper, Nancy, Prue, Roger, Rose, their parents, William Bankes, Augustus Carmichael, Paul Rayley, Charles Tansley, Lily Briscoe, and Minta Doyle. James and Cam, who 'ought to have been asleep hours ago' (p. 92) just before 11.00 p.m., have eaten their supper with Mildred in the nursery, whither she takes them on p. 52.

Bœuf en Daube: described on pp. 81–2. The holograph draft contains instructions for cooking this dish: 'You stand it in water for twenty four hours: you stir continuously; you add a little bay leaf, & then a dash of sherry: the whole never being allowed, of course, to come to the boil' (*OHD*, p. 129). A *daubière* is an earthenware pot from Provence in which the dish was cooked, hence the reference to an 'earthenware pot' on p. 85.

67 *Uncle James had brought her from India*: Woolf's paternal uncle, the jurist Sir James Fitzjames Stephen (1829–94), elder brother of Sir Leslie Stephen, was a prominent journalist, historian of the criminal law, and anti-democrat. He spent the years 1869–72 in India as legal member of the Viceroy's Council. 'To the end, Stephen remained among the staunchest supporters of a high-minded, visionary form of colonial domination' (*Oxford DNB*). With reference to the wild boar's skull, the chapter devoted to J. F. Stephen's time in India in his brother's life of him is disappointing: 'I shall have nothing to say about tiger-shooting [or wild boar shooting], though Fitzjames was present, as a spectator, at one or two of Lord Mayo's hunting parties' (Leslie Stephen, *The Life of Sir James Fitzjames Stephen Bart, KCSI: A Judge in the High Court of Justice* (London: Smith Elder, 1895), 237–97; quote from p. 245).

69 *as one might guard a weak flame with a newspaper*: a procedure which involves covering a fireplace with a sheet of newspaper in order to force a

draught up the chimney, thereby encouraging a 'weak flame' to draw more fiercely and (with luck) burn more strongly.

72 *Marlow*: town on the River Thames in Buckinghamshire, 30 miles west of London.

74 *X-ray photograph*: X-rays were discovered by Wilhelm Röntgen in 1895. Woolf attended a lecture on them, which included a demonstration of their revealing powers, on 9 January 1897 (*PA*, pp. 9–10).

79 *Neptune's banquet, of the bunch . . . and the torches lolloping red and gold*: known as Poseidon in Greek mythology, Neptune is the ancient Italian god of water. It is unclear whether there is an allusion to an actual picture or pictures in play here, though it is possible Woolf is thinking of *Neptune and Triton* (1620) by Gian Lorenzo Bernini (1598–1680), now in the Victoria and Albert Museum in London, a marble sculpture depicting Neptune calming the sea with his trident, while between his legs, Triton, his son, blows a conch shell. The late Roman Neptunalia was celebrated on 23 July and involved a huge banquet. This is likely to be the feast in question, but 'Neptune's banquet' might just be an allusion to the teeming fruits of the sea. Carmichael is again connected with Neptune on p. 169.

Bacchus is the usual name in Latin of the Greek god Dionysus. I have been unable to locate a picture or sculpture of Bacchus which precisely portrays him 'among the leopard skins and the torches lolloping red and gold', but there are a number of images of him which may be relevant here and from which Woolf may have assembled a composite Bacchus picture in her head, for example, *The Triumph of Bacchus and Ariadne* (1597–1602), a fresco at the Palazzo Farnese, Rome, by Annibale Carracci (1560–1609), in which Bacchus is portrayed with vine leaves hanging over his shoulder, and *A Dedication to Bacchus* (1889) by Sir Lawrence Alma-Tadema (1836–1912), featuring torches and a prominent tiger-skin and now in the Kunsthalle, Hamburg; the *Bacchus and Ariadne* of Giambattista Pittoni (1678–1767) may also be relevant here. It portrays vine leaves, a leopard skin under a red cloak, and a thyrsus, the distinctive Bacchic wand with a big pine cone on the end, which looks not unlike a torch.

80 *George Eliot . . . third volume of Middlemarch*: at this point in the manuscript there is yet another reference to the London Underground, where Woolf writes that Minta had left *Middlemarch* 'in the Tube' (*OHD*, p. 164). *Middlemarch* was published in four volumes in 1872 and Leslie Stephen published a life of George Eliot in 1902.

84 *the Mile End Road*: for Woolf, this thoroughfare was synonymous with the roughness and deprivations of the East End of London.

86 *square root of one thousand two hundred and fifty-three*: on this evidence, it is hard to tell whether Mr Ramsay is a rather good or a rather shaky mathematician, since the square root of 1,253, *to eight decimal places*, is 35.39774004. (My thanks to Dr Robin Knight for his help with this

infinite number.) 'He was a curious figure . . . sitting dead silent at the head of the family dinner table', Woolf wrote of her father. '. . . He would ask what was the cube root of such and such a number; for he always worked out mathematical problems on railway tickets . . . And mother would protest; no mathematics, she would say, at meals' (*MB*, p. 119).

Voltaire . . . Napoleon . . . Lord Rosebery; on Creevey's Memoirs: the multi-talented French man of letters Voltaire (1694–1778), whose real name was François-Marie Arouet, published *Candide* in 1759. Madame de Staël (1766–1817) was a noted critic, novelist, and letter writer. The character of the French soldier and emperor Napoleon Bonaparte (1769–1821) has been continually picked apart since his death and his psychology is discussed in the '1917' chapter of *The Years*, ed. Hermione Lee (1937; Oxford: Oxford University Press, 1992), 267; see also pp. 155 and 156 below. During his time in power, Napoleon redistributed aristocratic lands to a new class of landowner. Lord Rosebery was born Archibald Philip Primrose in 1847 and became the 5th Earl of Rosebery in 1868. He was Liberal foreign secretary in 1886 and prime minister for fifteen months in 1894–5. He resigned as Liberal leader in 1896 and he spent much of the Edwardian period as a cross-bencher with little sympathy for the reforming radicalism of Edwardian Liberalism. He died in 1929. Extracts from the journal and the selected letters of the Whig MP Thomas Creevey (1768–1838), together with letters which he had received from notables of his time, were published as *The Creevey Papers* in 1903. This volume includes Creevey's celebrated first-hand account of life in Brussels at the time of the Battle of Waterloo (1815).

the Waverley novels: were published by Sir Walter Scott (1771–1832) and concern the Waverley family. This group of novels includes *Waverley* (1814), the first in the series, *The Antiquary* (1816), *Old Mortality* (1816), and *The Heart of Midlothian* (1818), and is probably the sense of 'Waverley' in play here. But the term more generally applies to the Waverley Edition of all Scott's novels. Woolf recalled that her father always read aloud to his children, including 'that long line of red backs— the thirty-two volumes of the Waverley Novels, which provided reading for many years of evenings, because when we had finished the last he was ready to begin the first over again . . . My father always loved reading aloud, and of all books, I think, he loved Scott's the best' ('Impressions of Sir Leslie Stephen' (1906), repr. in *The Essays of Virginia Woolf*, ed. Andrew McNeillie (6 vols.; London: Hogarth Press, 1986–), i. 127–30; quote from p. 128). In fact, Woolf probably means the edition of thirty volumes (1834–71) which was supplemented by an edition of three further volumes (1841–7) as there has never been a thirty-two-volume edition of the Waverley Novels. Scott wrote on 'The Life of Napoleon Buonaparte' for the *Encyclopaedia Britannica* in 1827 and this may explain why the conversation has moved on from the Frenchman to the Scotsman and his novels. Nor was it only Woolf's father who was a Scott fan: 'For Scott she had a passion', Woolf wrote of her mother (*MB*, p. 97).

'*I—I—I.*': in the 'Present Day' chapter of *The Years* (1937), Peggy soon
tires of a young man speaking about himself at a party: 'She had heard it
all before. I, I, I . . . like a vulture's beak pecking, or a vacuum-cleaner
sucking, or a telephone bell ringing. I, I, I' Woolf, *The Years*, ed. Lee,
342). Similarly, in *The Waves* (1931), Louis says: 'I have signed my name
. . . already twenty times. I, and again I, and again I', and Bernard also
says 'I, I, I' in the same novel (Virginia Woolf, *The Waves*, ed. Gillian
Beer (Oxford: Oxford University Press, 1992), 138 and 141, 212), while
in *A Room of One's Own* (1928) Woolf remarks of men's writing: 'a
shadow seemed to lie across the page. It was a straight dark bar, a shadow
shaped something like the letter "I". One began dodging this way and
that to catch a glimpse of the landscape behind it' (Woolf, *A Room
of One's Own and Three Guineas*, ed. Morag Shiach (Oxford: Oxford
University Press, 1992), 130).

88   *Tolstoi . . . Anna Karenina*: among many other works, the Russian novelist
and moralist Count Leo Tolstoi or Tolstoy (1823–1910) published *War
and Peace* in 1865–9 and *Anna Karenina*, which describes how the married heroine's love for Count Vronsky leads ultimately to her suicide, in
1875–8.

89   *Come out and climb the garden path*: these words, the four verse quotations
on p. 90 and the three lines of poetry on p. 96 are taken from the first,
second, and fourth stanzas of 'Luriana, Lurilee' by Charles Elton (1839–
1900), a complete version of which was first published in *Another World
Than This . . . An Anthology* (London: Michael Joseph, 1945), 108, com-
piled by Vita Sackville-West and Harold Nicolson. In that version,
which, as John Shaw has discovered, Sackville-West copied down at
Virginia Woolf's dictation and then slightly altered to suit her taste, the
full poem reads:

> Come out and climb the garden path
> Luriana, Lurilee.
> The China rose is all abloom
> And buzzing with the yellow bee.
> We'll swing you on the cedar bough,
> Luriana, Lurilee.
>
> I wonder if it seems to you,
> Luriana, Lurilee,
> That all the lives we ever lived
> And all the lives to be,
> Are full of trees and changing leaves,
> Luriana, Lurilee.
>
> How long it seems since you and I,
> Luriana, Lurilee,
> Roamed in the forest where our kind
> Had just begun to be,

And laughed and chattered in the flowers,
Luriana, Lurilee.

How long since you and I went out,
Luriana, Lurilee,
To see the Kings go riding by
Over lawn and daisy lea,
With their palm leaves and cedar sheaves,
Luriana, Lurilee.

Swing, swing, swing on the bough,
Luriana, Lurilee,
Till you sleep in a humble heap
Or under a gloomy churchyard tree,
And then fly back to swing on a bough,
Luriana, Lurilee.

In 1939, Woolf told a correspondent that she used to hear her friend Lytton Strachey (1880–1932) reciting 'Luriana, Lurilee' (*Letters*, vi. 321). Charles Elton was a close friend of the Strachey family, having married a cousin of Lytton Strachey's father, and it was Lytton Strachey who gave a copy of 'Luriana, Lurilee' to Leonard Woolf when they were undergraduates at Trinity College, Cambridge. This information is taken from Elizabeth F. Boyd, 'Luriana, Lurilee', *Notes and Queries*, 208 (October 1963), 380–1. However, in 'Luriana, Lurilee' Revisited I: "A Garden Song": Leonard Woolf's Manuscript Copy: The "Right Version" of the Poem?', *Notes and Queries*, 250 (March 2005), 89–93, and 'Luriana, Lurilee' Revisited II: More Poems by Charles Elton', *Notes and Queries*, 250 (March 2005), 93–4, John Shaw has added greatly to our knowledge of Elton, his *oeuvre*, and the background to 'Luriana, Lurilee', and not least by recovering and publishing Leonard Woolf's own copy of the poem, which he had titled 'A Garden Song'.

91 *the Labour Party*: the Independent Labour Party (ILP) was founded in 1893 and first contested a general election in 1895. In 1900 the ILP joined forces with the Social Democratic Federation and the Fabian Society to form the Labour Representation Committee (LRC). The LRC changed its name to the Labour Party in 1906. Leonard Woolf joined the Fabian Society in 1916 and stood (unsuccessfully) for election in 1922 as a Labour Party candidate. He was an adviser to the Party on its response to the General Strike of 1926 and was secretary of its Advisory Committee on International Relations.

92 *that horrid skull again*: like Uncle James's opals, the skull seems to have been a gift from one of Mrs Ramsay's relations: 'What had possessed Edward to send them this horrid skull?' (p. 92).

95 *one of old Sir Walter's*: Mr Ramsay is reading chapter 31 of *The Antiquary* (1816), Sir Walter Scott's own favourite among his novels. Woolf wrote

an essay on *The Antiquary* in 1924 and when she praises 'the scene in the cottage where Steenie Mucklebackit lies dead' she reveals that she finds it no less affecting than Mr Ramsay: 'the father's grief, the mother's irritability, the minister's consolations, all come together, tragic, irrelevant, comic, drawn, one knows not how, to make a whole, a complete presentation of life, which, as always, Scott creates carelessly, without a word of comment, as if the parts grew together without his willing it, and broke into ruin again without his caring' ('The Antiquary', repr. in *Essays*, iii. 454–8; quote from p. 457). See also note to p. 86.

96 *Steer, hither steer your wingèd pines, all beaten Mariners*: the first lines of 'The Sirens Song' by William Browne of Tavistock (1588–1643), the opening poem of his *Inner Temple Masque* (1614):

> Steer, hither steer your wingèd pines,
> All beaten mariners!

'The Sirens Song' was anthologized by Sir Arthur Quiller-Couch in his *Oxford Book of English Verse 1250–1900* (1900).

97 *the poor old crazed creature in Mucklebackit's cottage*: this is Mucklebackit's grieving mother.

98 *Balzac*: the French novelist Honoré de Balzac (1799–1850) was the author of the *Comédie humaine* (1827–47), which comprises ninety-one separate but interconnected works of fiction.

Nor praise the deep vermilion in the rose: this line and the two lines of verse quotation below are from Shakespeare's Sonnet 98:

> From you have I been absent in the spring,
> When proud pied April, dressed in all his trim,
> Hath put a spirit of youth in everything,
> That heavy Saturn laughed and leaped with him.
> Yet nor the lays of birds, nor the sweet smell
> Of different flowers in odour and in hue,
> Could make me any summer's story tell,
> Or from their proud lap pluck them where they grew;
> Nor did I wonder at the lily's white,
> Nor praise the deep vermilion in the rose:
> They were but sweet, but figures of delight,
> Drawn after you, you pattern of all those.
> Yet seemed it winter still, and, you away,
> As with your shadow I with these did play.

TIME PASSES

103 *future to show . . . coming in from the terrace*: this links with p. 91, where

Bankes and Tansley have gone out on to the terrace to finish the discussion about politics which they had begun round the dinner table. See also third note to p. 103.

One by one the lamps were all extinguished: an allusion to the words of Sir Edward Grey (1862–1933), Foreign Secretary from 1905 to May 1916, who said in August 1914: 'The lamps are going out all over Europe; we shall not see them lit again in our lifetime'. See Introduction, p. xxv.

Virgil: the greatest of the Roman poets, Publius Vergilius Maro (70–19 BC), is the author of the *Eclogues*, the *Georgics*, and the *Aeneid*. Carmichael's choice of reading suggests he is engaged in some kind of *sortes Virgilianae*, that is attempting to divine the future by opening the works of Virgil at random and reading the first words which meet the eye—another method of trying to divine what the 'future' will 'show': see first note to p. 103.

downpouring of immense darkness began: there is an 'Outline' for 'Time Passes' in the manuscript which reads:

> [Tie?] *Ten Chapters*
> Now the question of the ten years.
> [Tie?]
> The Seasons.
> The Skull
> The gradual dissolution of everything
> This is to be contrasted with the permanence of—what?
> Sun, moon & stars.
> Hopeless gulfs of misery.
> Cruelty.
> The War.
> Change. Oblivion. Human vitality. Old woman
> Cleaning up. The bobbed up, valorous, as of a principle
> of human life projected
> We are handed on by our children?
> Shawls & shooting caps. A green handled brush.
> The devouringness of nature.
> But all the time, this passes, accumulates.
> Darkness.
> The welter of winds & waves
> What then is the medium through wh. we regard human beings?
> Tears. [di?]
> [Sleep th] Slept through life. (*OHD*, app. B, p. 51)

105   *their leaves fly helter skelter . . . and scatter damp paths*: see Introduction, pp. xxvi–xxvii.

108   *Prue Ramsay . . . with childbirth*: the sudden death of Prue Ramsay echoes that of Woolf's half-sister Stella Duckworth, who died on 19 July 1897,

possibly of a pregnancy complication, only three months after her wedding day. However, this premature death could be seen as yet another way in which the new, post-War order is marked: Mrs Ramsay was a martyr to motherhood; Prue has been spared a similar fate.

109 *an ashen-coloured ship*: in the holograph draft it is called a 'murderous looking ship' with a 'black snout' (*OHD*, p. 222), linking it, perhaps, to the wild boar's skull nailed to the nursery wall.

111 *the house would be sold at Michaelmas*: on p. 25 we learn that the house is rented, so this must mean that the lease was going to be sold, just as Leslie Stephen sold the Talland House lease after the death of his wife in 1895 (29 September).

once they had been coming . . . difficult these days: see the final lines of the fourth section of 'Time Passes'.

112 *a plate of milk soup for her*: see note to p. 47.

113 *Poppies sowed themselves among the dahlias*: see Introduction, p. xxv.

114 *Mrs Bast*: Woolf possibly borrows this surname from Leonard Bast in E. M. Forster's *Howards End* (1910).

116 *Then indeed peace had come*: the Armistice, which brought hostilities to an end, was signed on 11 November 1918 and the First World War was formally concluded with the signing of the Treaty of Versailles on 28 June 1919, suggesting very strongly that the end of 'Time Passes' and all of 'The Lighthouse' are set in September 1919.

THE LIGHTHOUSE

122 *'Alone' . . . 'Perished'*: these quotations (and others on pp. 136, 137, and 167) are from the final stanza of 'The Cast-away' (written 1799) by William Cowper (1731–1800). It concerns a seaman who is swept overboard during a fierce storm off Cape Horn in 1741. Although he is a strong swimmer, his ship is helpless to retrieve him in the face of the raging seas and he drowns with his shipmates looking back at him in horror. The last two stanzas read:

> I, therefore, purpose not to dream,
> Descanting on his fate,
> To give the melancholy theme
> A more enduring date,
> But Mis'ry still delights to trace
> Its semblance in another's case
>
> No voice divine the storm allay'd,
> No light propitious shone,
> When, snatch'd from all effectual aid,
> We perish'd, each, alone;
> But I, beneath a rougher sea,
> And whelm'd in deeper gulfs than he.

a moment of revelation: see p. 70.

124 *Here was Lily, at forty-four*: on page 45 we are told that Lily is 33, so the gap between 'The Window' and 'The Lighthouse' is either ten or eleven years. This is how we know that 'The Window' is set in either 1908 or 1909. But the fact that 'The Lighthouse' takes place in a post-war September suggests a minor error on Woolf's part with regard to Lily's age and a probable date of 1909 for 'The Window'. Interestingly, if Lily *is* 44 at the end, she is the same age at which Woolf had her vision of the novel while walking round Tavistock Square in 1926: see Introduction, p. xvi.

132 *Mrs Ramsay sat and wrote letters by a rock*: just as Mrs Flanders is doing on the beach at the beginning of *Jacob's Room*. Julia Stephen was a formidable letter writer.

135 *ten ships had been driven into the bay for shelter*: on p. 136 it says 'eleven' ships took refuge in this way.

136 *'We perished . . . each alone'*: see note to p. 122.

137 *But I beneath . . . than he*: see note to p. 122.

142 *Surbiton*: an outer suburb of Greater London in Surrey, now much more populous than it was in the early twentieth century.

143 *Rickmansworth*: in Hertfordshire, 17 miles north-west of London.

the taxation of land values and a capital levy: for a useful overview of this issue see 'New Liberalism and the Land', in C. F. G. Masterman, *The New Liberalism* (London: Leonard Parsons, 1920), 157–67. As Liberal Chancellor of the Exchequer from 1908, Lloyd George led a vigorous campaign from 1909 aimed at 'the "bursting of the land monopoly," ' (ibid. 160). It was known as the Land Campaign and was all part of the Liberals' opposition to the age-old privilege of the landed interest. In 1913–14 Lloyd George promised minimum wages for agricultural labourers and a rural house-building scheme.

145 *Raphael had treated divinely*: Raphael was one of the great painters of the Italian Renaissance. His full name was Raffaello Sanzio (1483–1520) and he made many paintings of the Madonna and Child.

Hampton Court: built on a site by the Thames 15 miles to the south-west of London which Thomas Wolsey had bought in 1514 (the year before he became cardinal and Lord Chancellor of England). Hampton Court Palace was handed over to Henry VIII four years before Wolsey fell from favour in 1529.

147 *a hand would be shoved up, . . . a blade would be flashed*: in 'The Passing of Arthur' (1869), the last of Tennyson's *Idylls of the King*, first published as a complete sequence of twelve books in 1891, there is a description of Sir Bedivere throwing Arthur's sword Excalibur into a lake at the command of the dying king only for it to be caught by the hilt by the Lady of the Lake before it touches the water. She brandishes it three times before drawing it down below the surface of the mere. See ll. 301–29.

148 *a wreath of white flowers*: such flowers, 'hyacinths or lilies' (below), are both associated with 'the fields of death' (p. 149). See notes to pp. 27 and 170.

149 *Piccadilly*: 'Extending from Piccadilly Circus to Hyde Park Corner, this is one of the two ancient highways leading westward out of London' (*London Encyclopaedia*, 613). It forms part of an obvious route into central London from the Brompton Road.

 Standard, News: two London evening newspapers.

154 *shapes of a world not realized*: there is a possible echo of 'Ode' ('There was a time . . .') (1802–4) by Wordsworth:

> Blank misgivings of a Creature
> Moving about in worlds not realised!
>
> (ll. 1457–8)

156 *the character of Napoleon*: see earlier references to Napoleon on pp. 86 and 155.

158 *colony of plantains*: that is, a colony of *Plantago major*, a common weed on Skye.

 he was growing famous: more details of this are given in the manuscript: 'It was said that a book he wrote in the 70s about travelling in Burma was a masterpiece . . . People were beginning to say that Mr Carmichael who had always been known to a few enthusiasts, was one of the finest translators of our time: & so on' (*OHD*, p. 330).

159 *Trafalgar Square grasping a big stick*: dominated by the Nelson Column, Trafalgar Square, at the north end of Whitehall (the thoroughfare where many Government offices, such as the Ministry of Defence, are located and off which runs Downing Street) has long been the focal point for mass and minor protests. The 'big stick' is likely to have had a placard attached to it.

160 *got his fellowship . . . he lived at Golders Green*: this probably means that Tansley, having become a Fellow of an Oxbridge college, subsequently took up a position in London, moving as a result to Golders Green, an area of outer north-west London which was subject to large-scale development at the beginning of the twentieth century following the extension of the Northern Line of the London Underground. In 1919 Golders Green would have been synonymous with the pleasures of leafy suburbia, but that is not quite how Woolf would have seen it.

162 *peg-top trousers*: in *Moments of Being* Woolf imagines the 'summer afternoon world' of around 1860 in which 'a stream of ladies in crinolines and little straw hats . . . are attended by gentlemen in peg-top trousers and whiskers' (*MB*, p. 97). Peg-top trousers were wide at the top and narrow at the bottom.

163 *say her name*: in the manuscript Mrs Ramsay's name is Sara (*OHD*, p. 6).

166 *Little bits of black cork had floated past*: perhaps a reference back to the possible torpedo incident after which the sea 'had boiled and bled', p. 109. The cork would have come from life-jackets.

169 *an old pagan god . . . in his hand*: Carmichael is again associated with Neptune or Poseidon, whose 'usual representation is with a trident (probably a fish spear)' (*Concise Oxford Companion to Classical Literature*, 445). See also note to p. 79.

170 *a wreath of violets and asphodels*: see notes to pp. 27 and 148. 'The colour [violet] indicates the love of truth and the truth of love. In the language of flowers the white violet is emblematic of innocence, and the blue violet of faithful love' (*Brewer's Dictionary of Phrase and Fable*, 1235). In church symbolism, violet stands for penitence.

A SELECTION OF OXFORD WORLD'S CLASSICS

TROLLOPE IN OXFORD WORLD'S CLASSICS

ANTHONY TROLLOPE

The American Senator

An Autobiography

Barchester Towers

Can You Forgive Her?

The Claverings

Cousin Henry

The Duke's Children

The Eustace Diamonds

Framley Parsonage

He Knew He Was Right

Lady Anna

Orley Farm

Phineas Finn

Phineas Redux

The Prime Minister

Rachel Ray

The Small House at Allington

The Warden

The Way We Live Now

Travel Writing 1700–1830

Women's Writing 1778–1838

WILLIAM BECKFORD	Vathek
JAMES BOSWELL	Life of Johnson
FRANCES BURNEY	Camilla
	Cecilia
	Evelina
	The Wanderer
LORD CHESTERFIELD	Lord Chesterfield's Letters
JOHN CLELAND	Memoirs of a Woman of Pleasure
DANIEL DEFOE	A Journal of the Plague Year
	Moll Flanders
	Robinson Crusoe
	Roxana
HENRY FIELDING	Jonathan Wild
	Joseph Andrews and Shamela
	Tom Jones
WILLIAM GODWIN	Caleb Williams
OLIVER GOLDSMITH	The Vicar of Wakefield
MARY HAYS	Memoirs of Emma Courtney
ELIZABETH INCHBALD	A Simple Story
SAMUEL JOHNSON	The History of Rasselas
	The Major Works
CHARLOTTE LENNOX	The Female Quixote
MATTHEW LEWIS	Journal of a West India Proprietor
	The Monk
HENRY MACKENZIE	The Man of Feeling

A SELECTION OF   **OXFORD WORLD'S CLASSICS**

SHERWOOD ANDERSON	**Winesburg, Ohio**
WILLA CATHER	**O Pioneers!**
JAMES FENIMORE COOPER	**The Last of the Mohicans**
STEPHEN CRANE	**The Red Badge of Courage**
THEODORE DREISER	**Sister Carrie**
F. SCOTT FITZGERALD	**The Beautiful and Damned** **The Great Gatsby**
BENJAMIN FRANKLIN	**Autobiography and Other Writings**
CHARLOTTE PERKINS GILMAN	**The Yellow Wall-Paper and Other Stories**
NATHANIEL HAWTHORNE	**The Scarlet Letter**
HENRY JAMES	**The Portrait of a Lady** **The Turn of the Screw and Other Stories**
JACK LONDON	**The Call of the Wild** **White Fang and Other Stories**
HERMAN MELVILLE	**Billy Budd, Sailor and Selected Tales** **Moby-Dick**
EDGAR ALLAN POE	**Selected Tales**
HARRIET BEECHER STOWE	**Uncle Tom's Cabin**
HENRY DAVID THOREAU	**Walden**
MARK TWAIN	**Adventures of Huckleberry Finn** **The Adventures of Tom Sawyer**
LEW WALLACE	**Ben-Hur**
EDITH WHARTON	**The Custom of the Country** **Ethan Frome**
WALT WHITMAN	**Leaves of Grass**
OWEN WISTER	**The Virginian**

The Oxford World's Classics Website

www.oup.com/uk/worldsclassics

- Information about new titles
- Explore the full range of Oxford World's Classics
- Links to other literary sites and the main OUP webpage
- Imaginative competitions, with bookish prizes
- Articles by editors
- Extracts from Introductions
- Special information for teachers and lecturers

www.oup.com/uk/worldsclassics

American Literature

Authors in Context

British and Irish Literature

Children's Literature

Classics and Ancient Literature

Colonial Literature

Eastern Literature

European Literature

History

Medieval Literature

Oxford English Drama

Poetry

Philosophy

Politics

Religion

The Oxford Shakespeare

A complete list of Oxford World's Classics, including Authors in Context, Oxford English Drama, and the Oxford Shakespeare, is available in the UK from the Marketing Services Department, Oxford University Press, Great Clarendon Street, Oxford OX2 6DP, or visit the website at www.oup.com/uk/worldsclassics.

In the USA, visit www.oup.com/us/owc for a complete title list.

Oxford World's Classics are available from all good bookshops. In case of difficulty, customers in the UK should contact Oxford University Press Bookshop, 116 High Street, Oxford OX1 4BR.